The Changing Adolescent Experience

The path adolescents take from childhood to adulthood is a product of social, economic, political, and technological forces. In the next century, these forces may facilitate youth's preparation to become healthy adults, or they may leave youth unprepared for adulthood. Knowledgeable projections are vital in shaping the agenda for research; for alerting educators, policy makers, and practitioners to new issues; and for formulating thoughtful responses to emerging dilemmas. This timely book focuses on the future of adolescence in postindustrial societies. The authors identify some ominous societal changes that will affect youth: unstable job markets, competition for public resources due to an aging population, and widening income gaps between "information workers" and low-skill workers. But they also observe numerous opportunities that may improve the lives of young people through the creation of new information technology, innovations in health-service delivery and criminal justice rehabilitation, and through the resourcefulness of a new generation. This volume examines these trends and other macrostructural changes that are likely to impact adolescents' lives and their futures as adults.

Jeylan T. Mortimer is Professor of Sociology and Director of the Life Course Center at the University of Minnesota. She is author of *Adolescents, Work, and Family: An Intergenerational Developmental Analysis* (with Michael Finch) and editor of *Youth Unemployment and Society* (with Anne C. Petersen).

Reed W. Larson is Professor of Human and Community Development, Psychology, and Educational Psychology at the University of Illinois at Urbana-Champaign. He is author of *Divergent Realities: The Emotional Lives of Mothers, Fathers, and Adolescents* (with Maryse Richards) and *Being Adolescent: Conflict and Growth in the Teenage Years* (with Mihaly Csikszentmihalyi).

The Changing Adolescent Experience

Societal Trends and the Transition to Adulthood

Edited by

JEYLAN T. MORTIMER

University of Minnesota

REED W. LARSON

University of Illinois at Urbana-Champaign

PUBLISHED BY THE PRESS SYNDICATE OF THE UNIVERSITY OF CAMBRIDGE
The Pitt Building, Trumpington Street, Cambridge, United Kingdom

CAMBRIDGE UNIVERSITY PRESS
The Edinburgh Building, Cambridge CB2 2RU, UK
40 West 20th Street, New York, NY 10011-4211, USA
477 Williamstown Road, Port Melbourne, VIC 3207, Australia
Ruiz de Alarcón 13, 28014 Madrid, Spain
Dock House, The Waterfront, Cape Town 8001, South Africa

http://www.cambridge.org

First published 2002

Printed in the United Kingdom at the University Press, Cambridge

Typeface Palatino 10/13 pt.   *System* LaTeX 2$_\varepsilon$ [TB]

A catalog record for this book is available from the British Library.

Library of Congress Cataloging in Publication data

The changing adolescent experience : societal trends and the transition to adulthood/
edited by Jeylan T. Mortimer, Reed W. Larson.
p. cm.
Includes bibliographical references and index.
ISBN 0-521-81480-4 – ISBN 0-521-89199-x (pb.)
1. Adolescence – Forecasting.   2. Teenagers – Social conditions – Forecasting.
3. Youth – Social conditions – Forecasting.   4. Twenty-first century – Forecasts.
I. Mortimer, Jeylan T., 1943–   II. Larson, Reed, 1950–
HQ796 .C4514   2002
305.235–dc21   2002025928

ISBN 0 521 81480 4 hardback
ISBN 0 521 89199 x paperback

Contents

Contributors

Ronald E. Anderson, University of Minnesota

Francis T. Cullen, University of Cincinnati

Elizabeth Fussell, Tulane University

Kate Hellenga, University of Illinois at Urbana-Champaign

Charles E. Irwin, Jr., University of California, San Francisco

Alan C. Kerckhoff, Duke University

Reed W. Larson, University of Illinois at Urbana-Champaign

Tracy Macdonald, University of California, San Francisco

Jeylan T. Mortimer, University of Minnesota

Elizabeth M. Ozer, University of California, San Francisco

Allison J. Ruth, The Catholic University of America

John Paul Wright, University of Cincinnati

James Youniss, The Catholic University of America

Preface

The Society for Research on Adolescence, in collaboration with the International Society for the Study of Behavioral Development, has sponsored a Study Group on Adolescence in the Twenty-First Century. With primary support from the William T. Grant Foundation, the Study Group commissioned the series of chapters included in this volume. Because critical information about the future of adolescence may reside not with adolescent researchers but with scholars knowledgeable about external institutions and changes that affect adolescence, we approached experts on the subjects to write these chapters. The scholars were asked to forecast major trends in their domains of study to promote an understanding of how such trends may influence adolescent development and the transition to adulthood during the next 25 to 50 years. As the kind of preparation adolescents need to enter adulthood is determined by the character of adult roles, the authors address broad societal transformations that affect both adolescent experience and the nature of adult roles for which adolescents will need to prepare themselves. Instead of making specific predictions, they identify key trends and possible scenarios. In addition to this book, the Study Group has produced two other volumes, one that deals with adolescence across regions of the world (Brown, Larson, & Saraswathi, 2002) and another that examines the influence of societal changes on adolescents' competence and well-being in four domains (Larson, Brown, & Mortimer, 2002).

We give special thanks to Suzanne Wilson, who played an invaluable role in coordinating the meetings of the Study Group. We also thank members of graduate seminars at the University of Illinois and the University of Wisconsin who provided helpful comments on earlier versions of the chapters. Added support for the work of the Study Group came from the Johann Jacobs Foundation, the Kellogg Foundation, and the Carnegie Adolescent Forum.

Members of the Study Group

Susan Nall Bales, *Frameworks Institute, Washington, DC, USA*
B. Bradford Brown, *University of Wisconsin, Madison, WI, USA*
Kathleen Thiede Call, *University of Minnesota, Minneapolis, MN, USA*
Marcelo Diversi, *Utah State University, Logan, UT, USA*
Jacquelynne Eccles, *University of Michigan, Ann Arbor, MI, USA*
Wendy Everett, *Institute for the Future, Menlo Park, CA, USA*
Frank Furstenberg, *University of Pennsylvania, Philadelphia, PA, USA*
Karen Hein, *William T. Grant Foundation, New York, NY, USA*
Michele Kipke, *National Academy of Sciences, Washington, DC, USA*
Helga Krueger, *Universität Bremen, Bremen, Germany*
Reed W. Larson, *University of Illinois at Urbana-Champaign, IL, USA*
Sharafuddin Malik, *International Council on Alcohol and Addictions, Cairo, Egypt*
Milbrey McLaughlin, *Stanford University, Stanford, CA, USA*
Vonnie McLoyd, *University of Michigan, Ann Arbor, MI, USA*
Jeylan T. Mortimer, *University of Minnesota, Minneapolis, MN, USA*
Anne Petersen, *W. K. Kellogg Foundation, Battle Creek, MI, USA*
Karen Pittman, *The Forum for Youth Investment, Takoma Park, MD, USA*
Michael Rutter, *Institute of Psychiatry, London, United Kingdom*
Madelene Santa Maria, *De La Salle University, Manila, Philippines*
T. S. Saraswathi, *Maharaja Sayajirao University of Baroda, India*
Michael Shanahan, *Pennsylvania State University, State College, PA, USA*
Rainer Silbereisen, *University of Jena, Jena, Germany*
Lawrence Steinberg, *Temple University, Philadelphia, PA, USA*
Suman Verma, *Government Home Science College, Chandigarh, India*
James Youniss, *Catholic University of America, Washington, DC, USA*

Steering Committee

Reed W. Larson (Chair)
B. Bradford Brown
Jeylan T. Mortimer

References

Brown, B. B., Larson, R., & Saraswathi, T. S. (eds.) (2002). *The World's Youth: Adolescence in Eight Regions of the Globe.* New York: Cambridge University Press.

Larson, R., Brown, B. B., & Mortimer, J. (eds.) (2002). Adolescents' Preparation for the Future: Perils and Promise (special issue). *The Journal of Research on Adolescence,* 12(1).

1

Macrostructural Trends and the Reshaping of Adolescence

Jeylan T. Mortimer and Reed W. Larson

The paths adolescents take from childhood into adulthood are shaped by broad demographic, institutional, and technological forces. In the next century, these societal forces may affect adolescent experience in ways that facilitate and enhance youth's preparation to become healthy adults or in ways that leave youth unprepared, even handicapped, for adulthood. Knowledgeable projections about how adolescent experience and preparation for adulthood are likely to be transformed in the future are vital for shaping agendas for research; for alerting educators, policy makers, and practitioners to new realities; and for formulating thoughtful responses to emerging dilemmas. This volume focuses on key societal phenomena that will influence the experience of adolescence in the future: demographic and economic trends, innovations in information technology, and alterations in key social institutions including those concerned with education, work, health care, and criminal justice.

Some ominous societal changes of the 21st century are addressed. Rapid population growth in some regions of the world induce crowding, environmental degradation, and resource scarcity that jeopardize investment in the next generation. In other regions where populations have stabilized or are shrinking, large aging cohorts compete with smaller and less powerful younger cohorts for resources. Across the world, technological and occupational changes have produced widening income gaps between "information workers" and low skill workers, with strong implications for the resources available to children in the succeeding generation.

Other quite promising societal changes are foreseen in these chapters. Cultural and economic globalization, information technology, new educational methods, and innovations in health-service delivery have the potential to enhance adolescents' lives in the future. They give young people access to diverse resources and present tremendous opportunities for youth to make choices among a wider variety of life options, thus enabling them to develop more fully their potentials.

This book examines adolescence in its worldwide context. Our comparative perspective highlights the ways in which the circumstances of adolescents in any single society are linked to trends that are common across societies. Although the social trends described in this volume affect all regions of the globe, special attention is directed to postindustrial societies, such as those in Europe, North America, and Japan. A companion volume, *The World's Youth*, focuses on the current state of adolescents in eight regions, including the developing world: the Arab states, Sub-Saharan Africa, Russia, India, Southeast Asia, East Asia, Latin America, and Europe and North America (Brown, Larson, & Saraswathi, 2002).

In this introductory chapter, we provide an overview of major societal changes that will influence adolescents in the future, and we consider some of the ways that they are likely to reshape adolescence in the decades ahead. We begin with a brief description of key macrostructural changes and then describe their impacts on adolescents' experiences.

MACROLEVEL CHANGES IN SOCIETY

Social scientists who study adolescence typically focus on the immediate contexts of their day-to-day experience, especially the family, school, and peer group, and, more recently, the workplace (Call & Mortimer, 2001). Neglected are the broader institutional forces and currents of societal change that affect the experiences adolescents have within these microsystems of development. It has been demonstrated, however, that societal changes can dramatically alter what happens within specific contexts (Elder, 1974). Modell (1989), for example, shows how dramatic changes in the dating patterns of U.S. adolescents in the early 20th century resulted from the increased availability of automobiles, as well as changing attitudes toward heterosexual relationships. In this section we introduce key macrostructural and institutional changes that are likely to impact strongly adolescents' lives in the future: patterns of demographic change; economic restructuring and globalization; institutional shifts, including school, work, and the links between them; criminal justice reforms; and trends in health-services delivery.

Demographic Change

To time travelers from the past, one of the most striking features of postindustrial societies – once they got beyond all our gizmos – would be the comparatively small number of children and youth and the large number of elderly. There is little doubt that this aging of the population will continue into the 21st century, changing society and bringing new issues to the fore. The nations of North America, Europe, and Japan have rapidly growing older populations that are dependent on economically active adults. In general, the economically active, adult population is shrinking relative to those who are economically dependent, including both younger and older generations. Therefore, investment in youth who will become the adults of the future deserves special attention.

An intergenerational contract, in which the older generation invests in the young, is the basis for social continuity in any society. Yet the exacerbation of competition between young and elderly in the distribution of resources is increasingly problematic in aging societies, especially those where the number of adults entering the productive labor force is shrinking. The following chapter by Fussell asks how this state of competition for scarce resources can be resolved. How can youth be enabled to move forward into adulthood, well equipped to deal with their economic and other adult roles, while the welfare of the elderly is not shortchanged? Her chapter suggests that postindustrial nations are at a crucial choice point; the future of young people – and ultimately society – hangs in the balance.

Fussell suggests that immigration from overpopulated to underpopulated societies may be a means to alleviate the labor shortages and resultant economic problems of aging nations. Indeed, that is a path being taken by the United States, where current immigration rates are high. But to date, receiving societies have been ambivalent about these new immigrants and their families, welcoming their labor but often posing restrictions on their continued residence and access to essential services (such as health care; see Ozer et al., this volume) and subjecting them to prejudice and discrimination. Immigrant adolescents may become exemplars of marginality: attached to the cultures and ways of life of their origin countries while at the same time attempting to be successful in their new environments, especially in school and work. Youth's increasing ethnic diversity may also exacerbate tensions between the dependent aging "majority" population and the younger "minority" population on which they will depend for their welfare, undermining the intergenerational contract.

At a more psychological level, changing demographic patterns create uncertainties for both majority and minority adolescents. Falling birth rates, delayed parenthood, divorce rates that have stabilized at high levels, and the proliferation of alternate lifestyles (e.g., cohabiting couples, single person households) can generate uncertainty for adolescents as they ponder their futures. For example, it is no longer realistic for an adolescent girl to expect to be supported as a homemaker by an employed husband to be and married for a lifetime. In the absence of clear guidelines, young men and women alike must navigate occupational choice and seek work-family balance in societies that are structured in many ways as if the "traditional" family still predominated (Johnson & Mortimer, 2000). Youth's responses to these dilemmas, in their own work and family behavior, will shape both the character of adolescence and the demographic realities of the future.

Economic Changes

The globalization of the economy, accelerated by new communication technologies, poses another set of changing realities, challenges, and opportunities for adolescents as they prepare for their occupational futures. Diminishing market barriers, increasing crossnational flows of goods and services, and growing global competition put pressures on businesses worldwide to decrease costs and reduce worker protections. This changing and more competitive business climate, coupled with rapid changes in the nature of work, make it increasingly likely that the future job market – for which adolescents are trying to prepare – cannot be accurately foreseen. Local job markets in the West can disappear in a year or two, as entire industries are suddenly exported to developing countries. Economic change is especially likely to affect young people because they are transitioning into the labor force, have relatively short tenures of employment, and limited job security.

This process of transition into the workforce, however, depends on how the institutions of education and work are organized and connected to one another within a nation. The chapter by Kerckhoff points out that some postindustrial societies provide well-constructed links between school and work, such as the apprenticeship system in Germany, Austria, and Switzerland. These give young people marketable educational credentials and provide clear institutional bridges into the labor market. In other nations, like the United States and Canada, young school-leavers must find their way into the full-time labor force mostly on their own.

The situation in these North American countries creates a context for relatively turbulent school-to-work transitions. The absence of institutional connections between school and work, and the provision of general rather than vocationally specific educational credentials, leaves youth ill-prepared. After finishing school, many American young people flounder from job to job, experiencing bouts of unemployment and many job changes. Turbulent transitions into the workforce are particularly prevalent among young people who do not obtain a four-year college degree, and this is likely to be even more true in the future.

As income differences between the highly educated (college or higher) and high school graduates grow, ever-increasing proportions of youth seek higher education, hoping to take their places as highly favored "information workers" in the global economy. However, large numbers of youth are not successful in completing the B.A. degree. Kerckhoff's proposals to strengthen the connections between school and work and to establish more occupationally relevant, educational credentials could ameliorate the economic strains of this period of life, especially for youth whose success in the educational system is limited.

While these recommendations are particularly pertinent to North American youth, whose bridges to work are the least structured among societies worldwide, they are increasingly germane in other nations as well. Links between school and work that have operated effectively in other postindustrial societies are under pressure in recent years as a result of global competition, technological change, and periodic economic recession. For example, traditional bridges between high schools and corporate employers are weakening in Japan, as economic recession has reduced the number of job openings. Many Japanese youth must find jobs on their own, like North American young people (Brinton, 2000). Similarly, German youth are responding to the tightening of labor markets by increasing the number of occupational qualifications they obtain, and by taking alternative and prolonged routes from education into the labor force (Mortimer & Krüger, 2000).

Accelerated technical and occupational change in the future may make it increasingly difficult for educational institutions to provide training that is fitted to a fluid and shifting labor market. For this reason, Kerckhoff and others have advocated closer communication between schools and employers. Fussell argues that the greatest need is not for more years of general postsecondary education but for better systems to match training to changing job opportunities.

Institutional Systems

Changes in service provision, in both governmental and nongovernmental sectors, represent another set of transformations affecting adolescent experience. Reviewing trends across nations of the world, Inglehart (1997) observes that postindustrial societies are experiencing a shift to "postmodern" values that include diminishing faith in the ability of large, hierarchical national bureaucracies to deliver social services. The demise of communist governments, the reduction of social welfare states in Northern Europe, and the diminution of welfare in the United States reflect a pessimism about the ability of big government to improve people's lives. In its place, governments are experimenting with privatization, public-private partnerships, voucher systems, and other alternative means to provide services. At the same time, the number of nongovernmental organizations aimed at addressing social service needs has been rapidly expanding (Salamon, 1995).

Provision of juvenile justice is one area where pessimism about the potential of government to ameliorate problems has won out, at least for the present. In the face of juvenile crime, including violent crime, the United States as well as a number of European societies have abandoned a liberal rehabilitative philosophy and have replaced it with one aimed at punishment and the protection of society from the perceived threat of juvenile offenders. The chapter by Cullen and Wright documents how increasing numbers of youth in the United States have been placed in the criminal justice system while diminishing efforts have been made to alter the conditions, both personal and social, that led to juvenile offenses. They argue that the change in philosophy may partly be due to the high numbers of Black and Hispanic youth in the adjudicated populations; the voting public is more likely to view these minority offenders as predators to be locked up than wayward youth to put straight. This crossgenerational racism echoes warnings from Fussell's chapter about schisms in the social contract between young and old.

The one ray of hope in this domain of government is that there have been a proliferation of experiments on alternative means of treating offenders and some, albeit uneven, use of research findings to shape policy. Many of the experiments in the United States have been based on the punitive philosophy, such as "scare straight" programs and boot camps, and the results have not been promising. But Cullen and Wright point to an increasing body of research that begins to identify the positive effects of specific rehabilitative programs for certain categories of offenders, including violent offenders. Their synthesis of the evidence suggests the merit of rethinking punitive strategies; rehabilitative interventions have the potential to reduce recidivism and other negative outcomes. One can hope, both for society and for the next generation, that the path of the future for the provision of juvenile justice will be toward "smart government" based on empirical evaluation of the outcomes associated with alternative treatments.

The trends in health care for adolescents reflect changes in governmental and nongovernmental systems that have been more responsive to the needs of youth. Focusing on the United States, the chapter by Ozer et al. shows that federal expenditures for adolescent health care have been increasing over the last decade. There is increased institutional momentum to create systems – such as the Children's Health Insurance Program (CHIP) – that deliver services to the young, including poor youth. They also point to increased use of the Internet and other information systems by health care providers to deliver information and supervise care that is fitted to the lifestyles of adolescents. For example, some health care providers are experimenting with the use of e-mail "ticklers" that prompt adolescents to get vaccinations or to make follow-up appointments for counseling on identified risk behaviors.

The future of health care for adolescents, however, is by no means secure. The efficacy of state-run medical systems of Europe and Canada is of continuing concern as rising costs of medical care collide with neoliberal fiscal conservatism. In the United States, the growing use of "managed care" is hardly a panacea. As Ozer et al. report, the patchwork system for financing medical care in the United States leaves many young people, especially minority youth in the age 15–25 age group, without health insurance. An optimist might predict that research knowledge will eventually lead to leaner but also smarter, more equal, and more customized delivery of educational, health, and criminal justice services to youth, but that outcome is by no means certain.

Again, the willingness of an aging majority population to devote resources to an increasingly minority young population looms as a threat to the health of future generations. Prospects of weakening the "social gradient in health" – the social class differences in health status that often emerge in late adolescence and early adulthood (Harley, 2001; Harley &

Mortimer, 2000; House et al., 1990) – are less likely under conditions of unequal access to health services.

Space did not permit us to include chapters on the many other institutional systems that provide services to youth, many of which are also experiencing fundamental change, crosspressures, and controversy. The institution of education may be considered a case in point. Across the world, educational institutions are under pressure as they attempt to cope with new knowledge about adolescent development, new conceptions of what this phase of life should be like, and constantly shifting global realities. For example, in an attempt to make secondary schools more responsive to the needs of adolescents, the Japanese government has cut back on school hours and has reduced the number of courses and tests required for graduation from high school; yet a private sector of supplementary *Juko* schools that make life stressful for many teens continues to flourish. Some important consequences of these trends are unintended and controversial, such as increasing socioeconomic disparities among youth in academic effort (Kariya and Rosenbaum, Forthcoming). In U.S. schools, issues of school choice, sex education, and drug education create battlegrounds on which debates between those promoting interventionist or noninterventionist philosophies, public versus private provision of services, and other controversies recur with adolescents' futures in the balance.

New Technology and Technology-Based Systems

Rapid technological change is yet another major factor that is certain to transform the lives of adolescents in the future. The increasingly rapid development and dissemination of new technologies, especially ICT (information and communication technologies) are restructuring the adolescent experience in pervasive and profound ways. Technological change underlies shifts in the occupational structure, educational demands, and the health care system, which we have discussed, as well as shifts in numerous other aspects of life that we have not discussed, from the kinds of entertainments adolescents' enjoy to their modes of relating to one another. In order to succeed in school and work, to have access to information of all kinds, and to participate broadly in the social and recreational adolescent subculture, adolescents must be computer literate and capable of regular retooling their technological knowledge as new technologies emerge.

Technological diffusion and its impact on adolescence are clearly global in character, with youth in remote corners of the world connected to one another and to information about how their more and less affluent peers elsewhere live. As the chapter by Anderson shows, young people throughout the world are increasingly online, despite a persistent digital divide in computer access crossnationally and socioeconomically. He also points out that the information available online is not well organized or evaluated, suggesting a critical need for adolescents to develop skills in navigating through this complex world. Extrapolating to the future, Anderson provides a glimpse of the potentials likely to arise as a result of ever-increasing speed and technological capacity, from digital implants that permit health and global positioning system (GPS) monitoring of youth, to cell-based computing devices, to improvements in instant translation that will allow adolescents to cross linguistic barriers and connect to ever-widening social worlds.

Technology's greatest impact, Boulding (1995) argues, consists of the human systems that develop around it. This is nowhere more true than with the Internet. Its physical capacities to store, retrieve, and exchange information are awe inspiring. But far more significant are the new communication patterns and life worlds that are evolving within it. Whereas Anderson examines the diffusion and increasing potentials of new technologies, Hellenga's chapter focuses on the evolution of the Internet as a new "social space" for adolescent life. She shows that the new worlds opened by – and being created by – youth alter adolescents' recreation and leisure time pursuits, peer relations, self-concepts, and, potentially, mental health. Increasingly, adolescents' communications with one another, even with close friends, are mediated by technology. With instant messaging, palm pilots, diverse portals to Internet chat rooms, multiple-player games, and other diversions, adolescents need never be alone. The buzz word is "connectivity," and it is clear that new generations of youth who have access to ICT will be connected to people and information as never before.

RESHAPING ADOLESCENCE

All of these macrostructural trends, in subtle and direct ways, are reshaping and reconstructing adolescence. As adult roles change in response to rapidly changing technologies, shifting occupational structures, and the increasingly global cultural and economic context, the requirements for effective preparation for adulthood change accordingly. At the same time, the system of supports available to youth – through governmental and nongovernmental systems, the Internet, families, and so forth – are also changing, altering the kinds of resources that they can draw on as they prepare to become adults.

The array of current and potential changes in adolescent experience are too numerous to do justice to here. They are observable throughout the modern world. In a separate volume, we examine the implications of change worldwide on key domains of adolescent functioning, including interpersonal skills, civic engagement, preparation for work, and well-being (Larson, Brown, & Mortimer, 2002). Here we focus on two general trends that affect all of these domains: the lengthening of the adolescent period and the increasing diversity among young people in the paths they take to adulthood.

Lengthening of the Adolescent Transition

The macroforces we have reviewed contribute to the delay of several transitions that typically mark the onset of adulthood. For many youth, the transition out of school occurs at older ages as they extend their years of education. Advances in technology require youth to attain more years of schooling to obtain the more desirable jobs. As Kerckhoff points out, appreciating economic returns make higher education increasingly attractive to adolescents as well as to their parents who are called on to provide continued support. Smaller family size and the growing affluence of the population have enabled the families of young people (at least those in the middle class) to invest in the development of their "human capital." While youth must postpone the economic rewards that derive from full-time labor force participation, their prospects for future economic well-being are enhanced. As a result, across postindustrial societies, the proportions of youth obtaining college and postgraduate degrees have been increasing over many decades, with no end in sight.

In addition to prolonged education, other key markers of the transition to adulthood have been postponed, including acquisition of full-time work, marriage, and childbearing. Fussell attributes these delays to the increased instability of entry positions in the labor market, to the erosion of arranged marriage in East Asia, and, across cultures, to growing individualism. Whereas the timing of these life transitions were socially scripted by cultural norms in the recent past (Modell, 1989; Modell,

Furstenberg, & Hershberg, 1976), contemporary society is less prescriptive. In Japan, over 50% of young women remain unmarried at age 30, most working, living with their parents, and enjoying freedoms not available to them were they to marry (Orenstein, 2001). But we should also stress that for many youth the situation is not so free. American youth who do not obtain college credentials often find themselves in a "revolving door" of low paying and unstable jobs, which are usually insufficient to support a family (Kerckhoff, this volume).

It must be emphasized, that although the various transitions marking adulthood have tended to occur at older ages, the ordering of the transition markers have also become more variable (Buchmann, 1989; Shanahan 2000), leading to greater complexity and uncertainty in the experience of this time of life. Fewer young people are becoming adults in what might be considered a traditional, normatively prescribed sequence of events, that is, leaving home and finishing their educations, acquiring full-time jobs, marrying, and having children. Instead, these sequences have become more variable or "disorderly" (Rindfuss et al., 1987). The growth of cohabitation is accompanied by a more frequent decoupling of marriage and childbearing (Fussell, this volume). There are more frequent reversals in trajectories, such as leaving home and then returning or entering full-time work and then reenrolling in school.

For some, this is a period of liminality during which their connections to social institutions are weak, ambiguous, and shifting. They frequently change jobs, housing, familial arrangements, social milieus, and lifestyles. The prolongation and unpredictable character of the late adolescent period give rise to increasing uncertainty about the ending of this phase. As young people go to school and postpone entry to adult roles for longer periods, up to and sometimes beyond the third decade of life, their experiences may become inconsistent, their age status blurred. They may be considered to be adults in some respects and may bear some responsibilities of adulthood (for example, being a parent) while they are still "adolescent" in other respects (e.g., living at home and still economically dependent, at least partially, on their parents).

As a result of these trends, a new phase of "postadolescence," "youth," or what Arnett (2000) has called "emerging adulthood" has been identified. Arnett considers this early 20-something phase as, above all, a period of individual volition, when young people explore different lifestyles, change residence more frequently than people in any other age group, and experiment with intimate relationships, types of work, and worldviews. However, the long period of transition to adulthood, with its numerous changes in life circumstances, may reflect constrained circumstances as much or more than individual choice. Indeed, the contemporary U.S. economy offers many contemporary young people who lack college degrees mainly nonstandard, "contingent" work that is temporary, part-time, or otherwise limited by contract (see Kerckhoff, this volume).

Thus, although some herald this new period as a time of unprecedented opportunity for identity development and human capital development prior to assuming full adult responsibilities, others worry that young people must make choices that will have lasting consequences for their life trajectories in work, family, and other spheres in the absence of adult guidance and institutional structuring (Kerckhoff, this volume; Hamilton, 1990). For many youth, this is a period of vulnerability, when low wages and lack of health care put them at risk. To make matters worse, it is an age period in which many risk behaviors peak (Arnett, 2000). This combination of experimentation, instability, and risk points to the second increasingly prominent feature in the reconstruction of adolescence.

Diversity in Adolescence and the Paths to Adulthood

We have already noted the increasing variability in the paths taken both within and out of adolescence and emerging adulthood. What remains to be emphasized is the ways in which differences in family wealth, and other inequities affecting access to resources, influence the paths young people take. Shaped within the competitive ethos of postindustrial capitalism, the new adolescence is a period of high stakes in which access to resources is critical in shaping both options and constraints. Multiple bases of inequality – related to gender, ethnicity, immigrant status, family socioeconomic status, and other factors – engender tremendous diversity in the capacity of youth to make choices and choose life paths.

Family income is a foremost factor in differentiating the paths taken through this transitional period. Family wealth affects adolescents' access to information technology and thus their development of ICT skills that are increasingly crucial to education, communication, and employment. As Youniss and Ruth (this volume) argue, "Denial of access, whether by design or neglect, is tantamount to relegating some youth to secondary status in the competitive job market." Family wealth also affects access to higher education – particularly in the United States – which affects the types of jobs young people eventually get. As

Kerckhoff points out, those without a college degree are more likely to find themselves in a low-paying and unstable labor pool, with limited options. Like the "upstairs borders," vagrants, and "maids" of the 19th century, they may find themselves stuck in situations that society may view as subadult. Based on recent societal trends, it is plausible to assume that the experience of transition to adulthood will become increasingly *differentiated* with growing economic inequality (Kerckhoff, this volume) and diminishing rates of social class mobility across generations.

Youth who are disadvantaged in one way are likely to be disadvantaged in others. In many cases lower family income is more frequent among ethnic minorities, including new immigrants, and the disadvantages of low income are magnified by other types of discrimination. We have already noted that the majority populations of many countries are ambivalent in their support of initiatives to enhance the lives of immigrant and minority youth. Cullen and Wright show that contact with the criminal justice system is a highly prevalent experience in adolescence and the transition to adulthood and, in the United States, it disproportionally affects minority youth, especially African American youth. As a result, difficulties of obtaining jobs following incarceration are compounded by minority status and discrimination.

This multiplication of disadvantage is also evident in the domain of health. Ozer et al. note the prevalence of comorbidities: disabling conditions, both mental and physical, often occur together. Adolescents who have learning disabilities and or mental and physical health problems that impair their abilities to climb the educational ladder will be disadvantaged. The growing difficulties in paths to adulthood as disadvantage and stressors accumulate pose daunting challenges to educators and youth service providers to enhance youth resilience under conditions of adversity.

Finally, if migration between societies quickens – as is likely – in response to worldwide differentials in population density, economic well-being, and standards of living (Fussell, this volume), increasingly diverse experiences of adolescence will coexist within single societies, as new cultural groups, with widely divergent economic and other resources, come in contact with one another and attempt to accommodate to the opportunities and constraints they face in their new homes. The growing diversity of societies, linked to expanding social inequality as well as to immigration, challenge youth to develop higher levels of empathy, tolerance, and interpersonal skills.

In sum, the dawn of the 21st century may be considered both the best of times and the worst of times for youth, a time of ominous trends as well as new opportunities. The great expansion of adult life patterns and options among which adolescents can choose presents an array of rich but often bewildering opportunities. Those who live in the more affluent, postindustrial societies and those who are positioned in the more advantaged social classes, ethnic groups, and other social locations within them can take advantage of expanding educational options, new technologies, and distance learning that will heighten both their human and their social capital as they enter the labor force and other adult roles. They will have a lengthened period for maturation and exploration that will increase the likelihood that they will make well-informed vocational choices and enter stable and satisfying intimate, and familial, relationships. They will become well equipped to contribute to the civic life of their communities.

But these same changes also create new "have nots." Other adolescents have less entrée to the rich options for personal development in this transitional period. They have fewer resources and less access to the manifold opportunities that would allow them to fully develop in this longer, more diversified, and often more competitive adolescence. Some youth leave school before obtaining the educational credentials needed to obtain jobs that allow economic sufficiency and health benefits, have little access to computers and other technological innovations, experience stigmatizing criminal justice attention, or bear children early and incur numerous psychological, social, and economic risks in doing so. Unless steps can be taken to level access to opportunities, many youth will become increasingly disadvantaged.

CONCLUSION: YOUTH'S AND ADULTS' ROLES IN SHAPING THE FUTURE

What is clear is that, across social strata, rapid social and institutional changes place a premium on youth's initiative, creativity, and ability to navigate a multidimensional labyrinth of choices and demands. For both rich and poor, the future puts greater responsibility onto their plates, requiring them to be volitional and agentic as they manage diverse components of fiscal, human, and social capital. Of foremost importance, they must be proficient in gathering information and putting it to use.

The concluding social policy chapter by Youniss and Ruth stresses the active role adolescents play in shaping both their individual futures and the future of society. They draw on dramatic historic examples of young people's important contributions to political change. The myriad choices of ordinary adolescents, little concerned with political struggles and having little awareness or exposure to social movement activism, also affect their societies' futures. Fussell shows that through their fertility decisions young people determine the future age structure of society, with its numerous ramifications. Adolescents are not passive recipients of macrosocietal change, they are actors within it. In some cases they create it. Adolescence is above all a period in which youth are required to be agents, to find their own paths, and, within the set of constraints and opportunities available to them, to mold themselves in ways that enable them to obtain the adulthoods they desire.

This new volitional adolescence, as Youniss and Ruth point out, shifts the role of parents and others who want to assist youth to that of providing support and guidance – in helping them to marshal resources to find their way in the labyrinth. The role of parents for the new adolescence is that of managers, who find information, make contacts, help structure choices, and provide guidance that helps youth avoid pitfalls and work their way through the myriad of choices (Furstenberg et al., 1999). This important contribution of parents creates another separation of "haves and have nots." Those youth who receive this type of navigational support from parents are likely to be highly advantaged over those who for whatever reason do not (i.e., parents are estranged, dead, too busy, or lack the knowledge or capability). A clear resource needed by young people in the 21st century is for help lines, advisors, career counselors, and enduring relationships with caring adults who can help them through the maze of information and options.

As several of the chapters in this volume attest, the macrolevel forces shaping adolescents' access to pathways of opportunity can be modified, arrested, or deflected by social interventions, including the actions of government and the leaders of key social institutions. Neither a Marxian economic determinism nor a Malthusian population determinism are tenable. As Fussell suggests, governments can affect the redistribution of wealth through welfare, taxation, and other policies, so as to ameliorate the economic distress of minority and immigrant populations, as well as other economically depressed segments of the population. Similarly, Kerckhoff notes that educational policy can either equalize or exacerbate the differences in knowledge, skills, and credentials that enable youth to succeed in the economic sphere.

An important social policy implication of these chapters is that increasing attention should be given to the needs of young people in their 20s. The lengthening of adolescence and the development of the liminal period of emerging adulthood intensify the need for support at this time of life. Whereas vocational psychologists have traditionally focused on the second decade of life as the critical period for the formation of vocational identity and career choice, serious occupational engagement and decision making are increasingly being postponed well into the third decade of life. This is also an age period when Americans are most likely to have no health insurance, a deficiency that must be addressed.

Youniss and Ruth point to the need to shift the focus of education to the learning of "re-programmable skills." It is becoming less important for secondary and higher education to provide a curriculum of fixed knowledge. Given rapid social, occupational, and technological change, successful young people (and adults) must be taught how to learn and continually relearn as they adapt to changing institutional structures. They must be provided the general knowledge and skills that will enable them to exercise agency as they attempt to achieve their goals in the context of ever-changing social realities. What is critical is that young people enjoy learning, know how to find information, and are able to think creatively in new situations.

As Youniss and Ruth point out, the positive and negative scenarios set forth by the authors of the chapters in this volume highlight the responsibility of adults to move adolescent futures in the more salutary directions. It is our hope that this volume will extend the boundaries of thinking about adolescence and adolescent futures, sensitize adolescent researchers to macrostructural variability and its impacts on adolescent experience, and increase awareness of growing inequalities. Young people have tremendous potential to shape productive futures for themselves and contribute to society if we give them the knowledge, opportunities, and support they need, and then stand out of their way.

References

Arnett, J. (2000). Emerging adulthood: A theory of development from the late teens through the twenties. *American Psychologist, 55, 5,* 469–480.

Boulding, K. (1995). Expecting the unexpected: The uncertain future of knowledge and technology. In E. Boulding & K. Boulding (eds.), *The Future: Images and Processes* (pp. 7–25). Thousand Oaks, CA: Sage Publications.

Brinton, M. C. (2000). Social capital in the Japanese youth labor market: Labor market policy, schools, and norms. *Policy Sciences, 33,* 3–4, 289–306.

Brown, B. B., Larson, R., & Saraswathi, T. S. (eds.) (2002). *The World's Youth: Adolescence in Eight Regions of the Globe.* New York: Cambridge University Press. In press.

Buchmann, M. (1989). *The Script of Life in Modern Society.* Chicago: University of Chicago Press.

Call, K. T., & Mortimer, J. T. (2001). *Arenas of Comfort in Adolescence: A Study of Adjustment in Context*. Mahwah, NJ: Lawrence Erlbaum.

Elder, G. H., Jr. (1974). *Children of the Great Depression*. Chicago: University of Chicago Press.

Furstenberg, F. F., Cook, T. D., Eccles, J., Elder, G. H., & Sameroff, A. (1999). *Managing to Make It: Urban Families and Adolescent Success*. Chicago: The University of Chicago Press.

Hamilton, S. F. (1990). *Apprenticeship for Adulthood: Preparing Youth for the Future*. New York: Free Press.

Harley, C. R. (2001). The social gradient in health: Social capital, human capital, and the transition to adulthood. Doctoral dissertation, University of Minnesota.

Harley, C. R., & Mortimer, J. T. (2000). Social status and mental health in young adulthood: The mediating role of the transition to adulthood. Biennial Meeting of the Society for Research on Adolescence. Chicago, March 30–April 2, 2000.

House, J. S., Kessler, R. C., Herzog, A. R., Mero, R. P., Kinney, A. M., & Breslow, M. J. (1990). Age, socioeconomic status, & health. *The Milbank Quarterly*, 68, 3, 383–411.

Inglehart, R. (1997). *Modernization and Postmodernization: Cultural, Economic, and Political Change in 43 Societies*. Princeton, NJ: Princeton University Press.

Johnson, M. K., & Mortimer, J. T. (2000). Work-family orientations and attainments in the early life course. In T. L. Parcel & D. B. Cornfield (eds.), *Work and Family: Research Informing Policy* (pp. 215–248). Thousand Oaks, CA: Sage Publications.

Kariya, T., & Rosenbaum, J. E. (Forthcoming). The incentive divide: Stratified incentives and life course behaviors. In J. T. Mortimer & M. Shanahan (eds.), *Handbook of the Life Course*. New York: Plenum Publishers.

Larson, R., Brown, B. B., & Mortimer, J. (eds.) (2002). Adolescence in the 21st Century [special issue] *Journal of Research on Adolescence*, 12 (1).

Modell, J., Furstenberg, F., & Hershberg, T. (1976). Social change and transitions to adulthood in historical perspective. *Journal of Family History*, 1, 1, 7–32.

Modell, J. (1989). *Into One's Own*. Berkeley: University of California Press.

Mortimer, J. T., & Krueger, H. (2000). School to work in the United States and Germany: Formal pathways matter. In M. Hallinan (ed.), *Handbook of the Sociology of Education*. New York: Kluwer Academic/Plenum Publishers.

Orenstein, P. (2001). Parasites in Prêt-à-Porter. *New York Times Magazine*, July 1, 30–35.

Rindfuss, R. R., Swicegood, C. G., & Rosenfeld, R. A. (1987). Disorder in the life course: How common and does it matter? *American Sociological Review*, 52, 6, 785–801.

Salamon, L. M. (1995). *Partners in Public Service: Government-Nonprofit Relations in the Modern Welfare State*. Baltimore: Johns Hopkins University Press.

Shanahan, M. (2000). Pathways to adulthood in changing societies: Variability and mechanisms in life course perspective. *Annual Review of Sociology*, 26, 667–692.

2

Youth in Aging Societies

Elizabeth Fussell

What will the future of youth in aging societies be? Some scholars view the unprecedented aging of the population in advanced industrial countries as a crisis for youth. Others look toward the reorganization of industrial society to post-industrial society and see great hope for the future, with youth playing an important role as the bearers of cutting-edge human capital. I suggest that the future of youth depends on the state of the intergenerational contract. This social contract commits adults to nurture and invest in youth and commits grown children to provide for their aged parents. This implicit agreement applies in both private families and in society at large through public welfare systems that provide, to varying degrees, support to the elderly and children. As more and more people live into old age, this arrangement potentially places a heavy burden on working-age adults and especially parents of young children, who are both contributing to pension systems, and possibly contributing to the care of their own parents, while raising their own children. The public aspect of this contract is manifested in the welfare state and labor market institutions that determine how earnings are redistributed from workers to economic dependents, and the private aspect through similar within-family exchanges.

The question I raise in this chapter is whether demographic circumstances and social arrangements in advanced industrial societies will be able to continue to support this intergenerational contract, or will the demographic shift in the age structure of the population cause the contract to break down? I draw on research from North America, Europe, and the economically advanced countries of East Asia. First I describe the process of population aging and examine the demographic basis for the argument that population aging increases competition between youth and the elderly. Advocates of this point of view argue that population aging will shift more social resources to the retired population and away from children and youth (Preston 1984). Though the intergenerational competition argument primarily applies to children ranging from ages 0 to 18, the ages of greatest economic dependency, it also applies to young adults (ages 19 to 29) or those in the phase of "emerging adulthood" when youth are preparing themselves for the full responsibilities of adulthood (Arnett 2000). In the next section I discuss research on why youth increasingly delay the assumption of (demographically measurable) adult roles. I argue that the new societal regime based on human capital endowments calls for a renewed commitment to investing in youth and minimizing the potential for intergenerational competition (OECD 2001). Indeed, the fortunes of future generations will be more equitably distributed within and between age segments of the population if the intergenerational contract is preserved and adapted to society's older age structure.

THE DEMOGRAPHICS OF POPULATION AGING

In order to understand how population aging may affect future youth cohorts, we must first understand what causes the population to age. The age structure of a population results from the fertility, mortality, and migration experience of a society over the previous eighty years or so. Fertility adds to the population by contributing new birth cohorts,[1] and mortality subtracts from the population by removing people from all age groups. In most advanced industrial countries, life expectancy is quite long because many causes of death have been minimized. Along with the decline in mortality, these countries have experienced a long-term downward trend in fertility to the point that their populations are no longer growing very quickly, and in some cases they are even shrinking. In 2000, all advanced industrial countries are projected to have below-replacement fertility (2.1 children per woman given age-specific fertility rates is the replacement level) with the exception of the United States (Figure 2.1). In other words, women are having fewer

---

[1] A birth cohort consists of all the people born within a defined period of time, usually five or ten years.

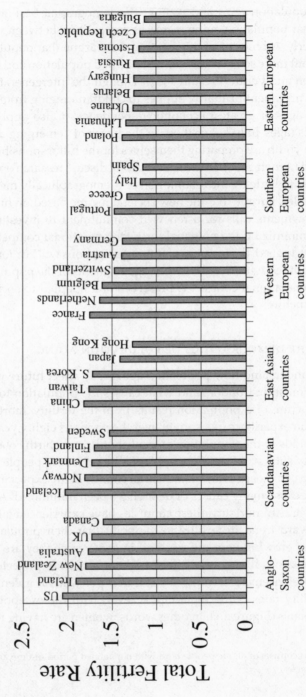

FIGURE 2.1. Total fertility rates in selected advanced industrialized countries, 2000. *Source:* U.S. Census Bureau International Database, 2001.

children than would be required in order to replace themselves and their male partners, making population decline inevitable unless sufficient numbers of immigrants compensate for falling fertility.

Once a population begins to decrease, the process is difficult to reverse since each birth cohort is smaller than the previous one and members of those smaller birth cohorts are unlikely to have more children than their parents on average. They are more likely to maintain low fertility levels, thus perpetuating the low fertility regime. This results in nearly rectangular, or even inverted, age-sex population "pyramids" (Figure 2.2). For example, in Italy, an extremely low fertility country, the age-sex structure of the population is narrowing at the bottom, which will result in a decline in total population after 2000 because those dying are not being replaced by newborns. In the United States, in contrast, there are bumps in the age-sex distribution as a result of the baby boom, the birth dearth, and the echo of the baby boom. These bumps are expected to even out (unless some other event causes a boom or bust in births) so that by 2050 there will be a nearly rectangular age-sex distribution assuming that the population continues to experience near replacement-level fertility.[2] But fertility rates ultimately depend on the behavior of future generations of youth.

The processes underlying the prolongation of the period of youth are poorly understood, but are certain to impact fertility levels in industrialized countries. Bongaarts and Bulatao (2000) argue that delays in family formation are a response to temporary social and economic conditions; therefore they expect that fertility will hover around the replacement-level over the long-term. Others view this type of forecast skeptically because there is no theoretical reason to argue that the long-run decline in fertility will end when replacement level fertility is achieved (Demeny 1997). Neither prediction is convincing without understanding the processes underlying the prolongation of youth and the delay in family formation.

The relationship between low fertility and the prolongation of the transition to adulthood clarifies the questions relevant for our topic, the future of youth. Is the delay in the transition to full adulthood a strategy for acquiring the resources necessary to begin family formation? If so, why does it take longer to acquire those resources today than in the past?

---

[2] Migration is less of an influence on the shape of the population pyramid because its effect is spread across two sexes and all the five-year age groups. This is because immigrants enter the pyramid at all ages, not just at age zero as in the case of infants.

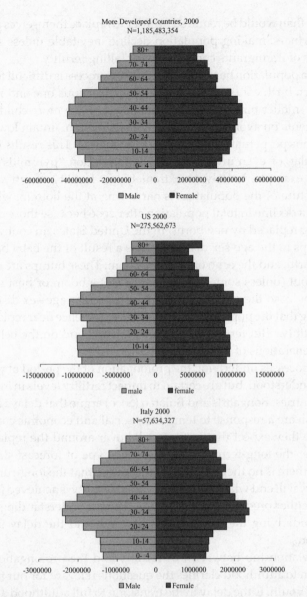

FIGURE 2.2. Age-sex population pyramids for the United States and Italy and for more developed countries, 2000 and 2025. *Source*: U.S. Census Bureau International Database, 2001. *Note*: The more developed countries and areas include all of North America and Europe (including the Baltics and the four European republics of the New Independent States) plus Japan, Australia, and New Zealand (U.S. Census Bureau, 2001). Each rectangle represents the size of the male or female population in a particular five-year age group.

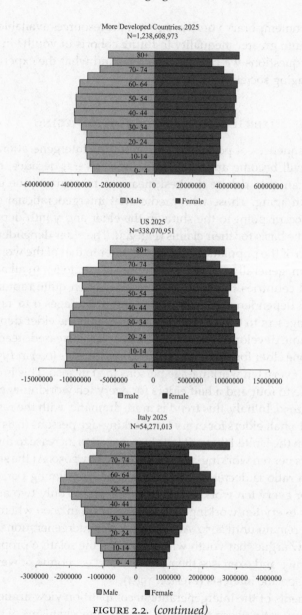

More Developed Countries, 2025
N=1,238,608,973

US 2025
N=338,070,951

Italy 2025
N=54,271,013

FIGURE 2.2. (*continued*)

Is it intergenerational competition or the new economic context in which youth are coming of age that has made this process more prolonged? Furthermore, what sectors of the youthful population are experiencing the greatest difficulties in making this transition? Does inequality between contemporary youth in terms of the resources available to them translate into greater inequality in future cohorts of youth? In answering these questions we can better understand what the experiences of youth in aging societies might be.

IMPLICATIONS OF POPULATION AGING

The consequences of population aging for the intergenerational social contract will become apparent in the next several decades, but until then we can only debate the best means of minimizing the effects of population aging. Those who predict that intergenerational competition will occur point to the shifts in the elder and youth dependency ratios as the basis for their claims (Fig. 2.3). The elder dependency ratio is the ratio of the population age 65 and older to that of the working age population, generally estimated as those ages 15 to 64. In all advanced industrial countries this ratio is increasing, often quite rapidly, while the youth dependency ratio is decreasing (those ages 0 to 14 divided by those ages 15 to 64). In Figure 2.3 we see that the elder dependency ratio in more developed countries (MDCs)[3] has increased steadily from roughly one elder for every ten working-age persons (0.1) in 1950 to two elders for every ten working-age persons (0.2) in 2000. This is expected to increase to four and a half elders for every ten working-age persons (0.45) by 2050. In Italy, this trend is more dramatic, with the ratio rising to six and a half elders for every ten working-age persons (0.65) in 2050, whereas in the United States it is only expected to increase to three and a half elders per ten working-age persons (0.35) by 2050. At the same time the youth ratio is decreasing in MDCs from four young persons ages 0 to 15 for every ten working-age persons (0.4) to only two and a half youth for every ten working-age persons (0.25) in 2000 where it is expected to remain until 2050. Advocates of the intergenerational competition view argue that youth will lose out as the relative proportion of elders grows and exercises their political and economic power in their own age-specific interests (Preston 1984).

Opponents of the intergenerational competition view argue that the dependency ratio doesn't simulate the actual mechanisms of the redistribution of resources. A society's ability to redistribute its resources

---

[3] The more developed countries and areas include all of North America and Europe (including the Baltics and the four European republics of the New Independent States) plus Japan, Australia, and New Zealand (U.S. Census Bureau 2001).

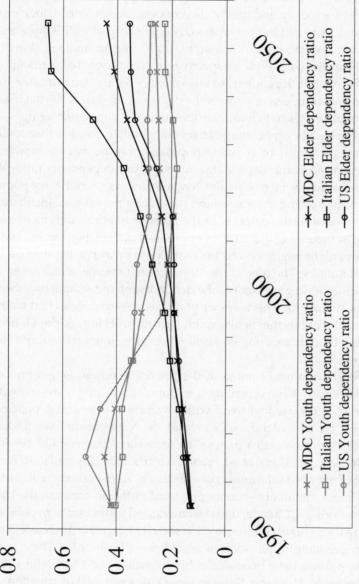

FIGURE 2.3. Youth and elder dependency ratios in more developed countries (MDC), Italy and the United States. *Source:* UN, World Population Prospects, 1998.

Ratio of Youth (0–14) or Elders (65+) to Working Age Population (15–64)

— MDC Youth dependency ratio
— Italian Youth dependency ratio
— US Youth dependency ratio
— MDC Elder dependency ratio
— Italian Elder dependency ratio
— US Elder dependency ratio

depends on the balance between the rate of growth of the productive capacity of a society and that of its economic dependents. Labor supply, that is, the working population, is only one part of this equation, along with capital, natural resources, trade, and technology (Keyfitz 1981; Binstock 1999). Both perspectives acknowledge that a changing ratio of economic dependents to working-age population is a cause for concern; the disagreement is over the degree of concern and what measures should be taken to minimize the impact of population aging.

The dependency ratio suggests several possible changes that could moderate the effects of an aging population on the balance between workers and economic dependents. An increasing dependency ratio can be altered either by increasing the denominator, the working-age population, or decreasing the numerator, the elderly population. Increasing the number of future entrants in the labor market through increased fertility or increasing the number of entrants in the labor market at all ages through immigration can lower the ratio by increasing the size of the denominator. The ratio is also diminished if the age of retirement is raised, thus adding workers to the denominator and subtracting them from the numerator. This measure points us toward policies that maintain a viable equilibrium between children, the working age population, and the retired by focusing on family formation, immigration, and the age of retirement.

As we have already noted in the previous section, long-term declines in fertility have contributed to population aging. Governments have tried to reverse that trend with a variety of pro-natalist policies. Germany, Japan, Finland, Norway, and the Netherlands have undertaken explicit pro-natalist policies by increasing the per-child benefit levels for each additional child. France, Austria, Hungary, and the Czech Republic have tried to be more cost-effective by focusing on specific birth orders, most commonly encouraging third births. In contrast, the UK, Sweden, Portugal, Canada, Italy, Denmark, and Spain ascribe to policies based on the rights of children to some social entitlements, therefore benefits are constant for all children regardless of birth order. The effects of these policies have been negligible (Blanchet and Ekert-Jaffé 1994; Gauthier 1996). However, Sweden received a great deal of attention in the 1980s when fertility levels increased above replacement level in response to a policy encouraging a shorter space between births, but this policy was not sustained in the face of economic reversals in the 1990s (Hoem 1993; Hoem and Hoem 1997).

Policies that facilitate the employment of young mothers through maternal leave with job protection and/or paid leave, child-care provisions, and paternity benefits may also impact the aggregate fertility level. These policies allow women to have additional births without worrying about the loss of income associated with their withdrawal from the labor market. Researchers have demonstrated that in countries with policies that minimize the penalty associated with having a young child, mothers are more likely to continue working (Gornick, Meyers, and Ross 1996). Thus maternal employment policies address two concerns that relate to population aging: they help to maintain a relatively large labor force by allowing women to continue working and they support fertility.

However, promoting fertility is not sufficient for countries that are facing population decline as a result of population aging. Some of these countries are considering more radical measures for countering population decline, namely recruiting international migrants to replace the population that they are "losing" as a result of low fertility rates (UN 2000; PDR 2000). This solution would mean reversing the anti-immigrant policies that exist in countries such as Germany, Japan, and Italy.

The countries aging most rapidly, such as Italy, Japan, and the Republic of Korea would need a level of migration much higher than that experienced in the recent past to offset population decline. For example, Japan would need 343,000, and Italy would need 251,000 immigrants annually to maintain their current population size (UN 2000). In contrast, the United States would need only 128,000 per year, a number far lower than recent rates of immigration (around 860,000 annually in the 1990s) (IOM 2000). Ironically, migration policy in the 1990s in the countries of the European Union (EU) has been focused on allowing greater movement within the EU but limiting immigration into the EU, especially from former colonies. This has had the effect of increasing *illegal* immigration from Eastern Europe and the Middle East to the Central European nations of Germany, Switzerland, and Austria and from North Africa and the Middle East to France (Massey, Arango, Hugo, Kouaouci, Pellegrino, and Taylor 1998). Meanwhile, net *legal* migration into the EU declined from over a million in 1990 to less than 400,000 in 1998 (Eurostat 1999). Whether they arrive legally or illegally, the presence of immigrants in industrialized countries is likely to increase in the next decades. Nations can welcome and invest in immigrant families, thus facilitating their incorporation into their new society, or they can marginalize them and perpetuate their status as second-class citizens.

Relaxing anti-immigrant policies may facilitate the slowing of population aging, an effect that may minimize intergenerational competition, but it will also create a more diverse youthful population. How immigrants adapt to their new homes depends on the policies of the receiving nations and the attitudes of residents toward their new compatriots. We can look toward the United States and see that future generations of youth will be far more racially and ethnically diverse in the next fifty years as a result of recent high immigration rates, but they will be geographically concentrated along race and ethnic lines (Massey 1995). Recent immigrants in the United States have been received with different degrees of welcome depending on their country of origin and the skills they bring with them (Tienda and Raijman 1999). Immigrants' "illegal" status, a sign of their reception in the host country, is one of the sources of disadvantage they carry with them.

Europe is confronting their anti-immigrant policies and sentiments as they face population decline by becoming more open to accepting those without shared ethnic or racial heritage as citizens. For example, in 1999 Germany adopted new legislation facilitating naturalization and providing citizenship to certain children born of immigrant parents. At the same time, immigrants there typically occupy lower socioeconomic status and their children are also disadvantaged in terms of their placement in the educational system (IOM 2000). Though there is variation between European countries, their immigrant policies are far from the pro-immigrant policies more typical of migration-based countries such as Australia, Canada, New Zealand, and the United States.

A third policy reform suggested by the elder dependency ratio is to raise the retirement age. This would mean reversing a trend (since the 1970s) toward earlier retirement in most of the Organization for Economic Cooperation and Development (OECD)[4] countries (OECD 1996). This is a controversial policy reform among those nearing retirement, especially for those with chronic health conditions or without economic resources to support themselves without a full pension. Employers may also object because older workers are often less productive and

---

[4] The OECD countries include Austria, Belgium, Canada, Denmark, France, Germany, Greece, Iceland, Ireland, Italy, Luxembourg, the Netherlands, Norway, Portugal, Spain, Sweden, Switzerland, Turkey, the United Kingdom, the United States, Japan, Australia, New Zealand, Finland, Mexico, the Czech Republic, Hungary, Poland, Korea, and the Slovak Republic.

more costly than younger workers. However, reforms can be made that make the transition from work to retirement more gradual, effectively raising the retirement age while still accommodating the limitations and needs of the oldest workers. The productivity of all workers, but especially older workers, can also be maintained through "lifelong learning" in which workers upgrade their skills, increasing productivity and labor force attachment. Indeed, given the increase in healthful life expectancy since the retirement ages were first established, raising the retirement age may be a first step in renegotiating the intergenerational contract.

Fears of population aging and decline are largely fears of the unknown: we have never before experienced these demographic circumstances. But we do know that population aging is practically irreversible, the best we can do is slow it by promoting fertility and immigration although these will not be sufficient to reverse it (Gauthier 1996; Le Bras 1991; UN 2000). Instead, in our new demographic regime, we must invest more in the smaller and more ethnically diverse cohorts of youth coming of age to ensure that they live healthy productive and reproductive lives and are full-fledged members of society. This requires adapting social institutions that embody the intergenerational contract to ensure that public and private monies are appropriately distributed across age segments of the population to ensure a baseline income for all families with children. In this way the new intergenerational contract should relieve some of the pressure on young adults in the labor force who shoulder the weight of both population reproduction and economic production. In the meantime, youth themselves have adapted their early life course to better assume their growing responsibilities, as we will see in the following sections.

YOUTH AND THE TRANSITION TO ADULTHOOD

We have seen that the aging of the populations of advanced industrial countries poses a potential threat to the intergenerational contract and the circumstances of youth. But as we will see, youth have also adapted to their new demographic and economic circumstances by delaying the transition to adulthood. In this section we ask the question, is the prolonged experience of youth a necessary strategy to acquire resources to complete the transition to adulthood? And why might it take longer to acquire those resources than in the past? To answer this question we consider the activities distinguishing stages of young adulthood. Adolescence spans most of the second decade of life and is a period of economic dependency and knowledge acquisition in which information is accumulated and problem-solving techniques are learned. Adulthood is the stage in which that knowledge is applied (Arnett and Taber 1994). Youth can be defined as the transition period between adolescence and adulthood or the period of "emerging adulthood" that covers the third decade of life (Arnett 2000; Furstenberg 2000). During this period youth have acquired basic life skills but are in a transitional stage in which they are applying those skills and acquiring more occupation-specific skills and self-knowledge. The prolongation of youth can be seen in the timing of transitions into adult roles over the course of the century and in cross-national perspective such that the transition period extends from roughly age 15 through the late 20s (Fussell and Furstenberg 2002; Fussell and Gauthier 2002).

Research on the transition to adulthood in the United States has focused on the spread between the mean age at the first transition (usually leaving school) to that at the last transition (usually becoming a parent). There was greater consensus about the normative ordering of youth transitions in the first half of the 20th century than in the second. Most men in the United States completed school, began work, left home, formed a new household, married, and had children in the standard order of the white-male life course. White women typically completed school, left home and married, and had children with labor force participation being exceptional at all ages (Modell, Furstenberg, and Hershberg 1976; Hogan 1981; Winsborough 1979; Shanahan 2000). The spread between the first and last transition shortened over the course of the century until the 1970s, when all of these transitions were generally compressed into a short period in the early 20s (Rindfuss 1991). The tension resulting from this condensed transition to adulthood was untenable for many (Modell et al 1976). The 1970s witnessed a reversal of trends such that the transition to adulthood came to be more individually determined and variable, with transitions to family roles generally being delayed until later in the life course (Buchman 1989; Shanahan 2000).

The compression of the timing of adult transitions and its reversal in the 1970s was witnessed in Europe as well as the United States, suggesting that pervasive structural and attitudinal changes underlie these common patterns (Monnier and Rychtarikova 1992; Lesthaeghe 1995). Since the 1970s, Japan and other East Asian countries have experienced a similar delay in age at marriage that is attributed to the erosion of the system of arranged marriage, as well as to rising educational attainment and increased labor market participation among women and to more individualistic values (Retherford, Ogawa, and Matsukura 2001). So what is driving all of these similar trends across a diverse set of countries? In the following sections of this chapter, I will review the literature and trends in each of the transitions to adult statuses, that is, the transition from school to work, home leaving, and family formation, to see how they help us understand why youth are taking longer to complete the transition to adulthood.

SCHOOL-TO-WORK TRANSITION

The school-to-work transition is critical for launching youth into adulthood because it provides them with the financial resources necessary to leave the parental home and start a family, two of the important markers of adulthood. The structural arrangements that guide this transition, or the absence of them, can significantly shape a young person's occupational and life trajectory (Kerckhoff, this volume). Education typically guides youth into occupations in advanced industrial countries. In the past half century, education has taken on a more important role as the demand for skilled workers increased. Today those who terminate their education at the secondary level have fewer well-paid employment possibilities and face greater risk of job loss than those who undertake vocational or professional education. The last decades of the 20th century have also seen the transformation of advanced industrial economies to post-industrial economies and a shift toward freer markets and fewer worker protections (Levy 1998). Thus the full-time, lifetime industrial employment that was commonplace during the post-WWII era is no longer certain; more flexible employment arrangements and the greater emphasis on human capital make the transition to employment more precarious, especially for those with less education. These changes suggest that the institutional arrangements that guided the occupational trajectories of the parents of youth do not necessarily apply to youth themselves.

The value of basic education is not under question, in fact, it is one of the most important predictors of economic success and it is now one of the most certain aspects of the life course (Levy 1998; Buchmann 1989). Indeed, in most of Western and Northern Europe primary and secondary education is nearly universal, and trends point in the same direction for other advanced industrial nations, though the countries in transition to market economies lag behind (UNESCO 1998). Furthermore, tertiary education is increasing throughout these countries, at both traditional and non-traditional school ages, as demand for professional and technical skills increases in the labor market and educational institutions

TABLE 2.1. *Rank order of countries according to percentage of men attaining at least a secondary education by birth cohort (1998).*

Birth Cohort 1934–43		Birth Cohort 1944–53		Birth Cohort 1954–63		Birth Cohort 1964–73		
Country	%	Country	%	Country	%	Country	%	Change[A]
Czech Rep.	86	Czech Rep.	90	Czech Rep.	92	Czech Rep.	93	7
Germany	86	Germany	89	Germany	90	Korea	93	51
Switzerland	83	Switzerland	87	Japan	90	Japan	92	32
US	80	US	87	Norway[B]	88	Norway[B]	92	23
Denmark	73	Denmark	83	US	87	Switzerland	92	9
Norway[B]	69	Norway[B]	79	Switzerland	86	Germany	89	3
Austria[B]	68	Canada	77	Austria[B]	84	Austria[B]	87	19
UK	64	Japan	77	Canada	81	Sweden	87	28
New Zealand	64	Austria[B]	76	Denmark	80	US	87	7
Canada	62	New Zealand	74	Korea	79	Canada	86	24
Netherlands	61	Hungary	72	New Zealand	78	Denmark	85	12
Japan	60	UK	72	Sweden	77	Finland[B]	82	39
Sweden	59	Sweden	70	Hungary	77	New Zealand	79	15
Iceland	55	Netherlands	68	Finland[B]	76	Hungary	79	45
Australia	54	Iceland	65	UK	72	France	75	28
France	47	Australia	61	Netherlands	70	Netherlands	73	12
Finland[B]	43	France	61	France	66	Belgium	71	34
Poland	43	Finland[B]	61	Australia	66	Australia	69	15
Korea	42	Korea	59	Iceland	65	UK	68	4
Belgium	37	Poland	56	Poland	61	Poland	63	20
Hungary	34	Belgium	53	Belgium	60	Greece[A]	63	36
Greece[B]	27	Italy	40	Greece[B]	51	Iceland	61	6
Italy	23	Greece[B]	39	Italy	50	Italy	52	29
Spain	17	Spain	27	Spain	39	Spain	50	33
Portugal	10	Portugal	14	Portugal	18	Portugal	25	15
Mean	54		66		71		76	22
Standard dev.	21		19		18		17	−4

[A] This column shows the absolute difference between the percentage of men attaining at least a secondary education in the latest (1964–73) and the earliest (1934–43) birth cohorts. Differences in means and standard deviations between these cohorts are also shown in the last column.
[B] Year of reference is 1997.
Source: OECD Database.

re-orient toward "lifetime learning" (OECD 1996, 1998). These all contribute to prolonging the period of skill acquisition in early adulthood.

The nearly universal agreement on the importance of secondary education is evident from the diffusion of secondary education evident in Tables 2.1 and 2.2, which show the rank order of countries according to the percentage of men and women attaining at least secondary education by birth cohort in 1998. Secondary education is now widespread among the youngest birth cohorts (1964–1973) in all countries, whereas in many countries among the oldest birth cohorts (1934–43) less than half

TABLE 2.2. *Rank order of countries according to percentage of women attaining at least a secondary education by birth cohort (1998).*

Birth Cohort 1934–43		Birth Cohort 1944–53		Birth Cohort 1954–63		Birth Cohort 1964–73		
Country	%	Country	%	Country	%	Country	%	Change[A]
US	79	US	88	Japan	93	Japan	95	41
Germany	66	Germany	78	US	89	Norway[B]	93	32
Czech Rep.	63	Czech Rep.	78	Norway[B]	88	Czech Rep.	91	28
Norway[A]	61	Norway[B]	78	Czech Rep.	84	Korea	91	78
Sweden	61	Japan	78	Canada	84	United States	89	10
Switzerland	60	Canada	77	Germany	84	Canada	88	29
Denmark	60	Sweden	76	Sweden	83	Sweden	88	27
Canada	59	Switzerland	72	Finland[B]	80	Finland[B]	86	46
Japan	54	Denmark	72	Denmark	79	Denmark	86	26
New Zealand	53	New Zealand	64	Switzerland	79	Germany	86	20
Austria[B]	46	Finland[B]	63	New Zealand	76	Switzerland	85	25
Finland[B]	40	Austria[B]	60	Austria[B]	71	Austria[B]	80	34
UK	39	Hungary	57	Hungary	68	New Zealand	79	26
Netherlands	39	Netherlands	51	Netherlands	65	Hungary	76	48
France	35	France	51	Belgium	61	France	76	41
Australia	35	Poland	50	Korea	61	Belgium	76	45
Poland	32	Belgium	49	France	61	Netherlands	75	36
Belgium	31	UK	47	Poland	56	Greece[B]	68	51
Hungary	28	Australia	43	Greece[B]	52	Poland	61	29
Iceland	27	Iceland	42	UK	51	Iceland	60	33
Greece[B]	17	Greece[B]	33	Australia	50	Australia	60	25
Italy	16	Italy	30	Iceland	50	Italy	57	41
Portugal	13	Korea	30	Italy	49	Spain	56	48
Korea	13	Spain	18	Spain	36	UK	55	16
Spain	8	Portugal	15	Portugal	21	Portugal	32	19
Mean	41		56		67		76	35
Standard dev.	20		20		18		16	−4

[A] This column shows the absolute difference between the percentage of women attaining at least a secondary education in the latest (1964–73) and the earliest (1934–43) birth cohorts. Differences in means and standard deviations between these cohorts are also shown in the last column.
[B] Year of reference is 1997.
Source: OECD Database.

the cohort attained at least a secondary education. Most of this change in educational attainment occurred as countries with low average secondary education attainment levels caught up to those with higher levels. Korea and Japan made the most remarkable advances among both men and women, but especially women who jumped from only 13 and 54 percent having at least a secondary education, respectively, to 91 and 95 percent having such education. Hungary, Finland, France, Belgium, Greece, Italy, and Spain also made significant advances as their educational systems caught up to those of their European neighbors.

Women's life courses have been even more affected by the spread of education then men's because education is not only an alternative to early marriage and childbearing; it has also opened doors for women in the traditionally male spheres of work and civic life. Among the oldest birth cohorts (1934–43), the inter-country sex difference in the percentage attaining at least a secondary education was 13 percentage points (a mean of 54 percent of men and 41 percent of women achieved a secondary education). This difference all but disappeared for the youngest birth cohorts (1964–73), although within-country differences remain. Clearly, the early life course of young adults in all these countries has changed radically between cohorts in the last fifty years as young adults everywhere spend more time in school.

Educational trends reflect the importance placed on increasing human capital as a means of increasing productive capacity throughout the advanced industrialized countries. However, some scholars, and youth themselves, have called this strategy into question now that secondary education is so widespread (Wyn and Dwyer 2000). They argue that in spite of the rhetoric that the new economy demands highly skilled workers, what is really needed are ways of making training more responsive to labor market demands (Heinz 2000; Wyn and Dwyer 2000).

Among industrialized countries there are different systems for channeling youth into occupations. In Western and Northern Europe, few teenagers work while attending school, and they combine the two only to a limited degree in their early and late 20s. In many of these countries, general and vocational education is organized in schools, so students do not enter into formal employment until completing their education. In the Anglo-Saxon countries, some youth receive on-the-job training in part-time or seasonal employment, but there are relatively few programs that channel them into jobs (Arum and Shavit 1995). In the Central European countries of Austria, Germany, and Switzerland, the vocational and educational training (VET) system tracks students from school into work (Kerckhoff this volume). But these programs are part of the old industrial structure and are not responsive enough to changes in labor demand, especially as information and communication technology changes production processes and, consequently, labor demand (Anderson, this volume). In the context of a rapidly restructuring economy none of these systems are effective enough at directing youth into the occupational fields in which demand is growing fastest.

Comparative studies have found that in Germany low-skill workers are less likely to experience unemployment and have higher relative wages than their counterparts in the UK and the United States as a result of the VET system (Nickell and Bell 1996; O'Higgins 1997). Voluntary training programs in the United States and the UK also improve youth's chances in the labor market, but they are criticized for limiting the occupational choices of youth (Arum and Shavit 1995; O'Higgins 1997). However, these programs are useful for giving youth a head start in the labor market, even if youth go on to choose different occupations over the long-run (Heinz 2000). So even while youth are structurally more vulnerable to fluctuations in the economy, government sponsored training programs can assist youth in finding stable employment in their first years in the labor market and keep them from experiencing long spells of unemployment and becoming discouraged workers.

However, instability in employment is an acknowledged feature of employment in economies restructuring from manufacturing to services. Growing numbers of jobs are now part-time instead of full-time, particularly for low-skill workers (Wyn and Dwyer 2000). Hand in hand with this shift is the widening wage gap between the highest and the lowest paid workers as the "new economy" jobs in the high technology or finance sectors are highly remunerated while wages in "old" industrial economy jobs stay the same (Levy 1998; Western and Healy 1999; Morris and Western 1999). Furthermore, there is more job changing early in the career and unemployment spells last longer than they did for earlier cohorts, again a sign of the effects of the new flexible economy in which the employer's commitment to workers is low (Berhardt, Morris, Handcock, and Scott 2001). Employment conditions in the United States and Europe differ because strong welfare states and industrial relations institutions in Europe make for more unemployment but higher wages, while the less regulated U.S. labor markets experience less unemployment but much lower wages at the bottom of the wage scale. In these ways, workers have borne the brunt of economic restructuring.

Youth face particular challenges as the newest entrants into the labor market. In a comparison of OECD countries, Gaude (1997) found that in absolute terms, youth unemployment rates (ages 15 to 19) vary more according to economic conditions than do adult rates, increasing more in recessions and always remaining higher than unemployment for other age groups. This reflects the fact that youth are less likely to be hired and are the first laid off during a recession. But youth unemployment rates have also risen in spite of the fact that increased educational participation and the diminished size of youth cohorts in these countries have lessened the supply of labor for entry level positions (O'Higgins 1997). This suggests that the effects of economic restructuring are felt more strongly by youth, drawing attention to the need for programs that match youth to jobs.

Institutions that assist in the school-to-work transition not only facilitate further transitions such as home leaving and family formation, they prevent youth from falling into bad work habits, crime, or other self-destructive behaviors that most frequently develop during adolescence and youth (Cullen and Wright, this volume). But we have seen that in the new economies of post-industrial nations, the path from school to work has more obstacles and fewer guideposts than in the past. The difficult employment conditions youth face – both the well-known instability of being "last hired, first fired" and the new instability of employment in the new regime of "flexible" employment relations – are important structural conditions underlying the prolongation of youth. Thus it is no surprise that youth feel so uncertain about their early employment that they are delaying taking on family responsibilities.

HOME-LEAVING

The instability of labor markets and more widespread pursuit of higher education discussed in the previous section are reflected in the more tentative movements of youth away from the parental home in some countries in the last thirty years. Greater participation in higher education has resulted in a shift toward earlier home leaving in order to live in non-family settings but more frequent returns to live with parents (Murphy and Wang 1998). Thus young people who leave home for higher education usually remain partially dependent on their parents, whereas those who find full-time employment or marry are more likely to be financially independent of their parents (Avery, Goldscheider, and Speare 1992; Goldscheider, Thornton, and Young-DeMarco 1993; Iacovou 1999). But the delay in entry into marriage and greater uncertainty in the labor market have resulted in a later age at home-leaving for those who are not going onto higher education – a finding that causes great concern in some countries but is par for the course in others.

Strong regional contrasts in the timing and pathway out of the parental household reflect greater or lesser individualist traditions and values, as well as differences in economic opportunities between countries and regions. Iacovou (1999) identifies two distinct models of home-leaving and household formation within Europe that divide along a roughly north-south axis,[5] similar to that identified by Hajnal (1982) in his study of pre-industrial household formation systems. In the Southern European model, young adults make direct transitions from living in their parent's home to forming their own independent families at a somewhat later age, usually in the mid- to late-20s. Rarely is there a period of independent living, which is due to both the tradition of multigenerational co-residence and shortages in the labor and housing markets (Sgritta 1999). In the Northern European model, young adults leave the parental home early but begin family formation relatively late. They are likely to spend an extended period of time living alone, with non-relatives, or in a cohabiting union before entering into marriage and parenthood, a pattern also seen in the United States, Canada, and Australia. Youth in the developed countries of East Asia[6] leave home much later than in Northern and Western Europe and North America since youth rarely leave home for higher education or employment, and it is common for young married couples to live with the husband's parents. Consequently, home leaving for men is much later than it is for women in these Asian countries (Yi, Coale, Choe, Zhiwu, Li 1994).

These regional contrasts illustrate that cultural patterns of family structure are closely tied to the timing of home-leaving, whereas widespread participation in secondary and tertiary education and labor market uncertainty are less important. Delays in home-leaving are most problematic in those countries where young people are encouraged to leave home and seek their own fortune, for example, the Northern and Western European countries and the diaspora of English-speaking countries. Prolonged education and the insecurity of early labor market experience conflict with this norm. Delays in home-leaving are increasingly problematic in Southern European countries where adult children are not leaving home until later ages than their parents did (Fussell and Gauthier 2002). Even though extended family residences are more common in Southern Europe, there is concern that youth do not have the economic opportunities to leave home and form their own families. Indeed, in these low-fertility countries, the contraceptive effect of living with one's parents may be more than the parents of today's youth would like! In Japan, there is speculation that multigenerational residences may

---

[5] Iacovou's north/south divide includes Denmark, the Netherlands, the UK, France, Belgium, and Luxembourg in the "north," and Italy, Spain, Portugal, Greece, and Ireland in the "south."

[6] The authors compared China, Japan, and South Korea with the United States, France, and Sweden.

be a strategy for families to cope with the economic recession, simultaneously serving as a private intergenerational transfer from the elder generation to young adults (Mason, The, Ogawa, and Fukui 1994). All told, the conflicts surrounding the experience of home leaving depend upon the cultural customs that govern the timing and meaning of leaving the parental home.

FAMILY FORMATION

Entering into marriage, or a marriage-like partnership, and becoming a parent have been increasingly delayed in advanced industrial countries. Since the 1970s in advanced industrial countries there has been a re-organization of the relationship between investments in personal development and investments in family formation that is still unresolved but is manifested in the period of "emerging adulthood." For some youth this is a time for personal growth, and, therefore, they refrain from taking on responsibilities for others. Other youth cannot reach the level of income and economic stability they feel is a necessary prerequisite to family formation in spite of their desire to do so. Indeed, in this period of rising inequality, youth's economic circumstances take on an even greater role in shaping their life courses (Oppenheimer, Kalmijn, and Lim 1997). But alongside these constraints there is also greater freedom to make one's own decisions. Both of these tendencies translate into a greater variety of pathways to family formation.

The greatest changes seen across all the advanced industrial countries are the delay in the age at first marriage, the de-coupling of marriage and childbearing, the rise in cohabitation in some countries, and the greater ease with which people dissolve marital unions. Some observers see this as a crisis in "the family," while others see it as evolution toward more diverse and egalitarian family forms (Popenoe 1993; Stacey 1993). A life-course perspective offers an alternative to the focus on value change as the causal factor, rather it asks, what is happening in the early life course to cause young people to make different choices than their parents did regarding family formation?

Later age at first marriage is often interpreted as a lesser commitment to marriage, however, it is more appropriately interpreted as less interest in marriage during the period of "emerging adulthood" because the vast majority of young people do marry eventually. Women's involvement in school and work may cause them to postpone marriage and childbearing, but there is little evidence that this is due to their economic independence (Oppenheimer and Lew 1995). Men are also choosing to enter family roles later, in fact, they marry later than women (Sardon 1993). Research in the United States points to men's instability in their early occupational trajectories as the reason for their later ages at marriage, particularly for those with less education and for African American men who face labor-market discrimination and are often geographically mismatched with employment opportunities (Lichter, McLaughlin, and Landry 1992; Oppenheimer et al 1997). Men's economic circumstances also affect the timing of women's marriage because men's ability to earn is often viewed as a necessary prerequisite to marriage (Smock and Manning 1997). Ideational changes also play a role, of course, as greater expectations for companionship in marriage, more gender-egalitarian values, increased market orientation, and greater emphasis on individual fulfillment combine to make family formation a more voluntary, rather than normative, decision (Lesthaeghe 1995).

Both the relaxation of norms surrounding marriage and the opportunity changes leading young people to delay marriage have led to the rise in cohabitation in some countries. With the exception of the Scandinavian countries, where cohabitation is a long-standing alternative to formal marriage, cohabitation in European countries and North America is a relatively new phenomenon whose meaning is still evolving, while it is extremely uncommon in East Asia (Rindfuss and VandenHeuvel 1990; Leridon 1990; Toulemon 1996; Retherford et al 2001; Schoenmaeckers and Lodewijckx 1999; Seltzer 2000). Indeed, in most countries where it is occurring, cohabitation is a precursor to marriage rather than a substitute, with the exception of Scandinavia. This interpretation is based on the lower rates of childbearing in cohabiting unions and the relatively quick exits into marriage for many couples (Thornton, Axinn, and Teachman 1995; Smock and Manning 1997; Lillard, Brien, and Waite 1995; Schoenmaeckers and Lodewijckx 1999). As in the case of marriage timing, men's economic circumstances are an important factor in determining whether and when a cohabiting union is converted into a formal marriage (Smock and Manning 1997; Liefbroer and Corijn 1999). In Southern European countries, where the Catholic tradition bans cohabitation and divorce, cohabitation is rare and generally limited to the separated or divorced who cannot legally marry (Iacovou 1999). Thus cohabitation is an alternative to marriage only in the Scandinavian countries; elsewhere it is not a substitute for marriage. Instead cohabitation satisfies the need for a marriage-like relationship in the early life-course when economic stability, particularly by males, has not been achieved.

Non-marital fertility is also linked to the delay in marriage since the longer a woman stays single the longer she is at risk of a non-marital birth. Non-marital fertility has increased in the United States such that in the early 1990s one-third of all births were non-marital, and most of those were to women in their 20s and 30s (Farley 1996). Such increases in non-marital fertility are related to labor-market downturns and the disadvantaged socioeconomic backgrounds of young men and women who become parents as well as a growing attitude that marriage is not a necessary prerequisite to childbearing (Pagnini and Rindfuss 1993; South 1999; Abrahamson 2000). In Europe the levels of non-marital fertility are still quite low, although rising, and these births mostly occur within cohabiting unions (Schoenmaeckers and Lodewijckx 1999; Kuijsten 1996). In contrast, the percentage of non-marital births to cohabiting parents in the United States has risen only recently to 40 percent, while the majority of non-marital births are still to single mothers (Bumpass and Lu 2000). Forming a family as a single mother, in a cohabiting union, or early in the life course has potentially negative consequences for both parents and children (O'Connor 1998; South 1999; Furstenberg forthcoming). For example, children born in cohabiting unions are more likely to experience the separation of their parents during their childhood (Wu, Bumpass, and Musick 2000; O 1997). This suggests that a new axis of inequality between children may be the age and marital status of their parents at the time of birth.

Delays in marriage and childbearing and increases in cohabitation and non-marital childbearing all seem to be partially rooted in the turbulence and uncertainty experienced in youth. The need for more years of education and the acquisition of skills to succeed in the labor market and the changing structures of employment underlie this uncertainty. But the ideology of youth that promotes a hiatus from adult responsibilities also contributes to this turbulence. Indeed, Hall (1993) has labeled these demographic changes as "reproductive individualism" to underscore the idea that family formation is increasingly an expression of individuality not conformity to the status quo.

Reviewing all the transitions considered here, we can see that the new life stage known as "emerging adulthood" helps us to understand the intersection of the structural and ideational changes that have brought about the changes in the timing and tempo of demographic events in the life course. But emerging adulthood has both positive and negative aspects: the greater expectations for human capital acquisition open greater possibilities for failure. Thus, as was seen most clearly in the discussion of the school-to-work transition, societies must create institutions that prevent people from falling between the cracks and that aid those who do. It is likely that the period of emerging adulthood will persist, making it all the more important to institutionalize support for those experiencing it.

FAMILY CHANGE AND THE FUTURE OF CHILDREN

Having reviewed the trends in the timing of these early adult transitions, it is important to consider the consequences of a greater diversity of paths in the early life course of today's youth for future cohorts of children. Some of the trends emerging from this process, such as the increase in single-parent families and higher rates of divorce and separation have harmful economic and emotional consequences for the children in these families (Seltzer 1994). Single-parent households are significantly associated with, though not necessarily the cause of, poverty, poorer school outcomes, and teenage pregnancy (McLanahan and Sandefur 1994). This is not only a result of the fall in income after divorce or separation, but also the lack of a second parent to offer emotional support and supervision. So is there a role for government and/or society to play in ensuring that children in precarious circumstances do not suffer unduly?

Research on single-parent households, the labor market, and the structure of welfare states shows that while each of these play an important role in determining the level of child poverty in advanced industrial countries, single-parenthood is *not* the most important factor (Oxley, Dang, Forster, and Pellizzari 2001; Bradbury and Jantti 2001). This research concludes that government efforts to regulate labor markets to create a wage floor do more to alleviate child poverty than increasing social transfers or somehow trying to manipulate family formation behavior (Bradbury and Jantti 2001). For example, they find that Swedish parents are able to earn enough to care for their children, therefore they are less dependent on social transfers to make up for shortfalls in their earnings. In contrast, large social transfers to the poorest families in the UK, Canada, and Australia compensate for parents' low market earnings. This difference results from the provision of welfare based on economic need (means testing) in the UK, Canada, and Australia, instead of citizen or worker entitlements as is done in Sweden. Means testing is typical of the welfare programs of the United States, the UK, Canada, and Australia, whereas universal or work-related entitlements are typical of many Western European countries. Thus, there is evidence that social transfers based on statuses, such as children and youth, the elderly, or employment, provide a more effective system of social transfers than one based on economic need.

Families, the community, the workplace, and the state all mediate the relationship between individuals and resources. These institutions also structure generational interdependence. In this review of the literature we have seen that the rise in single-parent families, the decline in wages, and differences in welfare benefits contribute to change in the relative well-being of children. Offsetting the adverse trends are the adjustments that youth make, such as having fewer children later in life and spending more time acquiring marketable skills. These promote child well-being because older parents and parents of fewer children have more resources to invest in each individual child. But young parents who forgo personal investments early in life have fewer resources to pass on to their children. Thus, the divergence of wages between those with a college degree or more and those with only secondary education is also a divergence in investments in children, particularly when public investments are scarce. In several instances in this discussion of the transition to adulthood it is clear that government programs have a critical role to play in easing the entry into adult statuses. Job training and placement programs and life-long learning can assist in the school-to-work transition, and programs that assist young families and particularly mothers in maintaining stable employment and rearing children are critical components of the public intergenerational contract.

RENEGOTIATING THE INTERGENERATIONAL CONTRACT

This chapter began by asking whether population aging will cause the intergenerational contract to break down. The demographics of population aging appear to overwhelmingly favor the elderly, but demographics are not the only factor shaping intergenerational accounting. Demographic policies can ease the dependency ratio by promoting fertility, raising the retirement age, or increasing immigration, but these cannot fully address the effects of population aging. The productive capacity of the economy is far more important, and the health of the economy ultimately depends on investments in children and youth to build human capital. Young adults have responded to their new economic circumstances by constructing a new life stage of "emerging adulthood," a period having both positive and negative aspects. On the positive side, young adults have time to gain more skills, experience, and self-knowledge. On the negative side, young people temporarily trade off family formation for occupational goals. This reorganization of the life course favors those who have the ability or privilege to build their human capital, but for those who lack such advantages, there are few institutionalized pathways to success in the new economy. Collective investments in these youth in particular would assist them in achieving a "successful" transition to adulthood and in contributing to the productive capacity of the economy. By way of conclusion, I revisit the debate over population aging and the intergenerational contract to illustrate how the debate reflects, or doesn't reflect, the demographic and social changes that we have reviewed in this chapter.

In 1984 Samuel Preston illustrated in his presidential address to the Population Association of America that the poverty rates of the elderly had decreased throughout the 1970s and those of children had increased, a trend that has continued in the United States through the 1980s and 1990s. Preston pointed out that this shift was brought about by two trends: the increase in children in single-parent, particularly female-headed, households that are more likely to be impoverished and the increase in the allocation of public monies to the elderly, both through program expansion and the demographic growth of the elderly population. Preston argues that "transfers from the working-age population to the elderly are also transfers away from children, since the working ages bear far more responsibility for child-rearing than do the elderly . . . [and] the sums involved are huge" (Preston 1984, pp. 451–452).

For many, Preston's argument was a rallying cry used not to encourage more public investment in children, but rather to justify decreasing public transfers to the elderly, especially as more industrialized countries face population aging (Thurow 1999; Peterson 1999; Lamm 1999). These "generational equity" advocates use the fact that pay-as-you-go social security programs transfer monies to the elderly from the paychecks of the working-age population to appeal to youth and workers to vote for privatization reforms to government pension programs both within the United States and the European Community (Walker 1993). They argue that by taxing all workers less, parents will be able to afford more for their children, but they do not advocate for more public investment in children nor in ensuring a baseline income for all families with children. The bottom line for the generational equity advocates is a shifting of the public intergenerational contract to a private one.

Advocates of "generational interdependence" argue that social security can be publicly supported with a few reforms as the population ages and the health of the economy varies, a more practical view given the uncertainty of long-run economic projections (Munnell 1999; Quadagno 1999; Walker 1993). The generational interdependence advocates argue that the growth in the productive capacity of the economy matters far more than the relative growth of different sectors of the population (Binstock 1999). As long as the economy is growing, the benefits of that growth can continue to be equitably redistributed (Vatter and Walker 1998). But even in economic hard times, there must be a safety net, especially if we don't want to lose a generation of children and youth. The generational interdependence advocates don't seek to pit one age group against another, but rather to promote solidarity and economic security across all ages, especially those at greatest risk of poverty.

Preston's argument for the 'diverging paths of America's dependents' was based on aggregate trends in poverty by age groups. The research testing Preston's thesis with individual-level data has found few conclusive empirical results, largely because it is difficult to model private and public intergenerational wealth flows (Cremer, Kessler, and Pestieau 1994). Research on Japan in the mid-1980s found little evidence of intergenerational inequality in per capita income, in spite of the rapid aging that country is experiencing (Mason, The et al 1994). The authors suggest that three-generation family households may offset the rise in public transfers to the elderly, but they are not able to show this with their model. Indeed, different national contexts have a diverse set of private and public intergenerational transfer systems making the comparative picture less clear, but this underlines the assertion that population aging does not necessarily override the social institutions that shape intergenerational relations.

A large body of research addresses the question of intergenerational conflict as a political response to changes in demographic circumstances. For example, Bengtsson and Fridlizius (1994) conclude that the public old-age pension program in Sweden needs to be supplemented with a private pension system because population aging and slow economic growth in the 1980s in Sweden eroded public support for social security. Walker (1993) argues that in the case of the UK, the ideology of individual rather than collective responsibility has been used to alter the social contract between generations, justifying the restructuring of the welfare system. He is concerned that this change in the public social contract will undermine the principle of reciprocity between generations in private relationships as well. The claim that generational conflict is a justification for privatization is echoed in research by Marshall et al (1993) who find stark differences between the public debates over intergenerational equity in Canada and the United States. In Canada, universal programs such as public health care, universal family allowances, and old-age pensions that are based on citizenship create collective solidarity rather than individualist conflicts and, thereby, ameliorate intergenerational inequities. In the United States in contrast, intergenerational conflict has been used to promote the privatization of the government's retirement pension program (Social Security). The "problem" of population aging is thus being used to promote a political agenda promoting the privatization of government social programs.

The implications of population aging are still unrealized, but clearly demand attention. One of the outcomes of the transformation of the age structure is that more individuals in society are living in households without children, as a result of both deferred and forgone childbearing and prolonged life expectancy. If we live in a world where people only pursue their individual self-interest, this may have dire consequences for children and youth. Fortunately, we do not live in that world. Instead we live in societies with social contracts. Clearly, the change in the age structure demands a renegotiation of the intergenerational contract – one that takes into account the distinct and common needs of children, youth, the working age population, and the elderly.

References

Abrahamson, M. 2000. "Case Studies of Surges in Nonmarital Births." *Marriage and Family Review*, 30(1-2):127–151.

Anderson, Ronald E. 2002. "Youth and Information Technology." This volume.

Arnett, Jeffrey Jensen. 2000. "Emerging Adulthood: A Theory of Development from the Late Teens through the Twenties." *American Psychologist*, 55(5): 469–480.

Arnett, Jeffrey Jensen, and Susan Taber. 1994. "Adolescence Terminable and Interminable: When Does Adolescence End?" *Journal of Youth and Adolescence*, 23(5):517–537.

Arum, Richard, and Yossi Shavit. 1995. "Secondary Vocational Education and the Transition from School to Work." *Sociology of Education*, 68(3):187–204.

Avery, Roger, Frances Goldscheider, and Alden Speare Jr. 1992. "Feathered Nest/Gilded Cage: Parental Income and Leaving Home in the Transition to Adulthood." *Demography*, 29(3):375–388.

Bengtsson, Tommy, and Gunnar Fridlizius. 1994. "Public Intergenerational Transfers as an Old-Age Pension System: A Historical Interlude?" In: *The*

Family, the Market, and the State in Ageing Societies. John Ermisch and Naohiro Ogawa, editors. Oxford: Clarendon Press.

Bernhardt, Annette, Martina Morris, Mark S. Handcock, and Marc A. Scott. 2001. *Divergent Paths: Economic Mobility in the New American Labor Market.* New York: Russell Sage.

Binstock, Robert H. 1999. "Scapegoating the Old: Intergenerational Equity and Age-Based Health Care Rationing." In: *The Generational Equity Debate.* Williamson, John B., Diane M. Watts-Roy, and Eric R. Kingson, editors. New York: Columbia University Press.

Blanchet, Didier, and Olivia Ekert-Jaffé. 1994. "The Demographic Impact of Family Benefits: Evidence from a Micro-Model and from Macro-Data." In: *The Family, the Market and the State in Ageing Societies.* John Ermisch and Naohiro Ogawa, editors. Oxford: Clarendon Press.

Bongaarts, John, and Rodolfo A. Bulatao, editors. 2000. *Beyond Six Billion: Forecasting the World's Population.* Committee on Population, Commission on Behavioral and Social Sciences and Education, National Research Council, National Academy Press. Washington, D.C.

Bradbury, Bruce, and Marcus Jantti. 2001. "Child-Poverty Across the Industrialized World: Evidence from the Luxembourg Income Study." In: *Child Well-Being, Child Poverty, and Child Policy in Modern Nations: What Do We Know?* Koen Vleminckx and Timothy M. Smeeding, editors. Bristol, UK: The Policy Press.

Buchmann, Marlis. 1989. *The Script of Life in Modern Society: Entry into Adulthood in a Changing World.* Chicago: University of Chicago Press.

Bumpass, Larry, and Hsien-Hen Lu. 2000. "Trends in Cohabitation and Implications for Children's Family Contexts in the United States." *Population Studies,* 54(1):29–41.

Cremer, Helmuth, Denis Kessler, and Pierre Pestieau. 1994. "Private and Public Intergenerational Transfers: Evidence and a Simple Model." In: *The Family, the Market, and the State in Ageing Societies.* John Ermisch and Naohiro Ogawa, editors. Oxford: Clarendon Press.

Cullen, Francis T., and John Paul Wright. 2002. "Criminal Justice in the Lives of American Adolescents: Choosing the future." This volume.

Demeny, Paul. 1997. "Replacement-Level Fertility: The Implausible Endpoint of the Demographic Transition." In: *The Continuing Demographic Transition.* G. W. Jones, R. M. Douglas, J. C. Caldwell, and R. M. D'Souza, editors. Oxford: Clarendon Press.

Eurostat. 1999. Demographic Statistics: Data 1960–99. Office for Official Publications of the European Communities, Luxembourg.

Farley, Reynolds. 1996. *The New American Reality: Who We Are, How We Got Here, Where We Are Going?* New York: Russell Sage.

Furstenberg, Frank F. 2000. "The Sociology of Adolescence and Youth in the 1990s: A Critical Commentary." *Journal of Marriage and the Family,* 62(4): 896–910.

Furstenberg, Frank F. Forthcoming. *Destinies of the Disadvantaged: The Life Course of Teenage Mothers and Their Children.* Cambridge, MA: Harvard University Press.

Fussell, Elizabeth, and Frank F. Furstenberg. 2002. "The Transition to Adult-hood in the United States during the Twentieth Century." Unpublished Manuscript. Tulane University, New Orleans, Louisiana. MacArthur Study Group on Transition to Adulthood.

Fussell, Elizabeth, and Anne Gauthier. 2002. "The Transition to Adulthood in Cross-National Perspective." Unpublished Manuscript. Tulane University, New Orleans, Louisiana. MacArthur Study Group on Transition to Adulthood.

Gaude, J. 1997. L'Insertion des Jeunes et les Politiques d'Emploi Formation. Employment and Training Papers, No. 1, Employment and Training Department, International Labor Organization, Geneva.

Gauthier, Anne H. 1996. *The State and the Family: A Comparative Analysis of Family Policies in Industrialized Countries.* Oxford: Clarendon Press.

Goldscheider, Frances, Arland Thornton, and Linda Young-DeMarco. 1993. A Portrait of the Nest-Leaving Process in Early Adulthood." *Demography,* 30(4):683–699.

Gornick, Janet C., Marcia K. Meyers, and Katherin E. Ross. 1996. Supporting the Employment of Mothers: Policy Variation across Fourteen Welfare States. Luxembourg Income Study Working Paper No. 139.

Hajnal, John. 1982. "Two Kinds of Pre-Industrial Household Formation Systems." *Population and Development Review,* 8(3):449–94.

Hall, R. 1993. Reproductive Individualism: Exploring the Relationship between Religion, Cohabitation and Divorce. The University of Western Ontario, Population Studies Centre, London, Ontario (Discussion Paper No. 93–9).

Heinz, Walter R. 2000. "Youth Transitions and Employment in Germany." *International Social Science Journal,* 164:161–170.

Hoem, Jan M. 1993. "Public Policy as a Fuel of Fertility: Effects of Policy Reform on the Pace of Childbearing in Sweden in the 1980s." *Acta Sociologica,* 36(1):19–32.

Hoem, Britta, and Jan M. Hoem. 1997. "Fertility Trends in Sweden up to 1996." Paper presented at the Expert Group Meeting on Below-Replacement Fertility, UN Population Division, New York, November 4–6.

Hogan, Dennis P. 1981. *Transitions and Social Change: The Early Lives of American Men.* New York: Academic Press.

Iacovou, Maria. 2002. "Young People in Europe: Two Models of Household Formation." *Annals of the American Academy of Political and Social Science,* March, 580:40–69.

International Organization for Migration. 2000. World Migration Report. New York: United Nations.

Kerckhoff, Alan C. 2002. "From Student to Worker." This volume.

Keyfitz, Nathan. 1981. "The Limits of Population Forecasting." *Population and Development Review,* 7(4):579–593.

Kuijsten, Anton C. 1996. "Changing Family Patterns in Europe: A Case of Divergence?" *European Journal of Population* 12(2):115–143.

Lamm, Richard D. 1999. "Care for the Elderly: What About Our Children?" In: *The Generational Equity Debate, John B.* Williamson, Biane M. Watts-Roy, and Eric R. Kingson, editors. New York: Columbia University Press.

Le Bras, Hervé. 1991. "Demographic Impact of Post-War Migration in Selected OECD Countries." *Migration: The Demographic Aspects*. Paris: Organization for Economic Cooperation and Development.

Leridon, Henri. 1990. "Extra-Marital Cohabitation and Fertility." *Population Studies*, 44(3):469–487.

Lesthaeghe, Ron. 1995. "The Second Demographic Transition." In: *Gender and Family Change in Industrialized Countries*, Karen Oppenheim Mason and An-Magritt Jensen, editors. Oxford: Clarendon Press.

Levy, Frank. 1998. *The New Dollars and Dreams: American Incomes and Economic Change*. New York: Russell Sage.

Lichter, Daniel T., G. K. McLaughlin, and D. J. Landry. 1992. "Race and the Retreat from Marriage: A Shortage of Marriageable Men?" *American Sociological Review*, 57(6):781–99.

Liefbroer, Aart C., and Martine Corijn. 1999. "Who, What, Where, and When? Specifying the Impact of Educational Attainment and Labour Force Participation on Family Formation." *European Journal of Population*, 15(1):45–75.

Lillard, Lee A., Michael J. Brien, and Linda J. Waite. 1995. "Premarital Cohabitation and Subsequent Marital Dissolution: A Matter of Self-Selection?" *Demography*, 32(3):437–457.

Marshall, Victor W., Fay Lomax Cook, and Joanne Gard Marshall. 1993. "Conflict over Intergenerational Equity: Rhetoric and Reality in a Comparative Perspective." In: *The Changing Contract Across Generations*. Vern L. Bengston and W. Andrew Achenbaum, editors. New York: Aldine de Gruyter.

Mason, Andrew, Yoke-Yun The, Naohiro Ogawa, and Takehiro Fukui. 1994. "The Intergenerational Distribution of Resources and Income in Japan." In: *The Family, the Market, and the State in Ageing Societies*. John Ermisch and Naohiro Ogawa, editors. Oxford: Clarendon Press.

Massey, Douglas S. 1995. "The New Immigration and Ethnicity in the United States." *Population and Development Review*, 21(3):631–652.

Massey, Douglas S., Joaquín Arango, Graeme Hugo, Ali Kouaouci, Adela Pellegrino, and J. Edward Taylor. 1998. *Worlds in Motion: Understanding International Migration at the End of the Millenium*. Oxford: Clarendon Press.

McLanahan, Sara, and Gary Sandefur. 1994. *Growing Up in a Single Parent Home: What Hurts, What Helps*. Boston: Harvard University Press.

Modell, John, Frank F. Furstenberg, and Theodore Hershberg. 1976. "Social Change and Transition to Adulthood in Historical Perspective." *Journal of Family History*, 1:7–32.

Monnier, Alain, and Jitka Rychtarikova. 1992. "The Division of Europe into East and West." *Population: An English Selection*, 4:129–160.

Morris, Martina, and Bruce Western. 1999. "Inequality in Earnings at the Close of the Twentieth Century." *Annual Review of Sociology*, 25:623–57.

Munnell, Alicia H. 1999. "America Can Afford to Grow Old." In: *The Generational Equity Debate*. John B. Williamson, Biane M. Watts-Roy, and Eric R. Kingson, editors. New York: Columbia University Press.

Murphy, Mike, and Duolao Wang. 1998. "Family and Sociodemographic Influences on Patterns of Leaving Home in Postwar Britain." *Demography*, 35(3):293–305.

Nickell, Stephen, and Brian Bell. 1996. "Changes in the Distribution of Wages and Unemployment in OECD Countries." *American Economic Association Papers and Proceedings*, 86(2):302–308.

O, Kravdal. 1997. "Wanting a Child Without a Firm Commitment to the Partner: Interpretations and Implications of a Common Behavior Pattern Among Norwegian Cohabitants." *European Journal of Population*, 13(3):269–298.

O'Connor, M. L. 1998. "Men Who Father Children Out of Wedlock Face Reduced Odds of Marrying and Increased Socioeconomic Hardship." *Family Planning Perspectives*, 30(5):248–249.

O'Higgins, Niall. 1997. The Challenge of Youth Unemployment. Employment and Training Papers, No. 7. Employment and Training Department, International Labor Office, Geneva.

Oppenheimer, Valerie Kincaide, and V. Lew. 1995. "Marriage Formation in the Eighties: How Important Was Women's Economic Independence?" In: *Gender and Family Change in Industrialized Countries*, Karen O. Mason and An-Magritt Jensen, editors. Oxford: Clarendon Press.

Oppenheimer, Valerie Kincade, Matthijs Kalmijn, and Nelson Lim. 1997. "Men's Career Development and Marriage Timing During a Period of Rising Inequality." *Demography*, 34(3):311–330.

Organization for Economic Cooperation and Development. 1996. Ageing in OECD Countries: A Critical Policy Challenge, *Social Policy Studies*, No. 20. Paris, France.

————. 1998. Education at a Glance, OECD Education Indicators. www.oecd.org/els/edu/EAG98.htm.

————. 2001. The Well-being of Nations: The Role of Human and Social Capital. Paris, France.

Oxley, Howard, Thai-Thanh Dang, Michael F. Forster, and Michele Pellizzari. 2001. "Income Inequalities and Poverty Among Children and Households with Children in Selected OECD Countries." In: *Child Well-Being, Child Poverty, and Child Policy in Modern Nations: What Do We Know?* Koen Vleminckx and Timothy M. Smeeding, editors. Bristol, UK: The Policy Press.

Pagnini, Deanna L., and Ronald R. Rindfuss. 1993. "The Divorce of Marriage and Childbearing: Changing Attitudes and Behavior in the United States." *Population and Development Review*, 19(2):331–346.

Peterson, Peter G. 1999. "How Will America Pay for the Retirement of the Baby Boom Generation?" In: *The Generational Equity Debate*, John B. Williamson, Biane M. Watts-Roy, and Eric R. Kingson, editors. New York: Columbia University Press.

Popenoe, David. 1993. "American Family Decline, 1960–1990. A Review and Appraisal." *Journal of Marriage and the Family*, 55(3):527–55.

Population and Development Review. 2000. "An Italian Statement on International Migration." 26(4):849–852.

Preston, Samuel H. 1984. "Children and the Elderly: Divergent Paths for America's Dependents." *Demography*, 21(4):435–457.

Quadagno, Jill. 1999. "Social Security and the Myth of the Entitlement 'Crisis'" In: *The Generational Equity Debate*.Williamson, John B., Diane M. Watts-Roy, and Eric R. Kingson, editors. New York, Columbia University Press.

Retherford, Robert D., Naohiro Ogawa, and Rikiya Matsukura. 2001. "Late Marriage and Less Marriage in Japan." *Population and Development Review*, 27(1):65–102.

Rindfuss, Ronald R., and Audrey VandenHeuvel. 1990. "Cohabitation: A Precursor to Marriage or an Alternative to Being Single?" *Population and Development Review*, 16(4):703–726.

Rindfuss, Ronald. 1991. "The Young Adult Years: Diversity, Structural Change, and Fertility." *Demography*, 28(4):493–513.

Sardon, Jean-Paul. 1993. "Women's First Marriage Rates in Europe: Elements for a Typology." *Population: An English Selection*, 5(1):119–152.

Schoenmaeckers, Ronald C., and Edith Lodewijckx. 1999. "Demographic Behaviour in Europe: Some Results from FFS Country Reports and Suggestions for Further Research." *European Journal of Population*, 15(3):207–240.

Seltzer, Judith A. 1994. "Consequences of Marital Dissolution for Children." *Annual Review of Sociology*, 20:235–266.

Seltzer, Judith A. 2000. "Families Formed Outside of Marriage." *Journal of Marriage and the Family*, 62(4):1247–1268.

Sgritta, Giovanni. 1999. "Too Late, Too Slow: The Difficult Process of Becoming an Adult in Italy." Paper presented at the Jacobs Foundation Conference on The Transition to Adulthood: Explaining National Differences. October 28–30, Marbach, Germany.

Shanahan, Michael J. 2000. "Pathways to Adulthood in Changing Societies: Variability and Mechanisms in Life Course Perspective." *Annual Review of Sociology*, 26:667–92.

Smock, Pamela J., and Wendy D. Manning. 1997. "Cohabiting Partners' Economic Circumstances and Marriage." *Demography*, 34(3):331–41.

South, Scott J. 1999. "Historical Changes and Life Course Variation in the Determinants of Premarital Childbearing." *Journal of Marriage and the Family*, 61(3):752–763.

Stacey, Judith. 1993. "Good Riddance to 'The Family': A Response to David Popenoe." *Journal of Marriage and the Family*, 55(3):545–547.

Tienda, Marta, and Rebeca Raijman. 1999. "Immigrants' Socioeconomic Progress Post-1965: Forging Mobility or Survival." In: *The Handbook of International Migration: The American Experience*. Charles Hirschman, Philip Kasinitz, and Josh DeWind, editors. New York: Russell Sage Foundation.

Thornton, Arland, William G. Axinn, and Jay D. Teachman. 1995. "The Influence of School Enrollment and Accumulation on Cohabitation and Marriage in Early Adulthood." *American Sociological Review*, 60(5):762–774.

Thurow, Lester C, 1999. "Generational Equity and the Birth of a Revolutionary Class." In: *The Generational Equity Debate*, John B. Williamson, Biane M. Watts-Roy, and Eric R. Kingson, editors. New York: Columbia University Press.

Toulemon, Laurent. 1996. "Cohabitation is Here to Stay." *Population*, 51(3): 675–715.

United Nations. 2000. Replacement Migration: Is it a Solution to Declining and Ageing Populations? Population Division, Department of Economic and Social Affairs, ESA/P/WP.160.

United Nations Educational, Scientific, and Cultural Organization. 1998. Primary and Secondary Education: Age-Specific Enrollment Ratios. Web site accessed May 10, 2001. http://unescostat.unesco.org/en/stats/statso.htm

United States Census Bureau. 2001. International Data Base. Web site accessed May 10, 2001. http://www.census.gov/ipc/www/idbnew.html

Vatter, Harold G., and John F. Walker. 1998. "Support for Baby-Boom Retirees – Not to Worry." *Journal of Economic Issues*, 32(1):79–86.

Walker, Alan. 1993. "Intergenerational Relations and Welfare Restructuring: The Social Construction of an Intergenerational Problem." In: *The Changing Contract Across Generations*. Vern L. Bengtson and W. Andrew Achenbaum, editors. New York, Adline de Gruyter.

Western, Bruce, and Healy K. 1999. "Explaining the OECD Wage Slowdown: Recession or Labor Decline?" *European Sociological Review*, 15:233–249.

Winsborough, Halliman H. 1979. "Changes in the transition to adulthood." In: *Aging from Birth to Death: Interdisciplinary Perspectives*, Matilda W. Riley, editor. Boulder, CO: Westview Press.

Wu, Lawrence, Larry Bumpass, and Kelly Musick. 2001. "Historical and Life Course Trajectories of Nonmarital Childbearing." In: *Out of Wedlock: Trends and Consequences of Nonmarital Fertility*. New York: Russell Sage Foundation.

Wyn, Johanna and Peter Dwyer. 2000. "New Patterns of Youth Transition in Education." *International Social Science Journal*, 52(2):147–159.

Yi, Zeng, Ansley Coale, Minja Kim Choe, Liang Zhiwu, and Lui Li. 1994. "Leaving the Parental Home: Census-based Estimates for China, Japan, South Korea, United States, France, and Sweden." *Population Studies*, 48(1):65–80.

3

The Transition from School to Work

Alan C. Kerckhoff

The pattern of labor force participation of young Americans has shifted greatly during the twentieth century. Entry into full-time work has occurred at increasingly older ages. A correlate, and to some extent a cause, of this change has been the tendency for young Americans to increase their levels of educational attainment. It would be a mistake to assume that young Americans make a one-time transition from school to work, but the longer they are in school, the later the transition to full-time work occurs. Work patterns of men and women have also become more alike during this century. Women are much more likely to continue full-time work after marriage and motherhood than was formerly the case.

The results of these and other changes are observable in the current labor force patterns of American youth, and they provide some suggestions about what we can expect the labor force participation of young Americans to be early in the twenty-first century. This chapter is an attempt to project from the observation of recent patterns some reasonable expectations for the foreseeable future.

The American pattern of transition from school to work is quite different from that found in many other Western industrial societies. In attempting to portray the current and possible future nature of the transition in the United States, I will make reference to some of those societal differences to highlight the nearly unique features of our own system. I will also use other societies' patterns of transition as examples of possible directions of change in the United States.

In attempting to use current patterns of education and labor force participation as a basis for estimating future patterns, it is useful to make some assumptions about the forces that generated the current patterns and the likelihood that those forces will continue to operate in the future. Therefore, after reviewing the current education and labor force participation patterns of American youth, a later section of this chapter provides a brief discussion of some of the forces I assume to have been important in generating the current patterns. A final section then presents a discussion of possible effects of changes in those forces on the education and labor force participation patterns of American youth in the early twenty-first century.

CURRENT PATTERNS OF TRANSITION FROM SCHOOL TO WORK

Labor force participation often begins early in adolescence on a part-time basis. It is common for high school students to have part-time jobs (Mortimer and Johnson 1999). The focus of this chapter is on full-time employment patterns, but early part-time work experience affects young people's full-time employment patterns, so some discussion of part-time employment is also necessary. The current patterns of full-time labor force participation of American youth vary considerably depending on the gender, ethnicity, and educational attainment of the individuals involved. Thus, to the extent possible, the discussion takes those factors into account. The transition of American youth from school to the labor force is discussed under the following five headings: educational attainment, getting a first job, the education-job association, discontinuous labor force participation, and job change and occupational mobility. In each section, some reference is made to how American patterns differ from those in some Western industrial societies.

Educational Attainment

Young Americans enter the labor force full-time at different ages, and they enter a wide range of jobs. Both of these variations are associated with the young workers' levels of educational attainment. In general, the higher the level of educational attainment, the older young Americans are when entering their first full-time year-round jobs and the higher the occupational status of the job entered. Few Americans enter the labor force full-time before the age of 18, because the great majority complete high school before doing so, and many are well into their 20s before becoming full-time workers.

Between 85% and 90% of Americans complete high school, and this rate has been relatively constant for many years. However, many more

Hispanics (37.2%) fail to graduate from high school or obtain a GED than either whites (6.4%) or blacks (11.7%) (NCES 1999b). Hispanics are thus disproportionately represented in the high school dropout labor force.

Whereas high school graduation rates have stayed quite constant, the proportion of high school graduates attending college has steadily increased during the past twenty years, from 50.7% in 1975 to 65.6% in 1998 (NCES 1999b). It is difficult to identify the source of the demand for higher education with any confidence. It is often argued that increases in enrollments in higher education are driven by employers' educational requirements when recruiting new employees, but it can also be argued that the employers' requirements are the result of the availability of young people with advanced schooling. More highly educated young people are available at least in part due to the robustness of the American economy in recent years. More can afford the earnings forgone by staying out of the labor force longer and can afford the additional costs of attending college.

Shifts in the nature of the available jobs undoubtedly add to students' motivation to obtain high education credentials. The American economic boom has been associated with a shift toward specialized high tech industries that need highly skilled workers. However, no single explanation of the increased demand is wholly convincing. The skills required by high tech industries are not taught in all college curricula. So, whatever the source of the demand, it is not at all obvious that the actual skill requirements of most high status jobs necessitate that workers have the kinds of schooling obtained in colleges and universities and required by many employers (Spenner 1988).

The very loose fit between the actual skill demands of many high status jobs and the substance of what is learned in college has led to the claim that employers pay for the credential and not any associated skill (Collins 1979). The loose fit between the skill demands of jobs and the educational credentials required by employers has also led to the charge that many workers are "overeducated" for the jobs they obtain (Rumberger 1981). The most basic result of this loose education-occupation linkage, however, is that the great majority of American youth, even those who obtain a college degree, enter the labor force with only very general skills that are not directly relevant to any particular kind of employment.

Because American higher education enrollments have been steadily increasing during the past twenty years, the average age at which

Americans have entered the labor force has tended to increase. Obtaining a higher education degree is much more common in the United States than in Europe (Shavit and Müller 1998). It is estimated that more than twice as many young Americans obtain a first university degree than do French, British, or German youth (OECD 1998; NCES 1999b). American minorities are much less likely than the white population to obtain a university degree, however. In 1998, 32.3% of American whites 25 to 29 years of age had a bachelor's degree or better, compared with 15.8% of blacks and 10.4% of Hispanics (NCES 1999c).

It is also important to remember that the American rates of enrollment in higher education are much higher than the rates at which higher education degrees are obtained. Although American higher education enrollment rates increased by an average of 1% a year between 1980 and 1995, the proportion of 25 to 29 year olds who had a bachelor's degree (or a higher degree) increased by only about 4% during those fifteen years (NCES 1996). That means that, although larger proportions of American students have entered higher education in recent years, increasingly large proportions of those who entered have failed to obtain a bachelor's degree.

In terms of educational attainment, one of the largest categories of American youth consists of those who can be referred to as "college dropouts." In 1998, 22.5% of Americans 25 to 29 years of age had only a high school diploma or GED, 27.3% had a bachelor's degree (or higher), and 33% had "some college" (NCES 1999b). The "some college" category includes those with an associate's degree (about 8% of the total), but even if they are considered separately, that still means that about one-fourth of all Americans 25 to 29 years of age are "college dropouts."

Thus, a large proportion of American youth "fall between the stools" because, although they have gone beyond high school and sought a higher degree, they have no tangible credential to show for it. The "some college" category includes about the same percentage of blacks (34%) and whites (31.8%) but a smaller percentage of Hispanics (22.1%) (NCES 1999b). These students make up a large proportion of those who enter the labor force between the ages of 18 and 22, but many of them have formal credentials that are no better than the credentials of high school graduates.

An important feature of the education system in the United States is the fact that Americans tend to define educational attainment wholly in terms of high school and college attendance and degrees. High school students are urged to stay long enough to graduate, and high school graduates are urged to go to college. Going to college means going to a four-year college to obtain a bachelor's degree. Nothing else is viewed as very meaningful.

Even programs leading to an associate's degree tend to be demeaned. Two-year colleges have been discussed in very negative terms as institutions serving a "cooling out function" (Clark, 1960) and as the embodiment of "the diverted dream" (Brint and Karabel 1989) of students who are not in four-year colleges. These discussions argue forcefully that programs offering credentials somewhere between a high school diploma and a college diploma serve to depress young people's attainments and have little or no value. Many educators seem to agree with these views. Throughout the United States, strong pressures are put on high school students to graduate and go to college. High school students are encouraged to think in terms of "college or nothing."

However, these demeaning views of post-secondary programs below the four-year college level ignore two important facts. One is the fact that there are huge time and money costs involved in moving from a high school diploma to a college diploma. Those costs discourage many students from going to college, but they also make it difficult for many who go to college to stay there long enough to obtain a bachelor's degree.

The other ignored fact is that post-secondary programs below the college level offer more to their students than is generally recognized (Dougherty 1987; Grubb 1997; Kerckhoff and Bell 1998; Monk-Turner 1990). Community college and technical institute credentials can play a very valuable role in young people's search for rewarding positions in the labor force (Reich 1993), but they are not widely honored by Americans.

Attempts have been made in recent years to strengthen the federal government's involvement in the school-to-work transition of non-college youth, to increase the visibility of post-secondary vocational schooling, and to standardize a set of nationally recognized vocational credentials (Borman, Cookson, Sadovnik, and Spade 1996). The Goals 2000 and School-to-Work Opportunities Acts have proposed a national system of credentials that certifies students' occupationally relevant skills. To date, however, the United States is far from having such a set of standards and credentials. In fact, support for community colleges appears to be declining (Hout 1996).

One of the problems Americans have supporting vocational post-secondary programs is the great variety of programs subsumed under that broad heading, everything from a six-week course in truck driving to a two-year associate's degree in business or an allied health specialty. The great variety of programs subsumed under the term vocational post-secondary education complicates the investigation of the labor force effects of attending such programs and obtaining one of the many credentials they award. It has been shown that members of the High School and Beyond senior cohort who took some kind of vocational post-secondary course had higher earnings levels five years after their senior year than did those who had taken no courses (Lewis, Hearn, and Zilbert 1993).

The value of post-secondary vocational credentials varies depending on the particular credential involved, and it often differs for men and women. Some (e.g., medical assistant) provide average earnings greater than those of workers with either a high school diploma or some college (Kerckhoff and Bell 1998). Vocational credentials are usually found to provide a greater earnings advantage for women than for men. This seems to be at least in part because men obtain vocational credentials associated with blue collar occupations more often, whereas women obtain credentials associated with white collar or allied health occupations more often. (See also Grubb 1997).

Although there is not widespread respect for vocational post-secondary schooling, a significant proportion of young Americans obtain some kind of vocational post-secondary certificate. Of the 1980 sophomores in the High School and Beyond study, 11% obtained a vocational certificate by 1992. Only 7.9% obtained an associate's degree, but 23.8% obtained a bachelor's or higher degree (NCES 1996).[1] Despite the fact that many Americans obtain them and there is evidence of their value in the labor market, however, vocational credentials are not emphasized by educators, and there is no national standardized system of certification such as found in most European countries. The American educational ideology tends to offer the high school graduate a very simple choice, "college or nothing." This narrow choice helps to explain the large proportion of young Americans who go to college but who end up with "some college" as their level of educational

---

[1] Members of the High School and Beyond sophomore class less often first entered four-year colleges (28.7%) than other (mainly two-year) post-secondary institutions (37.7%). However, by 1992, more members of the class had obtained a bachelor's or higher degree than had obtained a certificate or associate's degree (NCES 1996). Some unknown proportion of those who entered a two-year institution had transferred to a four-year institution and may have obtained a bachelor's or higher degree, so it is not possible to be sure whether the "dropout" rate is actually higher in the two-year institutions.

attainment. Many are encouraged to enter college who do not have the academic, economic, or personal resources to complete the four-year program.

The American educational system does little to shape the transition from school to work. Few American credentials have direct occupational relevance, and those that do are not highly respected. The postsecondary emphasis is generally "college or nothing," and that has two important results. It encourages many to go to college who do not obtain a degree (college dropouts), and it serves to demean those less-than-college credentials that are much more likely to have direct occupational relevance. As a result, leaving school and entering the labor force is an uncharted journey for most Americans.

Getting a First Job

One of the most difficult tasks when analyzing the transition from school to work is to define what is meant by "labor force entry" and "first full-time job." Adolescence is a period of many kinds of change and irregularities. The majority of students have jobs at some time during the high school years, and some of them engage in an intensive pattern of employment while still in school (Mortimer and Johnson 1999). Students whose family and academic backgrounds are predictive of relatively low later accomplishments are more likely to be heavily involved in work during high school. They are also more likely to perform relatively poorly academically and to drop out of high school before graduating (McNeal 1997).

Working while in school and leaving school at an early age have very different frequencies and meanings in some other Western industrial societies than they do in the United States. Adolescents as workers, even full-time workers, are much more commonly found in Great Britain than in the United States (MacDonald 1998). Young Britons often leave school before the age of 18 and enter the labor force. However, many young full-time British workers obtain vocational credentials on a part-time basis through colleges of further education. In Germany, about two-thirds of students experience a formal combination of work and schooling through the so-called "dual system" of apprenticeships during their late teen years (Müller, Steinmann, and Ell 1998). In contrast, American high schools do little to prepare students to take on particular work roles, and American students are often confused about how to look for a first job. For this reason, some scholars believe American schools should adopt some elements of the German apprenticeship system (Hamilton and Hamilton 1999).

For many young Americans there is a clear difference between "entering the labor force" and "obtaining a first full-time job." Especially for those with low educational levels, first jobs are often part-time or short-term. Even deciding what is a person's "first full-time job" is often difficult. Many studies of entry into the labor force actually do not focus on the *first* full-time job obtained. Young Americans often move back and forth between work and school, so many analysts consider the job obtained after *completing* one's education as one's "first job." This makes these studies more consistent with official documents that record the association between educational and occupational attainments at some age (e.g., NCES 1999c), but it does some violence to the actual process by which those attainments occur.

The kinds of employment opportunities available to high school dropouts, college graduates, and those with credentials that are between those two educational levels are quite varied. Very little can be said about the job market for high school dropouts except that they have little formal assistance in finding a job, and their choices are seldom very attractive. Their first jobs are more likely than the first jobs of those with more education to be part-time, temporary, or day laborer jobs (Kalleberg, Rasell, Hudson, Webster, Reskin, Cassirer, and Appelbaum 1997). Such jobs pay low wages, provide little job security, and offer few fringe benefits comparable to regular full-time jobs (Tilly 1996).

The labor markets for those with post-secondary schooling provide more attractive alternatives, and students often have more help in finding a job. The labor market for college graduates is based on institutional placement mechanisms and relatively clear definitions of what the graduate can reasonably expect. All colleges and universities have placement services, and employers use them to make contact with prospective employees. Jobs available to college graduates are largely white collar jobs, often in professional or managerial occupations. Those jobs usually provide employment security, good fringe benefits, and orderly career prospects.

There are major differences between the collegiate labor market and the labor market faced by high school graduates who are not college graduates, however. Grubb (1999) refers to the "subbaccalaureate labor market" (SBLM) as the labor market faced by those with just a high school diploma or post-secondary credentials lower than a bachelor's degree. He says that the SBLM is "a relatively free-market approach to the transition between schooling and work" (p. 174). By that he means that there are few institutional mechanisms available to assist in matching applicants and jobs. Those in the SBLM are not "on their own" as much as the high school dropouts, but they have less help in finding a first job than those in the collegiate labor market.

The SBLM is much more local than the collegiate labor market. Informal interpersonal ties are more important in getting information about jobs to prospective employees and helping employers screen prospective employees. Secondary schools seldom provide placement services for their students (McKinney, Franchak, Halasz, Morrison, and Fornash 1984). It is not even clear that non-college post-secondary schools are very effective in helping their students find jobs (Grubb, Dickinson, Giordano, and Kaplan 1992). The formal educational credentials of those with less than a bachelor's degree are seldom relevant to most hiring decisions. Instead, employers look for job-specific skills and general personal qualities that suggest the individual will be a dependable worker. Academic skills (e.g., verbal skills) are probably more important in obtaining the white collar (especially clerical) jobs women often obtain than the blue collar jobs most men obtain in the SBLM (Holzer 1996).

One of the problems faced by SBLM job seekers is employers' preference for workers who have work experience relevant to the particular jobs they seek to fill. This Catch-22 situation makes the initial job search especially difficult and forces many of these young people to accept temporary jobs, jobs with small firms, or undesirable working conditions (Borman 1991). Only after getting work experience can these young workers successfully compete for better jobs in larger firms. It may be that part-time work during high school provides some of these young workers with the kind of experience employers seek, however (Carr, Wright, and Brody 1996; Mortimer and Johnson 1999).

Searching for a job in the United States is additionally complicated because of the emphasis on local control of primary and secondary education. Even the basic American credential, high school graduation, can result from quite different kinds and qualities of educational programs. This is in sharp contrast to the situation in France where there is much greater central control and standardization of educational programs (Stevenson and Baker 1991). Despite the very non-specific nature of French credentials, French employers have a better basis for judging a prospective employee's work potential than do comparable American employers.

The process of labor force entry varies by level of educational attainment in most countries. However, those with secondary school credentials have a much more orderly entry in Germany than in almost any other Western industrial society. That is because the great majority of German adolescents take part in the dual system of schooling and job training and are qualified for particular kinds of employment when they complete that program (Müller, et al. 1998). School leavers are less qualified for particular jobs in either France or Great Britain. In Great Britain they tend to obtain qualifications through part-time post-secondary schooling (Heath and Cheung 1998), while in France job skills are more frequently obtained through on-the-job training (Goux and Maurin 1998).

College graduates are about the only American students who experience an orderly transition from school to work. The great majority of American students face a period of confusion and irregular work experience before they find a stable job. It is not the specific job skills college graduates bring to the transition that gives them this advantage, however. It is the institutional mechanisms available to them in making the transition, mechanisms not available to high school dropouts or those in the SBLM.

The Education-Job Association

Few longitudinal studies of educational and occupational achievement of young Americans focus on their entry into the labor force full-time. However, Arum and Hout (1998), in a recent study of labor force entry, report a strong association between levels of educational attainment and the level of the first jobs obtained by the National Longitudinal Study of Youth (NLSY) sample who were 26 to 34 years of age in 1990. Arum and Hout dealt with the problem of defining a first job by focusing on "the first job a person takes after leaving school for the last time" (p. 474).

They report that, even controlling for family background and ethnicity, those with no college credentials obtain much lower status first jobs than those with a four-year college degree. For both sexes, the average status level of the first jobs of high school graduates is much lower than the average first job level of college graduates. The college graduates are much more likely than those with a high school diploma to obtain a professional or managerial first job. Those with a two-year college degree obtain first jobs with mid-range status levels.

The association between educational attainment and earnings on the first job is weaker. Arum and Hout found essentially no difference between the first job earnings of those with two-year and four-year college credentials, although both earn more than high school graduates who, in turn, earn more than high school dropouts. Also, those with a four-year college degree are much less likely than any other attainment group to be unemployed. There is a significant gap between college graduates and all others on almost all measures of early success in the labor force.

The earnings of those with more education can also be expected to increase at a faster rate during their working lives. Of men who were 25 to 34 years of age in 1996, those with a bachelor's degree had annual earnings 54% higher than men with a high school diploma and 35% higher than those with some college. The differences were even greater for women. Women with a bachelor's degree had annual earnings 88% higher than women high school graduates and 48% higher than women with some college (NCES 1999b). The advantage college graduates have over high school graduates has steadily increased since World War II.

Both educational attainment and labor force participation differ appreciably by ethnicity and gender. Although 93.6% of whites and 88.2% of blacks 25 to 29 years old had completed high school in 1998, only 62.8% of Hispanics of those ages had done so. And, although 34.5% of white high school graduates 25 to 29 years old had at least a bachelor's degree, only 17.9% of black and 16.5% of Hispanic high school graduates had a bachelor's degree (NCES 1999b). Gender differences in educational attainment are not as great as ethnic differences. Women are at least as likely as men to graduate from high school, and they are more likely than men to obtain an associate's or a bachelor's degree. However, more men than women obtain advanced degrees (NCES 1999b).

Inequalities in labor force patterns by gender and ethnicity do not directly correspond to gender and ethnic differences in educational attainment. Many jobs are highly segregated by gender and ethnicity. In general, those jobs most often held by minority group members tend to be lower status than the jobs most often held by the white majority, and minorities' lower status jobs also have relatively low pay (Parcel and Mueller 1983). Jobs in which women are most frequently found are not particularly lower status jobs (many are white collar jobs with relatively high status) but they tend to have low earnings levels (Bielby and Baron 1986; Cohn 1985; Jacobs 1989; Marini 1989).

Although women and minorities have made some progress toward equality of job status and earnings in recent years (Fosset, Galle, and

Burr 1989), significant gaps remain, especially in earnings. Various explanations for these continuing gaps have been suggested, but it is not possible to explain them in terms of human capital differences (that is, differences in educational attainment and work experience). This is especially true for gender differences. Women generally have higher levels of educational attainment than men, and many of the jobs women hold are relatively high status, but women's earnings are considerably lower than men's. There is general agreement that jobs that come to be seen as "women's jobs" or "minorities' jobs" pay less even if they require relatively high levels of skill. (See Tomaskovic-Devey 1993 for a discussion of the explanations of these differences.)

Ethnicity is not as salient an issue in most European countries, but gender is a major basis for differences in both educational and occupational outcomes, and women are at a significant disadvantage. For instance, many more women than men leave secondary school early in Great Britain, and many more British men than women pass the demanding secondary school examinations that are a prerequisite to university admission (A-level examinations). In contrast, American women and men have very similar levels of educational attainment (Kerckhoff, Bell, and Glennie 2000). It is at the point at which educational qualifications are linked to jobs that American women are at a disadvantage. In Germany, that linkage mainly occurs during secondary school, and women are also at a disadvantage there. Secondary school girls are highly constrained in their choices of apprenticeships to those leading to female stereotyped jobs that tend to be low status and poorly paid (Mortimer and Krüger 2000).

Discontinuous Labor Force Participation

It is important for present purposes to recognize that those enrolled in higher education are not all 18 to 22 years old. Many older students in higher education are enrolled in advanced degree programs, but a large proportion of students enrolled in both two-year and four-year colleges are "adult" students. In 1989, 41.2% of those enrolled in higher education were 25 years of age and older. That proportion rose to 43.7% by 1997, although it is expected to fall back to 38.4% by 2009 (NCES 1999a). It has been estimated that about one-sixth of all college degrees are awarded to students who enroll after age 25 (Leigh and Gill 1997).

Many older students are working and going to school at the same time or are students who left school, worked for some time, and then returned to school. It is difficult to decide how to treat such older students in a discussion of "adolescence." Most definitions would view anyone over 25 years of age as well beyond adolescence. Yet, if we are to understand American patterns of educational attainment and labor force participation, it is important to recognize that the transition from school to work often takes place through several steps, and the last departure from school and entry into the labor force full-time may occur well beyond the ages usually covered by the term "adolescence."

The extended period of transition for some young Americans affects the school-to-work experiences of all young Americans, even those who make a single, early move from school into the labor force. Competition for positions in the youth labor market takes place among people of varied ages and with different amounts and kinds of educational and labor force experience. Those with intermittent schooling and labor force experience may be viewed favorably by some potential employers because they have continued to improve their qualifications, but they may be viewed unfavorably by other potential employers because they appear to be indecisive.

Nineteen percent of the men and 21% of the women in the National Longitudinal Study of Youth sample had moved from school to work, back to school, and back again to work at least once by the time they were 26 years old (Arum and Hout 1998). High school dropouts were least likely to make such a double move, and those who eventually ended up with a two-year post-secondary degree were most likely to do so. It is important to differentiate between dropouts and "stopouts" at all levels of educational attainment. About 64% of those who left four-year colleges after their first year returned within five years, although over half of them returned to a two-year college (Horn and Carroll 1998).

Intermittent labor force participation also occurs because of spells of unemployment and dropping out of the labor force. Although all young workers are exposed to the risk of unemployment, the risk is greater for those with lower educational attainment. Arum and Hout (1998) report a clear association between educational attainment and both unemployment and being out of the labor force. This is true for both men and women. The lower the level of educational attainment, the greater the likelihood the individual was unemployed at the time of the 1990 interview. (See Peterson and Mortimer [1994] for additional information about adolescent unemployment.) Women with lower levels of education are more likely to get married and/or become mothers at relatively young ages, and this also contributes to discontinuities of labor force participation. Overall, the lower the level of educational attainment, the less stable the individual's labor force experience. The instability can be due to returns to school, to unemployment, to job changes, or to competing activities.

There is more continuous labor force participation in most European countries than in the United States, especially for men. In Germany, this is largely due to the close linkage between schooling during an apprenticeship and a kind of occupation. Once in that occupation, returns to school are not at all common, although they do occur (Heinz 1999). British students often take part-time courses in colleges of further education after leaving full-time school, but they are much less likely than Americans to return to full-time school. In fact, schooling of any kind ends much earlier, on average, in Great Britain than in the United States. Kerckhoff, et al. (2000), found that only half as many Britons as Americans were in any kind of school program in their mid-20s, but that difference was largely due to the much greater tendency of British women than men to leave secondary school early and take no later courses.

Job Change and Occupational Mobility

As the previous discussion indicates, an almost unique characteristic of the labor force experience of American youth is the great amount of "turbulence" during the early years. By "turbulence" I mean frequent job changes and periods of unemployment. A major reason for this is the very general nature of American educational credentials. With few exceptions, American credentials do not provide guidance for either the youth or their potential employers with respect to appropriate locations for them in the labor force. Many young people work for extended periods in situations that both they and their employers expect to be temporary. This period of turbulence is likely to be more chaotic and extended the lower the individual's level of educational attainment, but it is a fairly common early labor force experience except for that minority of Americans with occupationally specific credentials (nurses, engineers, lawyers, etc). Even college graduates, who have been assisted by their college to find a first job, are likely to change jobs more than once during their early years in the labor force.

The very general nature of American educational credentials, together with the variation in the locally controlled programs through which those credentials are obtained, make the task of matching people with jobs a challenging one, especially in the SBLM. In most cases, the specific skills called for in a job need to be acquired after employment. Whatever the educational level of the employee, the employer often needs to provide on-the-job training programs in order to have an appropriately skilled work force. This poses problems for employers because once employees are trained they can move to other firms in which they can use their newly acquired skills. Training programs are thus often highly specific to the particular needs of the firms providing them in order to reduce the danger of such attrition. Another mechanism used to reduce the loss of skilled employees is to provide career ladders within the firm, often called "internal labor markets" (Althauser 1989). Opportunities for promotion up career ladders vary by a worker's seniority and effective contribution to the collective enterprise, but the availability of career ladders also varies by the size of the firm and the clarity of a hierarchical internal division of labor.

Employers seek employees with college degrees more because success in college suggests that an individual is "trainable" than because what is learned in college is directly useful in most jobs. College graduates can be assumed to be basically literate and numerate and able to learn the specific skills firms need. The fact that they persevered through four years of college also suggests that they have personal qualities that would make them dependable workers. In addition, college graduates are generally older than workers who have not gone to college, which makes them appear to be more likely to be ready for a continuing job commitment.

As a result of all of these conditions, the degree of "turbulence" in the early years in the labor force tends to be greatest for workers with lower levels of education. Employers are reluctant to invest very much in training them, they are often hired on a temporary basis, they are easily replaced, and few firms have job ladders for them to move up. There is also less stability of employment for women than men, in part due to women's attempts to combine work and family responsibilities (Tomaskovic-Devey 1993). Minority workers also experience less early employment stability, partly because of lower average levels of education and partly because they are often located in areas of high unemployment (Beggs, Villemez, and Arnold 1997).

This pattern of recruitment and firm-specific training puts a heavy premium on being a college graduate. It shuts off many less well-educated young people from access to the better jobs. There is an increasing tendency for the American labor force to be divided into high and low skill and high and low reward segments. During the early years in the labor force, high skill and high earnings jobs are generally available only to college graduates. Not only do these better jobs generally provide better wages and fringe benefits, but they also offer greater job security and better career opportunities. Those in low status jobs more frequently experience a great deal of early career turbulence, and they are usually in jobs with low pay levels, few if any fringe benefits, little job security, and few promotion opportunities.

European countries vary widely in these respects. The French educational system does not provide many occupationally-relevant credentials, so there is also a great deal of turbulence in the early labor force participation of young French workers (Maurice, Sellier, and Silvestre 1986; Goux and Maurin 1998). The pattern in Germany is quite the opposite. Because of the importance of apprenticeships during adolescence, young German workers are more easily recruited into jobs for which they are clearly qualified, and job stability is much greater than in either France or the United States (Müller et al. 1998). This does not mean that young Germans do not move between jobs once they are employed full-time (Heinz 1999), but there is much less movement than in either France or the United States, and even those who change jobs less often change occupations.

CONDITIONS AFFECTING THE CURRENT LABOR FORCE PARTICIPATION OF AMERICAN YOUTH

The previous section has outlined briefly the nature of the current labor force experiences of American youth. Those experiences vary by levels of educational attainment, ethnicity, and gender. If we are to use these current experiences as a basis for predicting the labor force experiences of American youth early in the twenty-first century, the simplest prediction would be that there will be no change, that what we now observe will continue to occur in the future. However, there have been some striking changes in some of these labor force patterns in the recent past. So, it may be useful to speculate about possible future changes. I do so based on estimates of the effects of current conditions on the labor force patterns just reviewed.

This discussion is necessarily speculative because no one knows what changes will occur, and social scientists are not very skilled at predicting social change. All we have is information about current social relations, educational institutions, industrial organization, and the state of the economy, and estimates of how these conditions affect the transition from school to work. Whether what is inferred from this information is wholly justified is at least questionable. At times, some perspective is sought here by making comparisons between conditions in the United States and conditions in other Western industrial countries. Although brief and partial, these comparisons help provide a broader base for the estimates made.

Most of this discussion is concerned with the nature of the American educational system and its relevance to the current labor force experiences of American youth. In addition, however, some demographic patterns and features of the current American economy are discussed. The goal is to suggest the effects of these educational, demographic, and economic conditions on the observed patterns just reported and to speculate about the effects of possible changes in those conditions.

Education and Occupational Outcomes

The American educational system plays a major role in shaping the transition from school to work in the United States. As indicated in the earlier discussion, our system affects the transition in different ways than the educational systems in other Western industrial countries.

Educational Attainments. Between 85 and 90% of Americans complete high school. Despite serious efforts to increase that proportion, it has been relatively constant for many years, and there is little reason to expect it to change in the foreseeable future. However, the proportion of high school graduates attending college for at least one year has steadily increased during the past twenty years, from 50.7% in 1975 to 65.6% in 1998 (NCES 1999b).

The tendency to leave secondary school at an early age is greater in Great Britain than in most other European countries. France and Germany, for instance, have secondary school completion rates as high as the United States. However, in no European country do as many students go to university level post-secondary institutions as in the United States, and many fewer obtain university level degrees (OECD 1998). This means that more Americans enter the labor force at relatively advanced ages, and many more American first job competitors have a university degree.

The education-occupation fit is highly varied in European countries. Most French students leave school with no specific job skills and must be trained by their employers, whereas most German students receive focused training for highly specific kinds of jobs while in school (Maurice, et al. 1986). Most British students' job skills are obtained through part-time programs after leaving secondary school (Kerckhoff 1993).

The majority of American students obtain either a high school diploma or a college bachelor's degree. Neither of those credentials has any direct relevance for specific placement in the labor force. This lack of occupational relevance of most American credentials shapes the whole process of transition from school to work.

Vocational Education. Post-secondary vocational education is not well-developed in the United States (U.S. Department of Education 1994). Most European countries' educational systems award a wide array of credentials, and those credentials are generally much more directly associated with specific jobs than are American credentials (Kerckhoff 2000).

As recently as twenty years ago, American high schools offered three curricula or "tracks," one of which was "vocational." Students learned basic skills that could be useful in a range of occupations. There has been a drastic reduction in the clarity of high school tracks, however (Lucas 1999). The American high school diploma is an even more general credential than it used to be.

This change in high school curricula has undoubtedly also contributed to students' (and educators') lack of knowledge about and interest in vocational post-secondary courses. Although enrollments in post-secondary institutions below the four-year college level are sizeable, there is little national recognition of the credentials they award. High school graduates continue to face a "college or nothing" view of further education.

School to Work. Young people in most European countries usually obtain their first full-time jobs at earlier ages than do Americans. A large proportion of young Britons leave school and enter the labor force full-time at age 16, although many obtain additional educational credentials on a part-time basis while working full-time (Bynner and Fogelman 1993). The majority of Germans enter the "dual system" in which they serve apprenticeships at the same time they obtain specialized schooling relevant to their jobs (Mortimer and Krüger 2000). Most complete their time in the "dual system" by age 19 .

The linkage between educational institutions and employers is also much closer in Europe, especially at the post-secondary level

(Rosenbaum, Kariya, Settersten, and Maier 1990). The German dual system is the most formal kind of linkage (Hamilton and Hurrelmann 1994), but many job-relevant British credentials are awarded through course work at colleges of further education arranged for by young people's employers (Kerckhoff 1993) and formally recognized by national organizations.

The American Uniqueness. Several features of the American educational system thus make the transition from school to work quite different from the transition in most European countries. They also make the transition difficult in general and especially disadvantageous for young people with relatively low levels of educational attainment.

(1) Due to the very general nature of American educational credentials and the decentralization of the educational system, neither American youth nor their prospective employers are provided much guidance in seeking a worker-job match.

(2) The very weak linkage between educational institutions below the college level and potential employers leaves most young people without institutional guidance or support in seeking positions in the labor force.

(3) The very large gap between the most common credential (a high school diploma) and the next generally recognized level of attainment (a college diploma) creates the basis for three important features of the American youth labor market: (a) Many young people enter the labor market after years of post-secondary schooling but with no post-secondary credentials (college dropouts). (b) The minority who obtain vocational post-secondary credentials are able to use them effectively only in a local labor market. (c) Those who do obtain a college diploma have a very great advantage in obtaining and keeping a good job.

The Economy

The American economy has recently experienced a record-breaking period of growth and vitality. Corporate profits have soared, there has been little inflation, and the unemployment rate has been at a very low level. All of these vital signs are the best they have been in a generation, and the federal budget has swung from deficit to surplus for the first time in decades. The educational investments young Americans make and the job opportunities they now have are significantly affected by the booming economy.

Employers can require high levels of educational attainment by their prospective employees because there are many highly educated people available. In order for a large proportion of young people to attend college, however, they need to have access to significant financial resources. Those financial resources are required both to pay the costs of higher education and to replace young people's forgone earnings during their years in college. To invest funds in higher education requires either that they currently have adequate resources or that they have confidence later earnings will justify assuming a significant debt. A booming economy makes all of this possible.

The booming economy also affects the job prospects of those with relatively low levels of education. Low unemployment rates mean that many employers need to organize their work force to provide jobs for less qualified workers whom they might not hire if they had alternatives. Because these are less desirable employees, employers do not want to make long-term commitments to them or invest a great deal in training them. Many of those workers are thus hired into "non-standard" jobs. These are often part-time, temporary, or on-call jobs (Kalleberg, Reskin, and Hudson 2000). The youngest workers, those with the lowest levels of education, minorities, and women are all over-represented in such jobs (Kalleberg et al. 1997).

Many of the jobs that are available to less well-educated young American workers are "derivative" in the sense that they depend on the ability of the college educated and more highly paid workers to pay for the services and products they produce. These jobs often involve personal services and the production of items usually purchased with discretionary funds (e.g., restaurant meals, recreation items, and services), and those jobs thus depend on other people having high incomes.

These non-standard and derivative jobs have assumed such importance in the lives of young people who have not graduated from college because many low-skill manufacturing jobs have been "exported" to less developed countries. What used to be a division of labor within the American economy has become a division of labor within the world economy. At the same time, within the American economy there has evolved a sharper division between high- and low-skill and high- and low-paid jobs.

Within the world economy, the United States has tended to specialize in financial and communications services and high technology manufacturing. Large segments of the American work force are required to be very productive in the performance of highly skilled tasks. This is one of the reasons why many American employers seek highly educated employees. The core occupations in those parts of the labor force call for high levels of skill and great flexibility in learning new tasks.

Large, complex corporations are most likely to be involved in the world economy. Those corporations not only seek college educated employees but they can afford to recruit those employees in a national labor market and to provide them with demanding training programs and career ladders within the corporation. Even in those large corporations, employees with less than a college degree are recruited locally (Grubb 1999), however, and they are more likely to have non-standard employment arrangements and are less likely to be offered firm-sponsored training programs or opportunities for career moves within the corporation. There is usually a sharp division between the work experiences of the core employees in these corporations and those who are viewed as "peripheral" (Kalleberg 1996).

The vitality of the American economy has thus made it possible for large proportions of our youth to continue in school after high school graduation, and it has provided jobs for an historic proportion of young Americans. However, the specialization of the American economy within the world economy has led to a growing division between high- and low-skill jobs, and that has provided a strong incentive for many young Americans to go to college. The great increase in the proportion of young people with post-secondary schooling would not have occurred without the combination of a demand for highly educated youth and an increase in the proportion of families that can afford the costs of higher education. For the rest of young Americans, however, although the booming economy has reduced the threat of unemployment somewhat, it has increased the prospect of what can be viewed as "bad jobs" (Kalleberg et al. 2000).

The labor force experiences of young people in most European countries have been rather different from those of young Americans. The labor markets of most European countries are more regulated than the American markets. The strong American emphasis on free enterprise and minimal government regulation has provided a basis for the recent booming American economy, but the same conditions are not present in Europe. State welfare policies in Europe provide protection against many of the negative effects of economic decline, but they also constrain some of the forces that have led to the booming American economy (Esping-Andersen 1990).

The last two decades of the twentieth century have been a period of economic problems in Europe, and youth unemployment rates have been consistently high (Furlong 1991; Layard, Nickell, and Jackman 1991; OECD 1998). However, unemployment has been less of a problem for young Germans than for French and British youth, except for those Germans with the lowest educational credentials (Brauns, Gangl, and Scherer 1999).

It seems likely that the German apprenticeship system is an important contributor to this European societal difference. An important part of the regulation of the German youth labor market occurs at the time apprenticeships are awarded. Not everyone can enter the apprenticeship of his or her choice (Mortimer and Krüger 2000), and employers are unlikely to award apprenticeships for occupations that do not have openings. So, rather than early labor force unemployment, young Germans may feel the pressure of employment constraints during the period in which they are being sorted into their adolescent apprenticeships.

The Demography of Youth

Another important feature of the context in which American youth move from school to work is the composition of the youth cohort making that transition. Two features are especially worth emphasizing, the size of the cohort and its ethnic composition. It is not necessary to speculate about these two features when anticipating the labor force experiences of American youth in the early twenty-first century, because they are already determined. The demographic characteristics of the American youth cohorts that will enter the labor force in the early twenty-first century are already known.

The post-World War II baby boom introduced a kind of ripple effect into the demography of the United States because the baby boomers had more children than the previous or following cohorts. There has also been a large in migration from Asia and Central and South America during the past few decades. As a result of these changes in immigration and reproduction, the size of the population making the transition from school to work has shifted recently, and it will continue to do so in the foreseeable future. In 1990, there were 26.8 million Americans 18 to 24 years old. That number dropped slightly to 24.9 million in 1995, but it rose to 28.3 million in the year 2000 and is expected to rise further to

30.1 million in 2010 (U.S. Bureau of the Census 1996). That is a one-fifth increase in the fifteen years from 1995 to 2010. Many more young Americans will make the transition from school to work in the early twenty-first century than were doing so in the last part of the twentieth century.

The ethnic composition of the cohorts making the transition is also changing. In 1990, 26.1% of Americans 18 to 24 years old were black or Hispanic, and in 1995 27.8% were black or Hispanic. In the year 2000, that proportion was 29.7%, and by the year 2010 it will be 33.7% (U.S. Bureau of the Census 1996). That is a 21.1% increase in fifteen years and a 29.1% increase in twenty years. Thus, the cohort making the transition from school to work will be much larger in the year 2010, and it will have a much larger minority ethnic component. The implications of those changes for early labor force experiences need to be considered.

The shift in the demography of American youth will not have a close parallel in Europe. Although European countries experienced a post-war baby boom, they also lost a larger proportion of their young male population in the war. In addition, they have not experienced the great in migration during recent decades the United States has had, nor will they have as large an in migration during the next decade. This is another feature of the greater state control in those countries.

THE TRANSITION FROM SCHOOL TO WORK IN THE EARLY TWENTY-FIRST CENTURY

The earlier discussion has shown that young Americans' current transition from school to work has a number of special characteristics, some of which distinguish it from the transition of young people in most European countries. Briefly, they are:

(1) There are few levels of educational attainment in the United States, and the two most salient credentials (high school graduation and college graduation) are widely spaced.

(2) Few American educational credentials have any direct occupational relevance, so there is seldom an obvious match between a student's educational credential and a particular job.

(3) On average, Americans are generally older than Europeans when they get their first full-time job.

(4) Access to good jobs (jobs with high status, good pay and fringe benefits, employment security, and promotion opportunities) in the United States is greater by far for college graduates than for those with less education.

(5) Especially for Americans with less than a bachelor's degree, there is usually an extended early period of "turbulence" involving frequent shifts between jobs and periods of unemployment.

(6) Americans are more likely than Europeans to shift back from full-time work to full-time school before settling into stable employment.

(7) American women have higher levels of educational attainment than men, and whites have higher levels of educational attainment than blacks or Hispanics.

(8) Given the same level of educational credentials, American women have lower earnings than men, and blacks and Hispanics have lower status jobs and lower earnings than whites.

The previous section has reviewed some features of the social and institutional context within which the school-to-work transition currently occurs. The nature of the American educational system and the vitality of the American economy have received the most attention. Assuming no changes in context, the most reasonable prediction for the foreseeable future is a continuation of the patterns described. Changes are almost certain to occur, but it is difficult at best to prophesy what they will be. In what follows, some estimates are made of the possible effects on the transition process of some changes that could occur in the educational system and the economy.

The previous section has also noted, however, that some demographic changes are already occurring, and those changes may alter the transition process even if the educational system and the economy remain as they are. This section is thus divided into three parts. The first deals with possible effects of the on-going demographic changes. The other two then deal with possible changes in the educational system and the economy and how they might affect the transition of young Americans from school to work.

In each of the three sections, it is possible to make very different kinds of projections for the future, and different combinations of those projections can lead to highly varied expectations for the twenty-first century. In conclusion, therefore, I present two general projections, one optimistic, one pessimistic.

Demographic Changes

The cohort entering the labor force in the year 2010 will be one-fifth larger than the cohort that entered the labor force in 1995, and it will also have a one-fifth larger proportion of black and Hispanic members. If nothing else changes, these demographic shifts are likely to alter the overall pattern of young Americans' entry into the labor force.

If blacks and Hispanics continue to have lower levels of educational attainment and if they continue to qualify for largely lower status and lower paid jobs, this should increase the number of candidates for low-skill jobs more than for high-skill jobs. If there are no major changes in the distribution of kinds of jobs or in discriminatory practices, this should worsen the job prospects of minorities because there will be more competition for the less desirable jobs than for the better jobs.

There have been major efforts recently to improve the educational opportunities and attainments of minority youth, however. To the extent these efforts are successful, minority youths may be increasingly able to compete with whites for at least moderately desirable jobs. And, if the economy continues to grow and more jobs are created, the fact that minorities will constitute a larger proportion of the youth population can serve to increase their visibility in the desirable jobs.

At the same time, if the economy does not continue to grow, the overall increase in the size of the cohort can increase competition for all entry jobs, even the better jobs. That competition, in turn, can increase employers' preference for more highly educated workers for those better jobs, and that, in turn, can increase the proportion of the cohort seeking higher education. If the recent pattern of higher education enrollments and successful completion of the bachelor's degree continues, this is also likely to increase further the proportion of future cohorts who are "college dropouts."[2] Over time, such an outcome could reduce the demand for higher education, but recent experience does not suggest that

---

[2] It is interesting to note that some projections of enrollments in four-year institutions of higher education and projections of the number of bachelor degrees are consistent with this speculation. Enrollments in higher education were 8.8 million in 1997, and they are expected to rise to 10.1 million by the year 2009. However, 1.160 million bachelor's degrees were awarded in 1997, and it is projected that only 1.275 million bachelor's degrees will be awarded in 2009 (NCES 1999a). Thus, although enrollments are expected to increase by 14.8%, the number of bachelor's degrees awarded is expected to increase by only 9.9%. That difference means that we can expect that a growing proportion of young people will be college dropouts.

it would. Instead, it seems more likely that any increase in the demand for highly educated workers will lead to increased college enrollments, even if, as expected, that leads to a lower rate of success in obtaining college degrees.

Changes in the Educational System

The two core features of the American educational system that provide a structural frame for the transition from school to work in the United States are the huge step from being a high school graduate to being a college graduate and the lack of occupational relevance of the major American educational credentials. From the perspective of European educational systems, the obvious missing piece is a set of standardized vocationally relevant post-secondary credentials awarded by well-established and respected institutions. It does not seem likely that such credentials and institutions will fully materialize in the foreseeable future, but changes in that direction may well occur, and it is worth speculating about what effect they could have if they should do so.

Two kinds of change appear to be possible. First, it is possible that recent efforts to increase the visibility of post-secondary vocational schooling and to standardize the credentials resulting from such schooling (Borman, et al. 1996) will be increasingly successful. Second, recent efforts to increase employers' contacts with sub-baccalaureate educational institutions (Rosenbaum, et al. 1990) may grow and become more coordinated. Such contacts should facilitate the matching of jobs and the knowledge and skills of young workers.

Should those two kinds of change occur, they would probably have the following effects:

(1) Employers would find it easier to recruit workers who already know something about the kinds of tasks they will be asked to perform on the job and who have at least some of the skills needed to perform them.

(2) High school students would be better able to make informed decisions about high school course selections, and they would have an alternative to the "college or nothing" choice once they graduate from high school.

(3) If many students choose to attend vocational post-secondary institutions and obtain vocationally relevant credentials, this would

very probably reduce the size of the "college dropout" segment of the cohort.

(4) With more young workers having some training for particular kinds of employment, successful worker-job matches would be more frequent, and the "turbulence" of the early years in the labor force would be reduced.

Changes in the Economy

Speculation here could go off in many different directions. I wish to consider only the possibility of a general economic decline. By this I do not mean an economic collapse or general depression but only a downward shift in the general health of the economy, one that would lead to the need for reductions in corporate expenditures and innovative investments. Developments during the last half of the year 2000 and the first half of the year 2001 make such an "adjustment" seem very likely. Such a change would have significant implications for workers of all ages, but it would have a greater impact on young workers than on older workers because they are less likely to have job security.

Possible effects of such a general downturn on the labor force experiences of young workers would include:

(1) Unemployment would almost certainly increase, and the increase would be especially large for the least secure workers: minorities and women and those with low levels of education and without specific job skills.

(2) There would be an increase in non-standard employment relations (part-time and temporary employment, etc.), and the same groups (the poorly educated, minorities, and women) would be increasingly likely to experience them.

(3) Competition for a reduced number of "good jobs" would become more intense which would lead to reductions in the current benefits associated with those jobs (earnings levels, job security, fringe benefits, and career opportunities).

It has also been argued that youth employment opportunities affect students' decisions about leaving school and entering the labor force. The so-called "warehousing effect" refers to the tendency for students to remain in school longer if employment opportunities are reduced (Grubb and Lazerson 1982). This effect has been observed in other countries as well. Raffe and Willms (1989) report that the higher the unemployment rates in areas of Scotland the more likely students are to remain in secondary school. It has also been argued that individual decisions about making the transition from school to work are affected by both one's experiences in school and opportunities for employment (Gambetta 1987). So, it may not be possible to project the effects on the labor force without also taking into account the possible effects on the internal workings of the schools.

A more intricate, but also more speculative, set of predictions can be made by assuming that the effects of an economic decline will vary depending on the level of education considered and depending on which labor market sectors are most affected (Shanahan, Miech, and Elder 1998). The boom in the American economy has occurred during a period in which there has been a sharp shift from the manufacturing to the service sector. That shift, of course, is one of the reasons for the great increase in demand for highly educated workers and a decline in attractive and secure employment opportunities for those with lower levels of education. If there is a decline in the American economy, the service sector (especially financial and high technology industries) will probably be most affected. That, in turn, could mean that the most immediate effect might be a worsening of the employment prospects of highly educated workers.

The boom period has been one of almost unimaginable prosperity for a segment of the American population, but it has also been a period of great inequality, much greater than in any other industrial country. American executives are paid hundreds of times as much as their employees, and there is more poverty (however defined) in the United States than in any other industrial country. Many American companies (especially the NASDAQ companies) are probably heavily over-extended.

One imaginable sequence following an economic decline is a degree of leveling of the pay differentials as well as a redistribution of investment capital into less speculative enterprises. That could also mean pulling back some of our global investments with an associated increase in investments in American industries and even increased employment opportunities for American SBLM workers.

However, the American free enterprise system is well-entrenched, both within the business world and in the political arena. The speculative spirit that has driven up the stock market to unimagined heights may not be flexible enough to shift gears if things go less well. Instead, there may be an increase in speculation, rather than an adjustment based on some image of economic cycles or equity. Recent corporate successes have involved large worker layoffs, huge investments in top management salaries, and constant upgrading of the technical foundations of the enterprise. It is not unreasonable to expect that any attempts to cope with even a modest economic decline will involve the same approaches.

TWO VIEWS OF THE FUTURE

Except for the demographic changes that are already known, there is no wholly reliable basis to predict any particular changes in the current conditions that affect the pattern of transition from school to work by American youth. I have suggested some of the possible effects of the demographic changes we know will occur, and I have suggested some possible effects of some *possible* changes in the educational system and the economy.

In the absence of a firmer basis for predicting these kinds of changes, it may be wiser simply to assume that the transition of American youth from school to work will remain much as it has been recently. However, I want to close this discussion by generating two possible scenarios for the future and deduce from them two rather different directions of change in the nature of the transition from school to work. One assumes that a number of changes will occur that will reduce the negative transition experiences of American youth, and the other assumes that changes will occur that will exacerbate those negative experiences. I will refer to them as optimistic and pessimistic scenarios. Both accept the reality of the demographic changes described and assume a modest decline in the American economy. They differ in their assumptions about changes in the educational system and about the adjustments that will be made to the demographic and economic changes.

The Optimistic Scenario

This scenario assumes the following:

(1) Vocational post-secondary programs will become more standard-ized and a national system of vocational post-secondary creden-tials will be established.

(2) Employers will more actively participate in the development of vocational secondary and post-secondary programs and establish on-going recruitment relationships with the schools that provide them.

(3) A larger proportion of students will obtain vocational skills in high school as well as vocational post-secondary credentials. Given these useful alternatives, fewer will feel impelled to go to college, and fewer will become college dropouts.

(4) The success of programs to improve the elementary and secondary educational opportunities of minority students will lead to more minority students completing high school and obtaining post-secondary credentials of all kinds.

(5) The economic decline will impact most heavily on high tech industries, reducing excessive speculation without having a major disruptive effect.

(6) The decline will bring about some reorganization of American firms and shift labor force recruiting somewhat so that there is less demand for college educated workers and greater demand for workers in the SBLM who have vocational skills and credentials.

(7) The economic reorganization, together with the increased academic and vocational skills learned by young members of minority groups, will make it possible for the economy to absorb the large future youth cohorts and their larger proportions of minorities.

This scenario assumes that the strong emphasis on going to college and restricting offers of good jobs to college graduates are due to two changeable conditions. One of these is the lack of adequate educational programs offering visibly marketable vocational skills and credentials at levels below the bachelor's degree. The other is excessive corporate investment in speculative high tech industries. According to this scenario, changes in the educational system that make it more like those in Europe and changes in the economy based on a more stable and continuous investment in a broad range of industrial arenas will have an overall positive effect. In particular, these changes will have a positive effect on the ability of young Americans to develop the skills needed to move more smoothly from school to work.

The Pessimistic Scenario

This scenario makes the following assumptions:

(1) There will be no significant changes in the core features of the American educational system. In particular, secondary and

post-secondary vocational programs will not be developed beyond their present condition.

(2) Employers will only occasionally involve themselves in the development of vocational programs, and few will establish continuing
recruiting relationships with schools below the college level.

(3) The "college or nothing" alternatives will continue to be the primary ones faced by high school graduates.

(4) The educational disadvantages of minority students will continue, and perhaps get worse, as the size of the minority youth
population increases.

(5) Because of American corporations' broad investment in and de-
pendence on high tech industries, any economic decline will be
pervasive rather than circumscribed.

(6) The speculative nature of the American economy and its long
period of success will make it difficult, if not impossible, for American corporations to adjust sensitively to the decline through internal reorganization.

(7) Using previously trusted methods (labor force reductions, speculative investments in new enterprises, offering decision makers
greater incentives and rewards), corporations will provide fewer
and less attractive opportunities to workers, especially young,
minority, female, and less well-educated workers.

This scenario makes many of the same assumptions as the optimistic
scenario about the conditions that produce the current emphasis on
going to college and restricting good job offers to college graduates.
But, in contrast to the optimistic scenario, it also assumes that those
conditions will not change.

The optimistic scenario assumes that the educational system will
change so as to make a greater range of marketable credentials available,
and it assumes that American corporations will be sufficiently flexible
to adjust to an economic decline by diversifying their investments and
altering their internal organization. Under those conditions, even the
huge demographic shift that is already under way and a modest economic downturn can be accommodated without major changes in the
American transition from school to work.

The pessimistic scenario assumes that the educational changes will
not occur and that the corporate world will be inflexible. Under the
pessimistic scenario, the combination of the demographic shift and a
modest economic decline will make the transition from school to work

much more difficult than it is at present. The pessimistic scenario thus calls for sharply increased youth unemployment, lower wages, and poorer job conditions for young American workers, especially for members of minority groups, females, and those who are less well-educated.

Of course, the future may well provide other combinations of the influences suggested here, not just one of these two contrasting combinations. In seeking to prepare for that future, each of us will need to decide just how optimistic or pessimistic we are.

References

Althauser, R. 1989. Internal Labor Markets. *Annual Review of Sociology* 15: 143–161.

Arum, R., and M. Hout. 1998. The Early Returns: The Transition from School to Work in the United States. Pp. 471–510 in Y. Shavit and W. Müller (Eds.), *From School to Work: A Comparative Study of Educational Qualifications and Occupational Destinations*. Oxford: Clarendon Press.

Beggs, J. J., W. J. Villemez, and R. Arnold. 1997. Black Population Concentration and Black-White Inequality: Expanding the Consideration of Place and Space Effects. *Social Forces* 76(September): 65–91.

Bielby, W. T., and J. N. Baron. 1986. Men and Women at Work: Sex Segregation and Statistical Discrimination. *American Journal of Sociology* 91(January): 759–799.

Borman, K. M. 1991. *The First Real Job*. Albany, NY: State University of New York.

Borman, K. M., P. W. Cookson, Jr., A. R. Sadovnik, and J. Z. Spade. 1996. *Implementing Educational Reform: Sociological Perspectives on Educational Policy*. Norwood, NJ: Ablex Publishing Corporation.

Brauns, H., M. Gangl, and S. Scherer. 1999. Education and Unemployment: Patterns of Labour Market Entry in France, the United Kingdom and West Germany. Arbeitspapiere, Nr. 6 – Mannheimer Zentrum für Europäische Sozialforschung.

Brint, S., and J. Karabel. 1989. *The Diverted Dream: Community Colleges and the Promise of Educational Opportunity in America, 1900–1995*. New York: Oxford University Press.

Bynner, J., and K. Fogelman. 1993. Making the Grade: Education and Training Experiences. Pp. 36–59 in E. Ferri (Ed.), *Life at 33: The Fifth Follow-Up of the National Child Development Study*. London: National Children's Bureau.

Carr, R., J. Wright, and C. Brody. 1996. Effects of High School Work Experience a Decade Later: Evidence from the National Longitudinal Study. *Sociology of Education* 69(January): 66–81.

Clark, B. R. 1960. The 'Cooling-Out' Function in Higher Education. *American Journal of Sociology* 65(6): 569–576.

Cohn, S. 1985. *The Process of Occupational Sex-Typing*. Philadelphia: Temple University Press.

Collins, R. 1979. *The Credential Society*. New York: Academic Press.

Dougherty, K. 1987. The Effects of Community Colleges: Aid or Hindrance to Socioeconomic Attainment? *Sociology of Education* 60(2): 86–103.

Esping-Andersen, G. 1990. *The Three Worlds of Welfare Capitalism*. Cambridge, UK: Polity Press.

Fossett, M. A., O. R. Galle, and J. A. Burr. 1989. Racial Occupational Inequality, 1940–1980: A Research Note on the Impact of Changing Regional Distribution of the Black Population. *Social Forces* 68(December): 415–427.

Furlong, A. 1991. *Growing Up in a Classless Society? School to Work Transitions*. Edinburgh: University of Edinburgh Press.

Gambetta, D. 1987. *Were They Pushed or Did They Jump? Individual Decision Mechanisms in Education*. New York: Cambridge University Press.

Goux, D., and E. Maurin. 1998. From Education to First Job: The French Case. Pp. 103–141 in Y. Shavit and W. Müller (Eds.), *From School to Work: A Comparative Study of Educational Qualifications and Occupational Destinations*. Oxford: Clarendon Press.

Grubb, W. N. 1997. The Return to Education in the Sub-Baccalaureate Labour Market, 1984–1990. ERE paper. *Economics of Education Review* 16(3): 231–247.

Grubb, W. N. 1999. The Subbaccalaureate Labor Market in the United States: Challenges for the School-to-Work Transition. Pp. 171–193 in W. R. Heinz (Ed.), *From Education to Work: Cross-National Perspectives*. New York: Cambridge University Press.

Grubb, W. N., T. Dickinson, L. Giordano, and G. Kaplan. 1992. *Betwixt and Between: Education, Skills and Employment in Sub-Baccalaurate Labor Markets*. Berkeley, CA: National Center for Research in Vocational Education.

Grubb, W. N., and M. Lazerson 1982. Education and the Labor Market: Recycling the Youth Problem. Pp. 110–141 in H. Kantor and D. Tyack (Eds.), *Work, Youth, and Schooling*. Palo Alto, CA: Stanford University Press.

Hamilton, S. T., and M. A. Hamilton. 1999. Creating New Pathways to Adulthood by Adapting German Apprenticeship in the United States. Pp. 194–213 in W. R. Heinz (Ed.), *From Education to Work: Cross-National Perspectives*. New York: Cambridge University Press.

Hamilton, S., and K. Hurrelmann. 1994. The School-to-Career Transition in Germany and the United States. *Teachers College Record* 96(2): 329–344.

Heath, A., and S. Y. Cheung. 1998. Education and Occupation in Britain. Pp. 71–101 in Y. Shavit and W. Müller (Eds.), *From School to Work: A Comparative Study of Educational Qualifications and Occupational Destinations*. New York: Cambridge University Press.

Heinz, W. R. 1999. Job Entry Patterns in a Life-Course Perspective. Pp. 214–231 in W. R. Heinz (Ed.), *From Education to Work: Cross-National Perspectives*. New York: Cambridge University Press.

Holzer, H. 1996. *What Employers Want: Job Prospects for Less Educated Workers*. New York: Russell Sage.

Hout, M. 1996. The Politics of Mobility. Pp. 293–316 in A. C. Kerckhoff (Ed.), *Generating Social Stratification: Toward a New Research Agenda*. Boulder, CO: Westview Press.

Jacobs, J. A. 1989. *Revolving Doors: Sex Segregation and Women's Careers*. Palo Alto, CA: Stanford University Press.

Kalleberg, A. L. 1996. Changing Contexts of Careers: Trends in Labor Market Structures and Some Implications for Labor Force Outcomes. Pp. 343–358 in A. C. Kerckhoff (Ed.), *Generating Social Stratification: Toward a New Research Agenda*. Boulder, CO: Westview Press.

Kalleberg, A. L., E. Rasell, K. Hudson, D. Webster, B. F. Reskin, N. Cassirer, and E. Appelbaum. 1997. *Nonstandard Work, Substandard Jobs: Flexible Work Arrangements in the U.S.* Washington, DC: Economic Policy Institute and Women's Research and Education Institute.

Kalleberg, A. L., B. F. Reskin, and K. Hudson. 2000. Bad Jobs in America: Standard and Nonstandard Employment Relations and Job Quality in the United States. *American Sociological Review* 65(2): 256–278.

Kerckhoff, A. C. 1993. *Diverging Pathways: Social Structure and Career Deflections*. New York: Cambridge University Press.

Kerckhoff, A. C. 2000. Transition from School to Work in Comparative Perspective. Pp. 453–474 in M. T. Hallinan (Ed.), *Handbook of Sociology of Education*. New York: Plenum.

Kerckhoff, A. C., and L. Bell. 1998. Hidden Capital: Vocational Credentials and Attainment in the United States. *Sociology of Education* 71(2): 152–174.

Kerckhoff, A. C., L. Bell, and E. Glennie. 2000. Comparative Educational Attainment Trajectories in Great Britain and the United States. Paper presented to the International Sociological Association, Research Committee on Social Stratification, Libourne, France.

Layard, R., S. Nickell, and R. Jackman. 1991. *Unemployment: Macroeconomic Performance and the Labour Market*. Oxford: Oxford University Press.

Leigh, E. E., and A. M. Gill. 1997. Labor Market Returns to Community Colleges: Evidence for Returning Adults. *Journal of Human Resources* 32(Spring): 334–353.

Lewis, D. R., J. C. Hearn, and E. E. Zilbert. 1993. Efficiency and Equity Effects of Vocationally Focused Postsecondary Education. *Sociology of Education* 66 (3): 188–205.

Lucas, S. R. 1999. *Tracking Inequality: Stratification and Mobility in American High Schools*. New York: Teachers College Press.

MacDonald, R. 1998. Youth, Transitions and Social Exclusion: Some Issues for Youth Research in the UK. *Journal of Youth Studies* 1(2): 163–176

Marini, M. M. 1989. Sex Differences in Earnings in the United States. *Annual Review of Sociology* 15: 348–380.

Maurice, M., F. Sellier, and J. J. Silvestre. 1986. *The Social Foundations of Industrial Power: A Comparison of France and Germany*. Cambridge, MA: MIT Press.

McKinney, F., S. Franchak, I. Halasz, I. Morrison, and P. Fornash. 1984. Increasing Job Placement Rates in Vocational Programs. *Research and Development Series*. Columbus, OH: National Center for Research in Vocational Education.

McNeal, R. 1997. Are Students Being Pulled Out of High School? The Effect of Adolescent Employment on Dropping Out. *Sociology of Education* 70(3): 206–220.

Monk-Turner, E. 1990. The Occupational Achievements of Community and Four-Year College Entrants. *American Sociological Review* 55(October): 719–725.

Mortimer, J. T., and M. K. Johnson. 1999. Adolescent Part-Time Work and Post-secondary Transition Pathways in the United States. Pp. 111–148 in W. R. Heinz (Ed.), *From Education to Work: Cross-National Perspectives.* New York: Cambridge University Press.

Mortimer, J. T., and H. Krüger, H. 2000. Transition from School to Work in the United States and Germany. Pp. 475–497 in M. T. Hallinan (Ed.), *Handbook of Sociology of Education.* New York: Plenum.

Müller, W., S. Steinmann, and R. Ell. 1998. Education and Labour-Market Entry in Germany. Pp. 143–188 in Y. Shavit and W. Müller (Eds.), *From School to Work: A Comparative Study of Educational Qualifications and Occupational Destinations.* Oxford: Clarendon Press.

NCES. 1996. *The Condition of Education, 1996.* Washington, DC: National Center for Education Statistics.

NCES. 1999a. *Projections of Education Statistics to 2009.* Washington, DC: National Center for Education Statistics.

NCES. 1999b. *The Condition of Education, 1999.* Washington, DC: National Center for Education Statistics.

NCES. 1999c. *Digest of Education Statistics, 1999.* Washington, DC: National Center for Education Statistics.

OECD. 1998. *Education at a Glance: OECD Indicators.* Paris: Organisation for Economic Co-Operation and Development.

Parcel, T. L., and C. W. Mueller. 1983. *Ascription and Labor Markets: Race and Sex Differences in Earnings.* New York: Academic Press.

Peterson, A. C., and J. T. Mortimer. (Eds.). (1994). *Youth Unemployment and Society.* New York: Cambridge University Press.

Raffe, D., and J. D.Willms. 1989. Schooling and the Discouraged Worker: Local-Labour Market Effects on Educational Participation. *Sociology* 23 (November): 559–581.

Reich, R. B. 1993. *The Work of Nations.* London: Simon and Schuster.

Rosenbaum, J. E., T. Kariya, R. Settersten, and T. Maier. 1990. Market and Network Theories of the Transition from High School to Work: Their Application to Industrialized Societies. *Annual Review of Sociology* 16: 263–299.

Rumberger, R. 1981. *Overeducation in the U.S. Labor Force.* New York: Praeger.

Shanahan, M. J., R. A. Miech, and G. H. Elder, Jr. 1998. Changing Pathways to Attainment in Men's Lives: Historical Patterns of School, Work, and Social Class. *Social Forces* 77(1): 231–256.

Shavit, Y., and W. Müller. (Eds.) 1998. *From School to Work: A Comparative Study of Educational Qualifications and Occupational Destinations.* Oxford: Clarendon Press.

Spenner, K. I. 1988. Technological Change, Skill Requirements, and Education. Pp. 131–184 in R. M. Cyert and D. C. Mowery (Eds.), *The Impact of Technological Change on Employment and Economic Growth.* Cambridge, MA: Ballinger.

Stevenson, D. L., and D. P. Baker. 1991. State Control of the Curriculum and Classroom Instruction. *Sociology of Education* 64(1): 1–10.

Tilly, C. 1996. Half a Job: *Bad and Good Part-Time Jobs in a Changing Labor Market.* Philadelphia: Temple University Press.

Tomaskovic-Devey, D. 1993. *Gender and Race Inequality at Work: The Sources and Consequences of Job Segregation.* Ithaca, NY: ILR Press.

U.S. Bureau of the Census. 1996. *Population Projections of the United States by Age, Sex, Race and Hispanic Origin: 1995 to 2050* (P25–1130). Washington, DC: Bureau of the Census.

U.S. Department of Education. 1994. *National Assessment of Vocational Education: Final Report to Congress.* Washington, DC: U.S. Department of Education.

4

Criminal Justice in the Lives of American Adolescents: Choosing the Future

Francis T. Cullen and John Paul Wright

Although most adolescents break the law – indeed, abstaining from involvement in at least petty delinquencies might be considered "deviant" – only a relatively small percentage of the youth population is brought into the criminal justice system in any given year. In the United States, for example, the Federal Bureau of Investigation (1999) compiles annual data on arrests for "Crime Index" offenses – an index composed of eight offenses that is meant to assess serious violent and property crime. A little over 4 percent of youths nationally are arrested for any Crime Index offense over the course of a year (Cook and Laub 1998). Perhaps more revealing, only a tiny percentage of juveniles in the United States – less than one-half of 1 percent of youths ages 10 to 17 – are arrested for violent offenses on the Crime Index (Snyder, Sickmund, and Poe-Yamagata 1996). Further, even among adolescents who are arrested, 44 percent are diverted from formal processing by the criminal justice system, with their cases handled informally (Stahl 1999).

Growing up in the United States, then, most youngsters do not have their lives decidedly circumscribed by the criminal justice system. They may experiment with illegal activities, but their criminality is not serious enough and persistent enough to draw sustained attention from enforcement officials or to prompt their incarceration. This observation is not advanced here as a prelude to our arguing that criminal justice interventions are of little consequence – as we will see shortly. Even so, it is perhaps a useful corrective to the intense media and popular representations which convey the message, implicitly if not explicitly, that drive-by gang shootings, wanton murders, and senseless school massacres are somehow both commonplace among adolescents and a sign that America is on the brink of moral collapse (see, e.g., Bennett, DiIulio, and Walters 1996; see also, Garland 1999). Hyperbole may garner headlines and sell books, but it can also stir up misplaced worries and cause us to choose unhelpful policies.

A judicious understanding of criminal justice in the lives of adolescents thus would start with the admonition not to exaggerate the extent to which youths are arrested and criminally sanctioned. But it would also lead us to examine more carefully how, from slightly different angles, the impact of criminal justice may be important and of concern to policymakers. Three considerations warrant attention.

First, as is well known, small percentages computed on a large base can result in a substantial *number* of cases. Thus, although a low percentage of adolescents are apprehended each year, the number of arrests is hardly inconsequential. The figures vary some from year to year, but the data from 1997 are instructive. For those under 18, there were over 2.8 million juvenile arrests. Of these, about 825,000 were for FBI Crime Index offenses; the rest were for "Non-Index" offenses, which are generally less serious legal violations. Almost 125,000 were for Crime Index violent offenses, including 2,500 for murder (Snyder 1998). Once in the criminal justice system, almost 1 million youths are processed each year by the juvenile court, with 10,000 cases sent to adult court for prosecution (Stahl 1999). It also is estimated that about 70,000 adolescents are behind bars in public juvenile facilities, with the average number of youths per state incarcerated standing at 1,351 (Moone 1997a). Privately-run facilities house another 39,671 juveniles, with almost 6 in 10 committed for a delinquent or status offense (as opposed to the commitment being tied to a youth's abuse, neglect, or emotional disturbance) (Moone 1997b).

Second, calculating annual figures can be misleading if we do not consider the *cumulative* or lifetime risk of significant contact with the criminal justice system. For example, although less than half of 1 percent of the nation's population was incarcerated in state and federal prisons on December 31, 1997 (Gilliard and Beck 1998), 5.1 percent of people in the United States will spend time in these prisons at some point in their lives (Bonczar and Beck 1997). Data on the risk of incarceration during the juvenile years is sketchy, but the chances of being sent to a state or federal prison – institutions typically reserved for those over 18 – is 1.1 percent by age 20. For African American males, however, the figure is a disquieting 7.9 percent (Bonczar and Beck 1997). These statistics, moreover, exclude time spent in municipal and county jails, which are used to detain the accused as they await court proceedings and to house those convicted of crimes in which the sentence is less than a year long. It is noteworthy that a 1993 census of jails estimated that the annual number of new admissions to local jails was nearly 10 *million* (Bonczar and Beck 1997).

Third, as the above discussion suggests, the impact of the criminal justice system is not spread evenly across society but rather is socially concentrated. "At the close of the twentieth century," observes Mauer (1999: 118), "race, crime, and the criminal justice system are inextricably mixed." Being a minority, especially from an inner-city community, dramatically increases one's prospects of significant contact with the criminal justice system (Snyder and Sickmund 1999a, 1999b; see also, Mann 1993). Thus, an analysis of statistics from Duval County, Florida, which contains Jacksonville, reported that a quarter of African American youths between the ages of 15 and 17 had been arrested in a four-month period (Miller 1996). Such figures are unusually high, but other studies of urban males find that upwards of a third are arrested by their 18th birthday (Tracy, Wolfgang, and Figlio 1985). In light of these statistics, it is perhaps not surprising to learn that in private and public residential juvenile facilities, 4 in 10 youths are Black and 1 in 5 are Hispanic (Gallagher 1999).

Such disproportionate contact with the criminal justice system extends into early adulthood, if not beyond. For example, among Black males 20 to 29, nearly 1 in 3 are under some form of supervision by the criminal justice system – that is, either behind bars or in the community while on probation or parole (Mauer 1999). In some places, the figures are even higher, with half the African American men in their 20s in Baltimore – to cite but one example – under formal legal supervision (Currie 1998). At birth, 3 in 10 Black males will face a prison sentence of a year or more in their lives (Mauer 1999). Specifically, among males, the lifetime likelihood of going to a state or federal prison – again, figures that do not include time spent in local jails or juvenile facilities – is 28.5 percent for African Americans, 6.0 percent for Hispanics, and 4.4 percent for whites; among females, the comparable figures are, respectively, 3.6 percent, 1.5 percent, and 0.5 percent (Bonczar and Beck 1997).

Scholars have differentially interpreted what these data mean. DiIulio (1994), for example, argues that justice is "color blind," and that the disproportionate presence of Blacks in the criminal justice system reflects their disproportionate involvement in serious and violent crime. In fact, the allocation of police and correctional resources to catch and incarcerate minority offenders is, in his view, a belated and much-needed investment of government resources in communities devastated by rampant criminality. Because criminal victimization is largely intra-racial and intra-class, locking up predatory offenders "saves Black lives." In contrast, other commentators characterize the high arrest and incarceration rates of poor African American youths as reflecting, at least in part, persisting racial discrimination. In the crackdown on crime, many adolescents who are not serious offenders are pulled, alongside predatory offenders, into the criminal justice system. The result of this "search and destroy" policy, as Miller (1996) calls it, is to foster antagonism toward criminal justice officials, to create as much crime as is saved, and to disrupt the life prospects of young Black males (see also, Mauer 1999; Tonry 1995).

It is beyond the scope of this chapter to settle this larger dispute. Nonetheless, there are two salient points to be faced. First, any discussion of "criminal justice in the lives of adolescents" – our topic here – is primarily a discussion of criminal justice in the lives of *minority* adolescents. White middle-class youngsters episodically have brushes with the law and some find their way to jail or prison, but most do not grow up with the expectation that contact with the criminal justice system will be a normal life event. For minority youths in the inner city, however, law enforcement officials are a common feature of the landscape, arrests can be witnessed all too often, and finding friends or family members – or oneself – behind bars is almost certain to take place in one's life course (Miller 1996).

Second, given the heavy presence of criminal justice in the lives of the most disadvantaged youths and in the most disadvantaged communities in the United States, it is critical to address the quality and effects of the sanctions that are imposed on adolescents by the legal system. What, in short, should be done with the youths brought within the criminal justice system – especially those that are confined in correctional institutions? The main point of this chapter is to show that two dramatically different answers have been offered to this question – answers that will frame the policy choices with regards to kids and criminal justice in the 21st century. One approach, *the punishment paradigm*, argues that the legal system should be used to punish youthful lawbreakers either to do justice and/or to control crime through deterrence (scaring offenders straight) or through incapacitation (locking up potentially chronic offenders so that they are physically unable to offend again). The second approach, *the rehabilitation paradigm*, wishes to implicate the criminal justice system in the social welfare task of improving offenders and their lives. "Programs," rather than the delivery of pain or the caging of youths, are held to change wayward adolescents for the better and thereby make society safer.

Deciding which approach to embrace is a complex task, complicated – as in other policy issues – by debates over core values and practical outcomes. Even so, in choosing the future, we have the benefit of looking to the past and of learning what has and has not proven effective. Indeed, the past two to three decades provide ample evidence with which to inform criminal justice policies as they relate to youths. We should confess "up front" that we are skeptical of the value of the punishment paradigm and cautiously optimistic about the value of the rehabilitation paradigm – views we convey in detail below. As a prelude to doing so, however, we will first provide a context for assessing the policy choices that confront us at the beginning of the 21st century by considering the "future" chosen by reformers in the U.S. at the very beginning of the 20th century.

As suggested thus far, this essay focuses predominantly on how criminal justice impinges on the lives of youths in the United States (for comparative discussions of juvenile justice, see Klein 1984; Mehlbye and Walgrave 1998; Winterdyk 1997). To a degree, the U.S. context and experience are exceptional. To be sure, most commentators suggest that youth crime has, despite periods of stability and decline, generally increased in Western Europe in the last quarter of the 20th century (Albrecht 1997; Weitekamp, Kerner, and Herberger 1998). As Europe has become more multicultural, there also has been a tendency – similar to the U.S. – to have ethnic, racial, and immigrant minorities disproportionately represented in the justice system (Mehlbye and Walgrave 1998; see also, Tonry 1994). European nations, however, lack the distinguishing feature of the juvenile crime problem in the states, especially among minority inner city youths: its disquieting lethality (see, more generally, Currie 1998; Zimring and Hawkins 1997).

Again, only a tiny fraction of American delinquents take the lives of others, and youth violence has been falling in very recent years in the U.S. (Blumstein and Wallman 2000). But the numerical count – as noted previously, 2,500 arrests for murder in 1998 – is shocking compared to the relative rarity of youthful homicides in other nations – or, for that matter, of murders in general. In 1996, for example, people *of all ages* in England committed fewer than 700 murders; in the United States the figure was close to 20,000 deaths from homicide (Langan and Farrington 1998). Currie (1998: 117) furnishes another revealing statistical juxtaposition by noting that in 1994, "an American male aged fifteen to twenty-four was 92 times as likely to die by violence as his Austrian counterpart."

Extreme acts of youthful violence are salient because they challenge the legitimacy of "juvenile justice" and, if publicized and politicized sufficiently, can trigger policy changes. When seemingly senseless episodes of lethal violence transpire – such as a recent case in the United States in which a 13 year old gunned down his teacher on the final day of the school year – the subsequent discourse inevitably laments that the "system was never designed to handle kids who kill." Prosecutors claim that they "have no choice" but to "treat this juvenile as an adult"; and where such efforts are frustrated by legal restrictions – such as a youth being too young to be transferred to adult court – calls are often made to expand the discretion of juvenile court officials to do so. Such cases are less frequent in other Western nations, precisely because violence is not as common. Still, they do occur, as was the case in England:

All this coincided with an exceptional crime in Merseyside, where a two-year-old boy was abducted from a shopping centre and murdered by two boys aged 10 and 11. It was a period of "public furore and massive media coverage" concerning criminal justice issues. In response, the Government decided to toughen its previous stance on criminal justice; and the courts became more punitive in their sentencing. (Bottoms, Haines, and O'Mahony 1998: 156; see also, Gelsthorpe and Fenwick 1997).

As this latter quote suggests, despite the distinctive features of juvenile crime and justice in the United States, there are common experiences that transcend the geographical and political boundaries separating America from other advanced industrial nations. As we will see immediately below, reformers in the United States developed a separate juvenile justice system – ostensibly for the purpose of rehabilitating wayward youths – in the beginning years of this past century. In the last quarter of the century, however, this social welfare approach to juvenile delinquents came under attack, both for its unjust legal treatment of youths and for its failure to "get tough" and curb youth predators from committing violent crimes. As Walgrave and Mehlbye (1998) point out, similar trends have characterized various Western nations (see also, Leschied, Jaffe, and Willis 1991).

Shortly after the creation of a distinct juvenile court in the United States, "separate jurisdictions and penal laws for children were established in the Netherlands (1905) [and] in the United Kingdom (1908). Belgium and France set up specific Children's Courts in 1912, which was done on an experimental basis in some cities in Germany already in 1908. Also in Denmark and in Italy, special attention was given to the position of children in penal justice" (Walgrave and Mehlbye 1998: 21). Similar to the United States, these systems of juvenile justice were based on a rehabilitative or "welfare approach: punishments are excluded, or are adapted to the specific needs of young people" (Walgrave and Mehlby 1998). But also like America, the hegemony of this model dissipated in the last quarter of the 20th century. The emphasis on the "welfare of the child" lost legitimacy as the effectiveness of rehabilitation was called into question. Again like the United States, reforms were initiated that, paradoxically, vacillated between trying to provide juveniles with more formal legal protections and justice on the one hand and trying to inflict harsher punishments on them on the other hand (Walgrave and Mehlbye 1998; see also, Matthews 1999; Leischied et al. 1991; Mehlbye and Walgrave 1998; Winterdyk 1997).

As Walgrave and Mehlbye (1998: 23) observe, the resulting ideological crisis has led officials in virtually every nation to "struggle with the welfare/justice balance." There has been a reluctance to abandon fully the idea that wayward youths should be "saved." But as in America, crime has often been politicized, and juvenile justice – especially the sanctioning of older, more serious offenders – has proven an attractive target for harsh rhetoric and, on occasion, punitive policies and practices. Thus, officials in Europe and elsewhere must – as in the U.S. – choose a future for their juvenile justice system. It strikes us that other nations have tended not to become so vigorous as the United States in their desire to exact harsh punishment on youthful criminals. Even so, the challenge remains as to whether the guiding thrust of these juvenile justice systems will be to rehabilitate and advance the welfare of youngsters or to be instruments that seek to inflict pain on juvenile "criminals," albeit justly and with an eye for advancing public safety. It is to these issues that we now turn.

THE PROGRESSIVE VISION

Poised at the front of a new century – the 20th – reformers in the "Progressive era" made a bold effort to choose a dramatically different approach to dealing with wayward youths. The justice system was faced with youthful offenders disproportionately drawn from poor, immigrant neighborhoods in the burgeoning inner cities. The social Darwinists suggested that such adolescents were of deficient stock and largely beyond redemption. An option might have been simply to embark on a campaign to lock up as many of the "dangerous classes" as was necessary and affordable. Instead, starting in 1899 in Cook County, Illinois (which includes Chicago), they took the path of creating a "juvenile court" whose explicit focus was to rehabilitate – not give up on – troubled youngsters. Although critical of their efforts in many respects, Platt (1969) termed these reformers the "child savers."

The inventors of the juvenile court rejected the idea that the state should stand as an *adversary* to delinquent youths. Instead, embracing the doctrine of *parens patriae*, they argued that the court and subsequently correctional officials should, as representatives of the state, act as kindly parents that were mindful of the best interest of their charges. In this view, youthful offenders should have no formal legal rights because they did not require protection from the parental, as opposed to adversarial, state. Much like parents, judges and other officials thus were accorded nearly unfettered discretionary powers to decide what should be done with the youths before them. The reformers believed that because the causes of crime were complex and potentially unique to each youth, adolescents entering the justice system should be studied carefully, the sources of their misbehavior diagnosed, and then a customized response developed on a case-by-case basis. Equipped with this knowledge, the court could then decide whether to divert an individual youth from the system, place the child in the community under supervision, or send him or her to a "reformatory." Adolescents who were institutionalized were not to be given a fixed sentence. Rather, they were to be kept in the reformatory until they were rehabilitated, which for particularly recalcitrant youths could extend until they reached the age of majority.

The Progressives wished, in essence, to *de-criminalize* the behavior of juveniles. Youths who committed "adult crimes" were not to be sanctioned like adults, but rather were – with few exceptions – to be kept within a juvenile justice system whose explicit purpose was to rehabilitate them. The de-criminalization of youth conduct, however, also justified the inclusion under the juvenile court of youths whose misbehavior and/or life circumstances would, if they were adults, have received no state intervention. To use contemporary language, these reformers believed that there were "risk factors" that would predict future criminality – parental abuse or neglect, truancy or running away from home – and that youths manifesting these risk factors required "early intervention." Accordingly, they expanded the jurisdiction of the juvenile court to cover "persons in need of supervision" (kids mistreated or not cared for by parents) and to cover "status offenses" (essentially deviant acts, such as skipping school, staying out late, and getting drunk, that adults can commit with impunity but which the "status" of youthfulness should prohibit). The logic, again, was for the state to intervene with and save youngsters on the pathway to serious criminal involvement – to provide the parenting that these juveniles' own parents could not furnish or undertook ineffectively.

This vision of saving youths either in or on the precipice of crime seemed noble and rational; by "doing good," the juvenile court would save troubled kids and make society safer. By 1917, all but three states in the United States had created legal structures similar to the juvenile court, and by 1945 all states had passed legislation mandating special juvenile courts and justice systems (Platt, 1969; Rothman, 1980). In the adult criminal justice system, the move toward rehabilitation was not so complete. Still, rehabilitation was elevated to the guiding philosophy, especially in the realm of corrections, where innovations emerged such as probation, parole, the indeterminate sentence, and the delivery of "treatment programs" both inside and outside the "correctional" institution.

This ambitious plan to save adolescents from a life in crime was beset by a range of problems: inadequate resources; the lack of trained personnel to deliver treatment services; a lack of criminological knowledge needed to diagnose and rehabilitate offenders; the abuse of discretion by judges and corrections officials; widely different penalties given to youths who had engaged in similar conduct; the inadvisability of mixing serious offenders with status offenders and kids whose only "offense" was being abused or neglected by their parents; the placement of youngsters in "reformatories" that more approximated harsh prisons; and so on (Platt 1969; Rothman 1980).

Even so, the rehabilitative ideal – the idea that juveniles should be reformed rather than punished – remained hegemonic until the mid-1960s. Until that time, problems were detected but were seen as fixable. Beginning in the middle part of the sixties, however, the very integrity of the Progressives' theory of individualized treatment came under sustained attack. In a series of rulings, the U.S. Supreme Court extended an array of legal protections to juveniles, in essence agreeing that the state was an adversary to youthful offenders and that juvenile reformatories dispensed more punishment than treatment. "Persons in need of supervision" – abused and neglected kids – were largely taken out of the juvenile system. The juvenile court still decided their fate but their day-to-day supervision was given to the child welfare division in states (Schwartz, Weiner, and Enosh 1999). The federal government also passed legislation seeking to prompt states to deinstitutionalize status offenders (Holden and Kapler 1995). Together, these changes re-criminalized youthful offenders both by extending them legal rights accorded to adult criminals and differentiating them from youths who committed status offenses or who suffered parental abuse or neglect.

Importantly, the attack on the Progressives' vision of the juvenile court came from those on the left and the right of the political spectrum. In large part, this odd coalition was inspired by the events in the prevailing social context, which created – at this particular juncture in time – a special sensitivity to long-standing problems in the juvenile justice system. The failure of the government to respond effectively to the disorder in the 1960s and early 1970s – which was punctuated by such notable events as the killings of students protesting the Vietnam War at Kent State, the massacre of inmates and guards in the Attica prison riot, and the scandals of Watergate – fostered a declining public confidence in government (Lipset and Schneider 1983). Yet the Progressives' vision of the juvenile court and of the rehabilitative ideal was predicated on a healthy *trust* in the state to do good – to act in the best interest of juveniles. It is instructive, therefore, that the reforms suggested by both liberals and conservatives focused on constraining the discretionary powers that had been accorded juvenile court judges and corrections officials. Those on the left and right agreed, albeit for different reasons, that the state could not be trusted to exercise its discretion in an appropriate way (Cullen and Gilbert 1982; Cullen, Golden, and Cullen 1983).

For liberals, the poverty of the juvenile system lay in the proclivity of state officials, under the guise of doing good, to act *coercively* toward youths. Rather than rehabilitate wayward kids, the system subjected youths – many of whom had done little wrong – to punitive intrusions into their lives, especially by placing them in inhumane juvenile "reformatories." Equally troubling, this excessive – indeed, repressive – social control was directed primarily at poor and minority youths, thus exacerbating existing inequalities. This is why they favored taking away discretion from state officials by giving youths an array of legal rights. Even better, they preferred a policy of "radical non-intervention" of the justice system leaving the kids alone whenever possible (Schur 1973). In contrast, for conservatives, state officials were not overly coercive but overly *lenient*. Equipped with a naïve, bleeding-heart ideology, judges and corrections officials – all in the name of rehabilitation – placed young predators back on the street. As one exposé's headline read: "Inside the Juvenile-Justice System: How Fifteen-Year-Olds Get Away with Murder" (Pileggi 1977). The state, in short, could not be trusted to protect the public. Its discretion to turn loose dangerous offenders – regardless of their age – had to be curtailed.

These criticisms contained important elements of truth: the juvenile justice system could be coercive and could allow serious offenders to return to the community to offend again. The difficulty, however, was that critics were better at scrutinizing the system and illuminating its failings than at articulating a coherent alternative that would prove more effective than existing practices rooted in the Progressives' rehabilitative ideal. As Miller (1996) understands, an important rationale underlying the founding of the juvenile justice system and the exercise of discretion was that judges and corrections officials would consider not just what an offender had done but also the nature of the offender's life circumstances:

In juvenile court, judges would, for the first time, consider issues that were dismissed as irrelevant to strict criminal court procedure. Issues associated with delinquency and crime – such as unemployment, health problems, emotional disturbance, disorganized communities, socially debilitating environments, poor education, family disorganization, and socioeconomic pressures – would all be fair game. (p. 90)

But with discretion fettered, the juvenile court would change its focus back to the offender's crime rather than to understand how the offender's circumstances had led him or her to break the law. The purpose, in short, would be to punish the crime, not to understand and save the wayward youth.

Moving away from the Progressives' paradigm of individualized treatment thus meant – and continues to mean – sacrificing an important policy consideration. The punishment perspective endorses a legalistic approach to offenders. In a very real way, the approach to offenders de-contextualizes and de-personalizes them. The only thing that matters are what criminal wrongs they committed and whether such conduct suggests that they might be dangerous in the future. Why they were moved to break the law and how their surroundings and emotional struggles may have contributed to their criminality are rendered invisible. Before the court, they are largely reduced to what they did – their crime – and, in turn, society is relieved of any responsibility for addressing the causes of their behavior. Because juveniles before the court are disproportionately poor and persons of color, this approach means that the role of the criminal justice system in investing in disadvantaged youthful offenders is ended. Instead, the role is narrowed to using punishment as a means of "doing justice" and controlling crime.

Moving away from the Progressives' rehabilitative paradigm also has entailed a *redistribution of power* within criminal justice as to who makes decisions over the lives of wayward youngsters. Under individualized treatment, legislators set only broad parameters as to the punishment delinquents would receive. Judges were invested with the discretion to decide whether youths should be sent home, supervised in the community, or sent to a reformatory. Corrections officials would then decide when such juveniles should be released from community supervision or from the institution. The goal, admittedly often not reached, was to base these decisions on the best interest of the child – on whether a youth had been rehabilitated. In the punishment paradigm, however, judges and corrections officials are largely stripped of their decision-making powers. The policy agenda is to standardize penalties by the seriousness of the crime committed, so as to ensure that offenders either receive equal sanctions before the court or experience certainty of punishment, which is held to foster deterrence. In this scheme, legislators pass laws that mandate what judges and corrections officials must do. Power thus reverts to politicians and, to an extent, to prosecutors who decide with which crime offenders will be charged. In the end, the question is whether troubled youths – and the community at large – will be better off having the fates of adolescents decided by legislators and prosecutors or by judges and corrections officials.

THE PUNISHMENT PARADIGM

Getting Tough with Juvenile Offenders

Between the mid-1970s and the late 1980s, rates of juvenile crime remained remarkably stable (Cook and Laub 1998). However, although property offenses remained level, violent crimes by juveniles – especially homicides – rose precipitously between 1988 and 1994. During this time, arrests for violence increased 60 percent for those between the ages of 10 and 17; arrests for homicide more than doubled (Cook and Laub 1998; Snyder 1998). In a much-publicized essay, DiIulio (1995) warned that these trends were reflective of a new generation of youthful offenders. No longer were we dealing with the kind of wayward kids depicted in *West Side Story* but with "super-predators," youths raised in "moral poverty" who "are perfectly capable of committing the most heinous acts of physical violence for the most trivial reasons.... They fear neither the stigma of arrest nor the pain of imprisonment. They live by the meanest code of the meanest streets, a code that reinforces rather than restrains their violent, hair-trigger mentality" (DiIulio 1995: 26). DiIulio predicted that, given the increasing size of the youth population in the years ahead, the United States would face in the next decade "an army of young male predatory street criminals who will make even the leaders of the Bloods and Crips ... look tame by comparison" (p. 25).

In reality, the juvenile arrest rate for violent crimes, including for murder, began a steady decline in 1994 that has continued throughout the decade (Cook and Laub 1998; Fox 2000; Snyder 1998; see also, Blumstein and Wallman 2000). Still, the disquieting jump in youth violence and its attribution to a crop of remorseless predators placed juvenile justice policy prominently on the political agenda (Bilichik 1998). A commonly proposed solution to this problem was to 'get tough' with juveniles – to punish them like adults and to put them behind bars. Symptomatic of this "temptation to increase punishment," as Donziger (1996: 134) calls it, was the following policy initiative:

During the debate over the 1994 federal crime bill, one proposal called for spending $500 million to build new juvenile institutions to hold 65,000 delinquent youths. At the time the proposal was made, *all* juvenile [public] facilities in the United States held a total of 63,000 youths, and only about 18 percent of those had been convicted of violent crimes. There was little discussion as to how the additional 65,000 beds would be filled, but it at least *sounded* as if something was being done about the juvenile violence problem. (Donziger 1996, p. 135; italics in the original)

This kind of thinking is a far cry from the idea that the juvenile court should try to "save" youths from a life in crime. It reflects a trend within criminal justice generally to use the infliction of pain on offenders as a means of controlling crime – what Clear (1994) calls the "penal harm movement" (see also, Beckett 1997; Mauer 1999). Within the adult justice system, for example, the number of inmates in state and federal prisons increased six-fold between 1970 and the century's end (Beck and Karberg 2001; Langan, Fundis, Greenfeld, and Schneider 1988). Including offenders in jail, the United States' incarcerated population now tops 2 million (Butterfield 2000). To keep offenders behind bars longer, legislators have passed an endless stream of mandatory punishment laws (Tonry 1996). They also have passed "three-strikes-and-you're out" laws, which require life imprisonment following a third felony conviction, and "truth in sentencing laws," which require offenders to serve a high proportion of the sentence assigned by the trial judge before any possibility of parole or early release (Ditton and Wilson 1999; Shichor and Sechrest 1996). States have tried as well to make prisons more discomforting by curtailing inmates' amenities – from permission to lift weights, to access to television, to support for college education (Finn 1996; Lacayo 1995).

The proposal to lock up an unprecedented number of young people, however, also is a continuation of an array of policies that, since the 1970s, has sought to toughen the justice system's reaction to adolescent offenders (Merlo 2000). Indeed, as Frazier, Bishop, and Lanza-Kaduce (1999: 167) observe, "get-tough reforms aimed at juvenile offenders have become commonplace in the United States" (see also, Feld 1998). For example, between 1988 and 1992 the percent of juveniles "waived" or transferred from juvenile court to adult court for prosecution increased 68 percent (Parent, Dunworth, McDonald, and Rhodes 1997; see also, Bishop 2000; National Criminal Justice Association 1997; Sickmund, Snyder, and Poe-Yamagata 1997). States have passed laws lowering the ages at which adolescents can be waived and broadening the crimes for which youths can be sent to adult court. Indeed, as Snyder, Sickmund, and Poe-Yamagata (2000: xi) observe, "between 1992 and 1997, all but six states expanded their statutory provisions for transferring juveniles to criminal court, making it easier for more juveniles to be transferred." Notably, "the purpose of transfer laws has not been to rehabilitate youthful violent offenders but rather to protect the public from them" (Parent et al. 1997: 1; see also, Bishop 2000). Similarly, by the end of 1997, 17 states had changed the legal purpose of the juvenile court to de-emphasize rehabilitation and to emphasize public safety, the imposition of certain sanctions, and/or offender accountability (Torbet and Szymanski 1998). The number of youths held in public juvenile facilities shows a trend consistent with this switch in justice philosophy: between 1984 and 1990, the institutionalized population rose 30 percent (Moon 1996). Further, Feld (1998) notes that numerous states have implemented laws mandating, based on the crime committed, determinate or mandatory minimum prison terms for adolescent offenders.

Does Punishment Work?

The punishment paradigm hinges on a clear conception of human conduct: behavior, including criminal behavior, is a matter of rational choice. Thus, youths will avoid crime if doing so is made sufficiently unpleasant – that is, if crime is made not to "pay." The solution to adolescent criminality is to increase the dose of punishment so that breaking the law becomes an unappealing choice.

This theory of crime and punishment, however, faces two problems. First, its understanding of crime is incomplete, if not incorrect. Research shows that there are a number of strong predictors of delinquent behavior, such as holding anti-social values, associating with delinquent peers, having an impulsive personality, and family dysfunction (Andrews and Bonta 1998). Punishing a wayward youth does virtually nothing to change these known predictors of criminal involvement. Even if the notion that "crime pays" were implicated in delinquent conduct, it would be only *one* cause of crime – among many – that tough punishment would potentially influence.

Second, the effectiveness of punishment – as any behavioral psychologists understands – depends on the negative stimuli being applied close in time to the targeted conduct, with certainty, and in an appropriately calibrated dosage. The justice system, however, has great difficulty applying punishments that could meet any of these criteria. Many delinquent acts that youths commit are not detected by law enforcement officials; punishments are applied many months after a youth is arrested; and the dosage of punishment can range from being too lenient to being overly harsh.

Relatedly, policy initiatives aimed at inflicting more stringent sanctions on delinquent youths can have unanticipated consequences. In Florida, for example, a 1994 "get tough" law aimed at facilitating the transfer of youthful lawbreakers to adult court did not lead to marked increases in the number of offenders actually waived to that court (Frazier et al. 1999). Similarly, research on the punishments received by adolescents in adult court as opposed to juvenile court illuminates a complex picture. Violent offenders waived to adult court do receive longer sentences. However, it appears that waived property offenders and persistent offenders are assigned *shorter* sentences than they would have received if they had remained under the jurisdiction of the juvenile court (Feld 1999). From the punishment perspective, results such as these are problematic, for they show how difficult it is to arrange a scheme of penalties that are applied as intended and in a way that might inhibit future criminal conduct.

Given these problems, it is perhaps not surprising that evaluations of deterrence-oriented programs with juveniles have revealed little support for the efficacy of "tough" criminal sanctions. In the 1980s and into the 1990s, jurisdictions implemented an array of programs aimed at increasing control over youths (and adult offenders). These included, for example, "scared straight" programs in which wayward adolescents were brought to prison and told by inmates, often in loud and graphic language, what ills would befall them were they to be incarcerated; "boot camps" in which offenders were subjected to military discipline while imprisoned; and "intensive supervision programs" in which offenders were closely watched in the community, with the threat of being sent to prison hanging over their head. Meta-analyses of evaluation studies report that these initiatives either had no effect or *increased* offender recidivism (Andrews et al. 1990; Lipsey 1992; Lipsey and Wilson 1998; see also, Cullen, Wright, and Applegate 1996; Finckenauer and Gavin 1999; MacKenzie 2000). We should also note that evidence from longitudinal studies is consistent in showing that contact with the criminal justice system can increase recidivism (Miller 1996). Finally, there is research suggesting that longer stays in prison are associated with higher recidivism rates (Gendreau, Goggin, Cullen, and Andrews 2000). Again, this kind of evidence is inconsistent with the punishment perspective's claim that "getting tough" deters criminal behavior.

The punishment perspective, however, has a fallback position: even if harsh sanctions do not deter, locking up – and thus "incapacitating" – super-predators saves crime because these offenders are "off the street." This claim is not without some merit. Life-course research demonstrates that there are youths who offend chronically and/or at a high rate (Le Blanc and Loeber 1998). Criminologists differ on how much future crime is prevented through a policy of incapacitation (see, e.g., Clear 1994; DiIulio and Piehl 1991; Mauer 1999; Sabol and Lynch 2000; Zimring and Hawkins 1995). Even so, it would strain common sense to argue that institutionalizing chronic, high-rate offenders is a foolish policy (Spelman 2000).

Three problems, however, temper one's enthusiasm for relying on incapacitation as a guiding principle for addressing the problem of youth crime. First, the vast majority of offenders arrested each year are not candidates for imprisonment due either to the low seriousness of their offense and/or to their lack of criminal history. For those adjudicated as delinquent by the court, 28 percent are placed in a residential facility. The remainder are either given probation (54 percent), given another sanction (e.g., restitution, fine) (13 percent), or are released (4 percent) (Stahl 1999; Torbet 1996). Beyond arguing that more offenders should be locked up, those endorsing incapacitation have little to say about what the justice system should do with the tens of thousands of offenders who will be returned by the court to the community.

Second, the policy of incapacitation is needlessly limited; it proposes to warehouse offenders but to do nothing to change them while they are within the confines of a juvenile institution. In the medical field, this would be tantamount to building hospitals to contain the sick but then to take no steps to treat the patients while they lay in their beds. Recall that in the Progressives' model, the purpose of imprisonment was for *both* social protection and rehabilitation. Release from juvenile reformatories was to be selective and based on offenders being cured of their criminal predispositions. The utility of institutions thus was linked not only to their ability to cage but also to their ability to provide the opportunity to improve the future life chances of offenders.

Third and relatedly, the effectiveness of incapacitation must be placed in an appropriate context. In computing how much crime would be saved from incapacitation, analysts assume that the alternative is that offenders would be roaming free on the streets. But the appropriate point of comparison should be how much crime incapacitation saves versus other possible policy alternatives – such as incapacitation plus treatment or community placement plus treatment. When this comparison is made, it is problematic whether incapacitation is, with most offenders, the most cost effective and most crime preventative strategy (see, e.g., Greenwood, Model, Rydell, and Chiesa 1996).

In closing, there appears to be a wide gap between the empirical support earned by a punishment-oriented policy and the confidence with which advocates argue that "getting tough" reduces youth crime. This is not to say that punishment has no effects. Although the magnitude remains unclear, a case can be made that criminal sanctions have a general deterrent effect – that those contemplating crime may be dissuaded by fear of suffering the sting of the criminal law (see, e.g., Nagin 1998). And, as stated, imprisoning chronically criminal youths will prevent crimes that might have been committed. Nonetheless, as a dominant model for the future, the limits of the punishment perspective are clear. It is based on a questionable theory of criminal behavior, applying it within the criminal justice system is difficult, and its effects on juveniles' crime are modest at best and counterproductive at worst. It also makes the disquieting choice, implicit if not explicit, to abandon youths once they have been arrested and given a stiff sentence. That is, once such adolescents enter the correctional system, the punishment perspective has no plan – other than heaping more punishments on them or subjecting them to "boot camp" discipline – to change offenders for the better.

THE LIBERAL PUNISHMENT PERSPECTIVE

As noted, in the 1970s, many liberals – the traditional supporters of the rehabilitative ideal – relinquished their allegiance to the Progressives' model of individualized treatment, which was most fully embodied in the juvenile court. They depicted judges as exercising their discretion inequitably, reformatories as being bastions of inhumanity, and the release from juvenile facilities as being conditioned on acquiescence to institutional rules rather than on youths being "cured" of their criminality. They also trumpeted a 1974 study by Martinson which ostensibly showed that "nothing works" in corrections to reduce recidivism. Taken together, these considerations led these liberals to argue that they should forfeit the optimistic but unattainable goal of "doing good" and substitute the pessimistic but realistic goal of "doing less harm." This is why they favored 1) giving youthful offenders an array of legal rights that would make the youths' conviction more difficult; 2) restraining the discretion of judges so that they would have to punish more equally (punish everyone committing a given crime the same); 3) trying to limit the number of offenders institutionalized; and 4) making sentences to reformatories "determinate" so that the release date would be set at the time of sentencing and would be contingent on the severity of the crime, not on the supposed rehabilitation of the offender (Cullen and Gilbert 1982).

Again, this approach made strange bedfellows of liberals and conservatives, because both groups were calling for the abandonment of the rehabilitative ideal and were seeking to constrain the discretion exercised by judges and corrections officials. The key difference, however, was that liberals wished to *decrease*, while conservatives wished to *increase*, the punitiveness of the juvenile justice system. In the intervening years, the juvenile justice system has not been fully dismantled, rehabilitation remains an integral goal of many states' systems, and some innovative policy initiatives have been undertaken that are, in the least, not exclusively punitive (see, e.g., Moon 1996). Even so, since the 1980s, the clear policy orientation – as we have reviewed above – has been decidedly in a conservative, punitive direction. Although a complex process, a main reason for this has been the redistribution of power in the justice system away from the back end of the system (judges and corrections officials) to the front end of the system (legislators and prosecutors). During this time period, crime and its control have been highly politicized issues (Beckett 1997). Legislators have seen "getting tough" – with adults and juveniles – as a way to secure political capital and advance their election prospects.

In this context, do liberal policy proposals that are punitively oriented have a future? We are skeptical that embracing punishment will produce a more humane or efficacious criminal justice intervention into the lives of adolescent offenders. Still, we will briefly review two policy proposals – abolishing the juvenile justice system and "restorative justice" – that view equitable sanctions, rather than well-designed rehabilitation programs, as the preferred basis for the state's reaction to wayward youths.

Doing Justice: Abolish the Juvenile Court

Feld (1998, 1999) makes a persuasive case for abolishing the juvenile court and for having one court system that has jurisdiction over both adults and adolescents. His abolitionist stance starts by repeating and documenting many of the criticisms voiced by liberal critics of rehabilitation in the 1970s: there is disparity in punishment in the system that works to the disadvantage of minorities; the rights of youthful offenders are not fully protected; juvenile reformatories do not reform; and, in general, rehabilitation programs do not have a meaningful effect on recidivism. Rather than retain the masquerade that the juvenile court could be a means of doing good, "states should uncouple social welfare from social control, try all offenders in one integrated criminal justice system, and make appropriate substantive and procedural modifications to accommodate the youthfulness of some defendants" (Feld 1999: 19). The lynchpin to his policy proposal – what makes it liberal rather than conservative – is that he wishes to treat youthfulness as a formal mitigating factor in the punishment an offender would receive. Thus, he advocates for a "youth discount" in which juveniles would receive a shorter penalty because of their presumed immaturity in social developments. "A 14-year-old offender might receive," says Feld (1999: 23), "23–33 percent of the adult penalty; a 16-year-old defendant, 50–66 percent; and an 18-year-old adult, the full penalty, as currently occurs."

There are four problems that mark Feld's abolitionist stance. First, it is far from clear that a legalistic, rights-oriented approach to reforming the criminal justice system leads to a more just and more humane system (Cullen and Gilbert 1982; Griset 1991; Tonry 1996). For example, under determinate sentencing, which Feld favors, judges merely apply the punishment listed in the statute for the crime committed – ostensibly evenly to all offenders regardless of race, class, or gender. This approach seemingly would reduce disparities in punishment, which occasionally occur. Under this system, however, prosecutors gain in power since they decide whether to plea bargain and decide with what crime an offender will be charged. Whether a system that vests so much power in prosecutors produces better outcomes for youths is problematic.

Second, Feld's advocacy of a "youth discount" – the key to his proposal not devolving into a reform that exposes young offenders to the full weight of the adult system – seems politically naïve. One imagines that in the face of a well-celebrated heinous crime committed by a juvenile, thoughts of "punishment discounts" for delinquents would be dismissed. The risk of his system leading to far greater punishment of youths – an adult system with few, if any, discounts – seems a likely and disturbing prospect.

Third, like other liberals concerned with "doing justice" for youthful offenders, Feld largely ignores the *utilitarian* goal of the criminal justice system – the expectation that the system will control crime. To a large extent, Feld believes that punishing in a just manner is the core function of the legal system, not controlling lawlessness. Unfortunately for those of his persuasion, this is *not* the view of the American public or, for that matter, of the nation's policymakers (Cullen, Fisher, and Applegate 2000). The popularity of "get tough" policies lies not only in the promise of revenge but in the promise of reducing the threat criminals pose to public safety. Feld's approach, however, has virtually no answer as to what to do to reduce youth crime. Giving punishment discounts is unlikely to be a politically feasible response, especially when doing so can be readily depicted as teaching young "super-predators" that crime pays.

Fourth, the abolitionist's position to divorce criminal justice from social welfare assumes that a system stripped of a human services orientation will somehow be preferable. But why would one expect that youths in the juvenile justice system will be better off if the goal is avowedly to punish them – to inflict pain on them – rather than to save them, to improve their lives? Whatever the failings of the rehabilitative model, it drew in numerous workers whose occupational goal was to "help kids," and it reified the idea that "doing good" for youthful offenders was a legitimate correctional goal. Rejecting rehabilitation in the name of punishing "justly" ignores the potential costs of stripping from juvenile justice the good will of its workers and the impulse to seek a better life for the youths – mostly poor and minority – that the state brings under its control.

Restorative Justice

"Restorative justice," an increasingly popular idea within criminal justice, seeks to offer an alternative approach to traditional ways of reacting to offenders (see Braithwaite 1998, 1999; Van Ness and Strong 1997). This perspective rejects the philosophy of retributive justice in which the state, on behalf of the victim, exacts a just measure of pain from the offender. Instead, its focus is on rectifying the harm that a criminal act has caused. In this scheme, the state, acting as a mediator, brings the offender, victim, and interested community parties together, usually in some form of conference. In this meeting, the offender is called on to accept responsibility for the harm he or she has caused. Victims are able to express their anger and identify their injury. The sanction that is developed is oriented toward having the offender repair the harm he or she has caused to the victim and, secondarily, to the community (e.g., through restitution, community service). In exchange for remorse and reparation, the victim and community are to accept the offender back into the community, ideally in a way that repairs the harms the offender may have suffered in his or her life. Typically, the goal of restorative justice is to keep the offender in the community and thus to obviate the need for incarceration.

Restorative justice is increasingly being used to inform how youthful offenders are processed within juvenile justice (Bazemore 1999a; Levrant, Cullen, Fulton, and Wozniak 1999). Indeed, restorative justice is shaping justice policies and practices not only in the United States but also in many nations (see Bazemore and Walgrave 1999; Bonta, Wallace-Capretta, and Rooney 1998; Braithwaite 1998, 1999). Some good may come of this approach, because it has the potential to conceptualize offenders not merely as purveyors of bad acts but as people who are driven to break the law for complex reasons. Even so, restorative justice may also prove to be a reform that creates as many problems as it solves.

First, advocates of restorative justice make much of the fact that it is a "balanced" approach, one that demands accountability from offenders in exchange for supportive reintegration into the community. Underlying this "balance," however, are two incompatible interests: 1) the interests of conservatives to see restorative justice bring more justice to victims, who often have been ignored and not received justice as their cases have been processed by a bureaucratic legal system; and 2) the interests of liberals who see restorative justice as a means to punish offenders in a nicer way – that is, with forgiveness and certainly not in prison. It remains to be seen how this latent tension will be resolved. Will restorative justice remain balanced, or will it become a reform that ultimately inflicts increasing amounts of "responsibility" – that is, harsher sanctions – on offenders with little restoration given in return (Levrant et al. 1999)?

Second and relatedly, restorative justice is best suited for minor offenders – those with whom victims may be willing to meet and for whom prison is not an appropriate penalty. In particular, it is not clear how restorative justice would deal with recalcitrant offenders who, after promising to repair harm, either ignore the conditions of their sanction (e.g., do not pay restitution) or, still worse, choose to recidivate. That is, once restorative justice fails, what is the next option? Is it more of the same or a reliance on harsher punishment?

Third, because restorative justice is a sanction-based perspective, it is limited in scope and, in the end, potentially unscientific. Advocates of restorative justice have a faith, rooted in precious little evidence, that "restorative" sanctions – such as offenders making public displays of remorse at victim-offender conferences and offenders making restitution and or doing community service – have the capacity to transform criminals into non-criminals (Levrant et al. 1999). Although the application of these sanctions may have some benefits, the restorative focus narrows the kinds of interventions that might be employed (i.e., interventions, such as behavior programs, that are offender-oriented and have nothing to do with restoring victims will not generally be considered). Further, the perspective risks being non-scientific because it starts with the realm of sanctions it wishes to impose and then, working backwards to the offender, presumes that these sanctions will change the offender's behavior. It fails to ask, initially, what causes criminal behavior and then, subsequently, what interventions are able to target these criminogenic predictors for change (for an alternative view, see Bazemore 1999b; Braithwaite 1998, 1999).

At present, research on restorative justice programs remains in its beginning stages, often raising more questions than it answers. It seems clear that, in general, these programs are supported by offenders and victims who participate in them and find the process and outcomes "satisfying" (Braithwaite 1998; Schiff 1999). More problematic, however, is whether restorative justice interventions are able to reduce recidivism. Rigorous, randomized experimental tests of these programs are in short supply, and existing studies provide conflicting results (Kurki 2000; Schiff 1999; Sherman, Strang, and Woods 2000). When positive results are reached, it is difficult to discern whether reductions in recidivism are due to the "restorative" aspect of the program or to some other feature of the intervention – such as the services offenders received or the fact that participation is voluntary (Bonta et al. 1998; Latimer, Dowden, and Muise 2001). Further, two recent meta-analyses of programs with a restorative justice orientation report that these interventions have, at best, a modest overall impact on recidivism (Gendreau and Goggin 2000; Latimer et al. 2001). These latter results are not surprising to us, because, as noted above, the behavioral science underlying restorative justice provides, at best, a partial understanding of criminal behavior (in contrast, see Andrews and Bonta 1998).

It is possible that the socio-cultural context in which restorative justice is implemented will shape whether this initiative does more good than harm. If used in communities or nations characterized by low crime and homogeneity, restorative justice may provide creative ways to sanction less serious offenders. The challenge faced by restorative justice is whether it can provide politically feasible and scientifically viable answers to the more daunting problem of serious chronic offending.

THE REHABILITATION PERSPECTIVE

In the early 1970s, a team of researchers embarked on an effort to collect and assess evaluation studies on the effectiveness of correctional treatment programs (see Lipton, Martinson, and Wilks 1975). They tracked down 231 studies that had a treatment and control group and that were published between 1945 and 1967. One of the authors, Robert Martinson (1974), conveyed his interpretation of the results of this analysis in what would become one of the most important and most cited social science essays, "What Works? Questions and Answers About Prison Reform." Martinson concluded that "with few and isolated exceptions, the rehabilitative efforts that have been reported so far have had no appreciable effect on recidivism" (1974: 25).

This finding – presented in seemingly cautious scientific language – soon was interpreted as showing that "nothing works" in correctional rehabilitation. Most academic studies, of course, are greeted with skepticism and criticism. And in this case, a few commentators did urge caution, pointing out, for example, that almost half of the treatment-intervention studies reviewed by Martinson showed that recidivism was reduced and that many of the programs evaluated had little "therapeutic integrity" (see, e.g., Gendreau and Ross 1979; Palmer 1975). But these more judicious voices were largely ignored. Martinson's "nothing works" conclusion was taken by academic criminologists and policy-makers as the "final word" to be uncritically accepted. To a large extent, this ready acceptance of rehabilitation's ostensible ineffectiveness was triggered by the fact that many people – as noted above – had already come to reject the Progressives' model of individualized treatment. Martinson's study did not so much change their minds as confirm "what they already knew" (Cullen and Gendreau 2000; Cullen and Gilbert 1982).

Now a quarter century after Martinson's essay appeared, it is difficult to convey the enormous impact of his message. But some sense of the essay's effects in the 1970s can be grasped from Adams's (1976: 76) contemporaneous appraisal that the "Nothing Works doctrine . . . has shaken the community of criminal justice to its roots . . . widely assorted members of the criminal justice field are briskly urging that punishment and incapacitation should be given a much higher priority among criminal justice goals." After all, in the face of hard empirical evidence confirming that rehabilitation "did not work," how could faith in the paradigm of offender treatment – no matter how noble its goals – be sustained?

For those who would prefer a criminal justice system in the 21st century that seeks to save rather than merely punish adolescent offenders, this question remains to be confronted. Is it possible for correctional interventions to change youths for the better? Can these interventions work with serious offenders? Beyond these questions, even if rehabilitation does in some sense "work," will the public – often characterized as seeking vengeance – support a criminal justice response to offenders that takes seriously the Progressives' challenge of reforming wayward youths? The following discussion addresses these questions.

Does Rehabilitation Work?

It would seem a rather simple matter for researchers to agree whether rehabilitation does, or does not, "work" to reduce recidivism. A number of reviews have been conducted on treatment program effectiveness, but interpreting the results of these analyses has been the occasion for disagreement rather than agreement. Andrews et al. (1990: 374) note, for example, that "reviews of the literature have routinely found that at least 40 percent of the better-controlled evaluations of correctional treatment services reported positive effects." But what are we to make of this finding? One might conclude that there are many programs that are effective with offenders, and that these should be used as models for future programming. One might also conclude that rehabilitation is a "hit or miss" affair, an enterprise characterized more by chaos than by reliable, replicable results that could be used to develop effective programs across diverse social settings. In short, is the glass half-full or half-empty?

An important measure of clarity to this debate was introduced by the use of the technique of "meta-analysis" to quantitatively synthesize the evaluation literature (see Hunt 1997). A meta-analysis starts by computing for each study the statistical relationship, ranging from $+1.0$ to -1.0 between the treatment intervention and the outcome variable – in our case, recidivism. Then, it computes the average "effect size" of treatment across all studies. This approach can also explore what factors may "condition" the effect size. For example, does the effect size vary by the quality of the methodology employed or by the type of offender studied?

A number of meta-analyses have now been conducted on the extant body of evaluation studies, with many of them evaluations undertaken with juvenile samples and cross-culturally (see, e.g., Andrews et al. 1990; Lipsey 1992, 1999; Redondo, Sanchez-Meca, and Garrido 1999). Across these assessments, Losel (1995) estimates that the average effect size is .10. In practical terms, this means that if a control group had a recidivism rate of 55 percent, the treatment group's recidivism rate would be 45 percent (for the computation of this statistic, see Rosenthal 1991).

Again, one might quibble as to whether a 10 percent reduction in recidivism is substantively important. Three considerations are relevant to this concern. First, when one considers that the comparable reduction for deterrence-oriented programs is zero (if not an increase in recidivism), this savings in crime achieved by treatment appears more noteworthy. Second, research shows that the decrease in criminal participation from rehabilitative interventions is achieved among *serious and violent* juvenile offenders (Andrews et al. 1990; Lipsey 1999; Lipsey and Wilson 1998). It is one thing to depress rates of shoplifting, quite another to put a dent in chronic offending and predatory crimes. Third, the focus on a 10 percent reduction in recidivism is misleading for the following reason:

there is considerable *heterogeneity* in the effect size according to the type of intervention that is used. That is, the reductions in recidivism are far higher – 25 percent and upwards in recidivism reduction – for some rehabilitation programs than for others (Andrews et al. 1990; Lipsey and Wilson 1998). Again, in practical terms, this means that if a control group had a recidivism rate of 62.5 percent, the treatment group's recidivism rate would be 37.5 percent.

Notably, scholars are attempting to develop a theory of the "principles of effective correctional intervention" (see, e.g., Andrews 1995; Andrews and Bonta 1998; Gendreau 1996). They suggest, for example, that programs are most effective when they: 1) target for change the known predictors of recidivism (e.g., anti-social values, pro-criminal associates, anti-social personality characteristics); 2) use cognitive-behavioral treatment strategies as opposed to non-directive and psychodynamic approaches; 3) focus primarily on high-risk offenders; 4) take into account the learning styles of offenders; 5) are conducted in the community rather than in an institution; 6) are delivered by a trained staff; and 7) involve relapse prevention or "aftercare."

The challenge, of course, is whether these principles can be followed in a typical criminal justice agency that processes youthful offenders. Two considerations merit our attention. First, it is important to note that research on correctional interventions has developed to the point where the "technology" exists to make meaningful impacts on the lives of youthful offenders, including serious offenders (see also, Henggeler 1997). In the past, this knowledge did not exist; the Progressives and successive generations largely conducted rehabilitation programs based on hunches or, at most, on theories of criminal conduct for which there were scant empirical support. What differs now is that the knowledge to intervene more effectively with adolescent offenders is not beyond reach.

Second, while the issue of how best to transfer this "technology" or knowledge remains a daunting question, it is instructive that the "principles-of-effective-treatment" movement is gaining headway in the United States. When these principles are presented to audiences comprised of criminal justice practitioners and officials, the response most often is quite receptive (personal communication, Edward Latessa). Indeed, when faced with the question – "Why aren't you doing what works?" – many of those in juvenile justice are willing to reconsider current ways of doing things. They are not wed to the irrationality of pursuing ineffective policies when effective intervention strategies are at hand.

Does the Public Support Child Saving?

Research on public opinion about the criminal sanctioning of offenders consistently reveals that citizens favor interventions that are *both* punitive and rehabilitative (see, e.g., Applegate, Cullen, and Fisher 1997; Cullen et al. 2000; Roberts and Stalans 1997). This finding contravenes the popular conception, often portrayed in the media, that the public is clamoring exclusively for draconian measures to deal with law breakers. Instead, it appears that people want a balanced approach to criminal justice interventions, one that exacts a measure of pain, incarcerates the dangerous, and does its best to reform offenders and return them to the community less predisposed to victimize again.

But what about juvenile offenders? What role does the public want criminal justice to play in the lives of adolescents? For a number of years, commentators have questioned whether "rehabilitation is dead" in the public's eyes (Cullen et al. 1983; Moon, Sundt, Cullen, and Wright 1999). In fact, the results for juvenile delinquents parallel those for adults – with one noteworthy exception: although punitive toward youthful offenders – especially violent criminals – citizens are even more supportive of the rehabilitation of juveniles than they are of adults (Moon et al. 1999). They also strongly endorse a range of early intervention programs with youths at-risk for criminal involvement (Cullen et al. 1998). Belief in child saving, it seems, is alive and well.

For example, a 1998 sample of Tennessee residents were asked "what should be the main emphasis of juvenile prisons." In a forced-choice response, almost two-thirds chose "rehabilitation" as opposed to punishing the adolescent criminal (18.7 percent) or using juvenile prisons to protect society from the future crimes a young offender might commit (11.2 percent). Further, about 9 in 10 members of the sample stated that it was a "good idea" to treat offenders who are in the community and/or who are in jail. Further, 3 in 4 respondents believed that rehabilitation programs should be "available even for juvenile offenders who have been involved in a lot of crime" (Moon et al. 1999). These findings are consistent with studies conducted in other states (Cullen et al. 2000).

CONCLUSION: CHOOSING THE FUTURE

In an essay commenting on the "decline of the rehabilitative ideal," Francis Allen (1981) keenly observed that, concrete criticisms aside, the shattering of the hegemony of the Progressives' paradigm of individualized treatment in the 1970s reflected the weakening of two interrelated beliefs: a belief in the malleability of offenders, and a belief that the state could represent a social consensus of the American citizenry and serve broader social purposes. In short, people became less convinced that the government had the know-how and competence to change criminals for the better. This situation was exacerbated, suggested Allen (1981: 30–31), by the issue of race:

...public pessimism about the capacities of penal programs to achieve reform... requires further analysis, but there is reason to suspect that in part it is related to a widespread perception of the American crime problem as one principally of race. It is hardly coincidental that the decline in public support for the rehabilitative ideal accompanies rising percentages of noncaucasian inmates in the prisons. Optimism about the possibilities of reform flourishes when strong bonds of identity are perceived between reformers and those to be reformed. Conversely, confidence in rehabilitative effort dwindles when a sense of difference and social distance separates the promoters from the subject of reform.

Allen's analysis is not without flaws – for example, the public's faith in rehabilitation declined but nonetheless remained firm – but he raises issues that might help us to think more clearly about what future role criminal justice should play in the lives of wayward adolescents. We have made the case that the empirical support for rehabilitative interventions is growing and should guide how we process youths in the criminal justice system. Yet we also understand that social science data are but one consideration – usually a small consideration – in the formulation of criminal justice policy. In addition to rational analysis, fundamental cultural beliefs are likely to shape what policy future is chosen.

In this regard, a conservative punishment perspective rests on the belief that offenders are not malleable and that the tools the state has to reform offenders are ineffectual. In this view, offenders are not portrayed as abused and troubled – as needing help – but as "super-predators" drawn from and reaping most of their havoc on the inner city. The racial identity of these criminals is left implicit but is not hard to fathom. For these offenders, talk of "malleability" seems senseless. The state is left to try to scare them straight or, still better, to use its resources to do the one thing that it can do effectively: store them away in prisons for years to come. As James Q. Wilson (1975: 235) asserted in his now-famous statement, "Wicked people exist. Nothing avails except to set them apart from innocent people." If Hillary Clinton could argue that ensuring a child's welfare "takes a village," this perspective would argue that, with juvenile justice, "it takes a prison" to ensure society's welfare.

The liberal punishment perspective is pessimistic about the malleability of offenders and is fearful of what the state might do if given the leeway to try to change people. This abiding pessimism underlies its hope that the law might serve to give youthful offenders a measure of justice and a measure of protection from the power of the criminal justice system. It especially sees the need to protect the major clientele of the system: disadvantaged minorities, mainly young males. Its approach is minimalist: don't let the state try to reform offenders and don't let the state punish offenders (at least not too much).

In a decided contrast, the rehabilitation perspective is optimistic about both the malleability of offenders and about the ability of the *people* who work in criminal justice – as opposed to the ill-defined concept of "the state" – to develop programs that invest in and improve the life prospects of offenders. Admittedly, the Progressives of a century ago were *overly* optimistic about the ease with which offenders can be changed. Such a task is difficult and replete with failure. Even so, the contemporary rehabilitation perspective – now rooted more firmly in scientific criminology – is persuaded that offender change is attainable and a worthy goal for we, as a people, to pursue. In particular, given the disproportionate involvement of the poor and minorities in the juvenile justice system, it seems inexcusable to acquit "the state" of any obligation to invest resources to "save" these youthful offenders.

In reality, elements of these competing perspectives will be found in state and local juvenile justice systems across the United States. This assessment can be made of juvenile justice systems in most advanced industrial nations (Mehlbye and Walgrave 1998). At issue, however, is which paradigm will shape most fully the destiny of juvenile justice policy in the 21st century. We can offer two competing prognostications or "futures" for youths ensnared in the criminal justice system – one that focuses on punishing adolescents and a second that focuses on saving them.

Punishing Adolescents

Perhaps the safest prognostication is that the conservative punishment perspective will continue to eviscerate, little by little, the juvenile court invented by the Progressives. This "future" seems likely because of the principle of inertia: things just have to keep going in the current direction. An inordinate effort or cataclysmic series of events will be needed to reverse paths and to revitalize the rehabilitation or welfare model.

A conservative, "get tough" future might not just "plod along," however; it might gain strength if social change leads to the continued polarization of society – in America or elsewhere. Predictions of sustained socio-economic cleavages come, disturbingly, from the political left and right. On the left, there is the warning that persistent racial divisions and inequities are not closing but are widening and being reified (Hacker 1992; Massey and Denton 1993). In America's inner cities, an entrenched underclass – caught in the midst of deteriorating neighborhoods and buffeted by concentrated disadvantage – is socially, culturally, and politically isolated from "mainstream" society (Wilson 1987; see also, Anderson 1999). In the near future, at least, there is little prospect for their participation in the larger social order. On the political right, the analysis differs but the endpoint is similar. Thus, in their controversial *The Bell Curve: Intelligence and Class Structure in American Life*, Herrnstein and Murray (1994) argue that it is the very openness of the United States – for example, the "democratization of higher education" – that is fostering inequality. In an increasingly open-class society, a meritocracy based on "cognitive capacity" is inevitable. As time progresses, the more intelligent rise to the top of the socio-economic ladder; the "stupid" among us fall to the bottom rungs of society. Social Darwinism, in short, becomes a reality.

We have just described, of course, two underlying views on the origins of inequality: one that attributes inequality to social causation, the other to self-selection. Regardless of the merits of these competing positions, both perspectives predict the greater isolation of urban minorities from the "rest of society." If this transpires, it is conceivable that these inner-city residents – especially because they are marked by comparatively high levels of violence that may be fueled further by projected increases in their youth population (Fox 2000) – will be portrayed, even more so than today, as "dangerous classes" (see also, Gordon 1994). This portrayal could have salient consequences (Gordon 1994). Thus, Herrnstein and Murray's analysis of crime may be faulty in other respects (see Cullen, Gendreau, Jarjoura, and Wright 1997), but they may be prescient in alerting us to the risk that we are headed toward a "custodial state." "When a society reaches a certain overall level of affluence," they write, "the haves begin to feel sympathy toward, if not guilt about, the condition of the have-nots" (p. 523). But this emotion can change as the affluent become "increasingly frightened of and hostile toward the recipients of help"; they can lose "faith that remedial programs work" (p. 523). In this scenario, resources are reallocated from assisting the disadvantaged

to keeping those populating the dangerous class in "their" neighborhoods, where they can be policed, frisked, monitored, and, if necessary,
confined. Indeed, as noted above, Allen (1981) has warned that as social distance, exacerbated by racial division, widens, offenders can be
seen as virtual aliens that are beyond redemption. Harsh policies are
the likely result when the objects of our "justice" are seen as members
of a dangerous class – as "wicked people" – with whom we have no
connection and for whom we have no responsibility.

The punitive future envisioned by conservatives, however, is not en-
sured. Indeed, it is likely to confront three stubborn realities that, taken
together, promise to temper, if not undermine, its realization. First, the
punishment paradigm is testing the limits of how tough we wish to get
with our children. The extensive popularity of Hillary Clinton's (1996)
It Takes a Village is a testament to the nation's abiding belief that *all of
us* have a collective responsibility to save from undue hardship *all of the
nation's children*. We have not, in short, lost our bonds to and sense of responsibility for the young, even for those that live apart from us socially
and culturally. It is instructive that, as we have reported, there remains
widespread faith among Americans that juvenile offenders can change
and should be the object of efforts to rehabilitate them. These cultural
beliefs are strong and enduring, and they reflect a common sense of purpose with regard to delinquent kids. Again, if Allen's (1981) insights are
correct, then these cultural beliefs will restrain further attempts to move
away from a juvenile justice system devoted to the welfare of "wayward
youths."

Second, simplistic "get tough" policies are running up against another obstacle: the evidence suggests that they are not effective in reducing crime – that is, they "don't work." Failure is not necessarily a
recipe for policy change, but it does make policy initiatives vulnerable
to criticism and, eventually, to revision. In the U.S., for example, by the
early 1990s "boot camps" for youthful offenders had achieved the status
of a panacea that promised to "build character" and show delinquents
"discipline." The research studies demonstrating that these programs
were ineffective did not immediately stop the implementation of boot
camps (Cullen et al. 1996). Still, after several years of negative findings
and publicity of these failures in the media, boot camps have now lost
their appeal and are being abandoned as a policy initiative (Blair 2000).

Third, and related to the previous two points, correctional systems
face the problem of "legitimacy deficits" and concomitantly the constant task of showing – or at least rationalizing through ideology – their

legitimacy (Sparks 1994). In the past, "get tough" rhetoric has served this purpose by arguing that harsh sanctions were achieving "law and order," but its capacity to persuade may be waning. Especially in the realm of juvenile justice where "kids" are involved, the prospect of continuing to warehouse increasing numbers of youths – mostly poor and/or people of color – raises the question of "what is wrong" with the justice system and, more broadly, with the prevailing social order. The "custodial state" that Herrnstein and Murray see on the horizon might be an efficient way to control underclass youths, but it runs the risk of making the stark admission that the government has forfeited any concern for its "disadvantaged" citizens. As Piven and Cloward (1971) understood some years ago, welfare potentially functions to "regulate the poor" – to bolster the legitimacy of the state and to calm the poor's impulse for insurgency. In the absence of a welfare approach – were a custodial state to take hold – the crass exercise of the state's power – backing the haves over the have-nots – would be unmasked and could well deepen feelings of injustice and of anger toward the government and its officials. If Marxist commentators are correct, this is a risk that the state cannot afford to take because such a movement could call into question the fairness of capitalist America – not only to the poor but to others committed to "equality" – and cost some politicians their jobs.

Saving Adolescents

The onward march of the punishment paradigm thus is not an inevitability. At least some ideological space exists in which to carve out progressive reforms (Dionne 1996); after all, even those on the right are now speaking of "compassionate conservatism." But if a progressive agenda is to emerge, its viability, we suspect, ultimately will hinge on its ability to build on the pervasive sentiment that children – even troubled and troubling ones – have not fully chosen their fates and deserve a chance to have a meaningful life.

For this reason, we do not believe that a liberal punishment approach that stresses doing justice and preventing harm – but not "saving" or changing offenders for the better – will guide progressive reform efforts. It would be unpersuasive to argue that a lack of legal rights is the main problem confronting youths at-risk for crime and will prompt a movement to renovate juvenile justice. More likely, a variant of this view – restorative justice programs – will continue to spread and gain popularity in the U.S. and in other Western nations. Restorative justice is

appealing because it promises to punish youths – to hold them accountable – but in a constructive way. In this model, adolescent offenders
restore harm (e.g., by making restitution), and in exchange they typically avoid incarceration. Advocates of restorative justice also contend
that the process of restoring harm – a process in which offenders acknowledge their guilt and compensate their victims – will help reform
or save offenders. We do not believe that this last contention is built on
sound criminology or on what is known about why offenders change,
but that may be beside the point as long as people believe that restorative
justice has such benefits. In the end, restorative justice is an attractive
package because it seemingly offers something for everyone – victims,
the community, and offenders.

Another possibility, however, is that the vision articulated by the
Progressives over a century ago will be revitalized. These reformers had
a bold design for the juvenile justice system: it should be like Hillary
Clinton's "village" – a place where everyone was working to save troubled children. It became fashionable to critique the Progressives' system,
but it is clear that attempts to move away from it arguably have caused
much more harm than good. In this context, it is not farfetched to suggest
that reformers should embrace a future that, in essence, embraces the
central message of the Progressives. In choosing this future, reformers
would state directly that the justice system is not simply an instrument of
punishment but an instrument for social welfare. When troubled youths
come within its reach, it has an obligation to the offenders and to the
public to rehabilitate these adolescents – to save their lives and to save
the public from preventable future victimization.

We favor this option of reaffirming rehabilitation, both because we
are persuaded as to its effectiveness and because there is strong public
support for treating youthful offenders. However, even if this is not the
future chosen by progressives, there is a large need to pursue juvenile
justice policies in which the well-being of adolescent offenders is not rel-
egated to secondary importance (Merlo 2000). The main message of this
chapter is that the growing salience of the punishment paradigm has
moved us decidedly in this uncaring direction. Its ready embrace has
made criminal justice an ineffectual, if not counterproductive, force in
the lives of too many adolescents. The choice to do more of the same or,
even worse, to make the system still harsher is disquieting – and clearly
within the realm of possibility. In the United States and, increasingly,
elsewhere, there is thus an urgency to balance a desire and, at times, need
to "get tough" with the realization that reforming youthful offenders,

especially serious ones, requires an investment into their lives. The challenge, in short, is to loudly proclaim that criminal justice has a special mandate when it comes to our youths – a mandate unflinchingly trumpeted by Progressive reformers a century ago but that rings true today: to care about wayward adolescents and to save them from a life in crime.

References

Adams, S. 1976. "Evaluation: A Way Out of Rhetoric." In R. Martinson, T. Palmer, and S. Adams (Eds.), *Rehabilitation, Recidivism, and Research* (pp. 75–91). Beverly Hills, CA: Sage.

Albrecht, H.-J. 1997. "Juvenile Crime and Juvenile Law in the Federal Republic of Germany." In J. A. Winterdyk (Ed.), *Juvenile Justice Systems: International Perspectives* (pp. 233–69). Toronto: Canadian Scholars' Press.

Allen, F. A. 1981. *The Decline of the Rehabilitative Idea: Essays in Law and Criminology.* Chicago: University of Chicago Press.

Anderson, E. 1999. *Code of the Street: Decency, Violence, and the Moral Life of the Inner City.* New York: W. W. Norton.

Andrews, D. A. 1995. "The Psychology of Criminal Conduct and Effective Treatment." In J. McGuire (Ed.), *What Works: Reducing Reoffending* (pp. 35–62). West Sussex, UK: John Wiley.

Andrews, D. A., and J. Bonta. 1998. *The Psychology of Criminal Conduct* (2nd ed.). Cincinnati: Anderson.

Andrews, D. A., I. Zinger, R. D. Hoge, J. Bonta, P. Gendreau, and F. T. Cullen. 1990. "Does Correctional Treatment Work? A Clinically Relevant and Psychologically Informed Meta-Analysis." *Criminology* 28 (August): 369–404.

Applegate, B. K., F. T. Cullen, and B. S. Fisher. 1997. "Public Support for Correctional Treatment: The Continuing Appeal of the Rehabilitative Ideal. *The Prison Journal* 77 (September):237–58.

Bazemore, G. 1999a. "The Fork in the Road to Juvenile Court Reform." *Annals of the American Academy of Political and Social Science* 564 (July): 81–108.

Bazemore, G. 1999b. "After Shaming, Whither Reintegration: Restorative Justice and Relational Rehabilitation." In G. Bazemore and L. Walgrave (Eds.), *Restorative Juvenile Justice: Repairing the Harm of Youth Crime* (pp. 155–94). Monsey, NY: Willow Tree Press.

Bazemore, G., and L. Walgrave. (Eds.). 1999. *Restorative Juvenile Justice: Repairing the Harm of Youth Crime.* Monsey, NY: Willow Tree Press.

Beck, Allen J., and Jennifer C. Karberg. 2001. *Prison and Jail Inmates at midyear 2000.* Washington, DC: U.S. Department of Justice, Bureau of Justice Statistics.

Beckett, K. 1997. *Making Crime Pay: Law and Order in Contemporary American Politics.* New York: Oxford University Press.

Bennett, W. J., J. J. DiIulio, Jr., and J. P. Walters. 1996. *Body Count: Moral Poverty . . . and How to Win America's War Against Crime and Drugs.* New York: Simon and Schuster.

Bilichik, S. 1998. "A Juvenile Justice System for the 21st Century." *Crime and Delinquency* 44 (January):89–101.

Bishop, D. M. 2000. "Juvenile Offenders in the Adult Criminal Justice System." In M. Tonry (Ed.), *Crime and Justice: A Review of Research, Vol. 27* (pp. 81–167). Chicago: University of Chicago Press.

Blair, J. 2000. "Boot Camps: An Idea Whose Time Came and Went." *New York Times* (January 2):wk3.

Blumstein, A., and J. Wallman (Eds.). 2000. *The Crime Drop in America*. Cambridge, UK: Cambridge University Press.

Bonczar, T., and A. J. Beck. 1997. *Lifetime Likelihood of Going to State or Federal Prison*. Washington, DC: U.S. Department of Justice, Bureau of Justice Statistics.

Bonta, J., S. Wallace-Capretta, and J. Rooney. 1998. *Restorative Justice: An Evaluation of the Restorative Resolutions Project*. Ottawa, Ontario: Solicitor General Canada.

Bottoms, A., K. Haines, and D. O'Mahony. 1998. "England and Wales." In J. Mehlbye and L. Walgrave (Eds.), *Confronting Youth in Europe: Juvenile Crime and Juvenile Justice* (pp. 139–215). Copenhagen, Denmark: AKF Forlaget.

Braithwaite, J. 1998. "Restorative Justice." In M. Tonry (Ed.), *The Handbook of Crime and Punishment* (pp. 323–44). New York: Oxford University Press.

Braithwaite, J. 1999. "Restorative Justice: Assessing Optimistic and Pessimistic Accounts." In M. Tonry (Ed.), *Crime and Justice: A Review of Research, Vol. 25* (pp. 1–127). Chicago: University of Chicago Press.

Butterfield, F. 2000. "Prisons Grow at a Lower Rate." *Cincinnati Enquirer* (August 10): A2.

Clear, T. R. 1994. *Harm in American Penology: Offenders, Victims, and Their Communities*. Albany, NY: State University of New York Press.

Clinton, H. 1996. *It Takes a Village – And Other Lessons Children Teach Us*. New York: Touchstone.

Cook, P. J., and J. H. Laub. 1998. "The Unprecedented Epidemic in Youth Violence. In M. Tonry and M. H. Moore (Eds.), *Crime and Justice: A Review of Research, Vol. 24 – Youth Violence* (pp. 27–64). Chicago: University of Chicago Press.

Cullen, F. T., B. S. Fisher, and B. K. Applegate. 2000. "Public Opinion About Punishment and Corrections." In M. Tonry (Ed.), *Crime and Justice: A Review of Research, Vol. 24* (pp. 1–79). Chicago: University of Chicago Press.

Cullen, F. T., and P. Gendreau. 2000. "Assessing Correctional Rehabilitation: Policy, Practice, and Prospects." In J. Horney (Ed.), *Criminal Justice 2000: Vol. 3, Changes in Decision Making and Discretion in the Criminal Justice System* (pp. 109–75). Washington, DC: U.S. Department of Justice, National Institute of Justice.

Cullen, F. T., P. Gendreau, G. R. Jarjoura, and J. P. Wright. 1997. "Crime and the Bell Curve: Lessons from Intelligent Criminology." *Crime and Delinquency* 43 (October):387–411.

Cullen, F. T., and K. E. Gilbert. 1982. *Reaffirming Rehabilitation*. Cincinnati: Anderson.

Cullen, F. T., K. M. Golden, and J. B. Cullen. 1983. "Is Child Saving Dead? Attitudes Toward Juvenile Rehabilitation in Illinois." *Journal of Criminal Justice* 11 (1):1–13.

Cullen, F. T., J. P. Wright, and B. K. Applegate. 1996. "Control in the Community: The Limits of Reform?" In A. T. Harland (Ed.), *Choosing Correctional Interventions That Work: Defining the Demand and Evaluating the Supply* (pp. 69–116). Newbury Park, CA: Sage.

Cullen, F. T., J. P. Wright, S. Brown, M. M. Moon, M. B. Blankenship, and B. K. Applegate. 1998. "Public Support for Early Intervention Programs: Implications for a Progressive Policy Agenda." *Crime and Delinquency* 44 (April): 187–204.

Currie, E. 1998. *Crime and Punishment in America*. New York: Metropolitan.

DiIulio, J. J., Jr. 1994. "The Question of Black Crime." *The Public Interest* 117 (Fall): 3–32.

DiIulio, J. J., Jr. 1995. 'The Coming of the Super-Predators." *The Weekly Standard* (November 27):23–28.

DiIulio, J. J., Jr., and A. M. Piehl. 1991. "Does Prison Pay?" *The Brookings Review* 9 (Fall):28–35.

Dionne, E. J. 1996. *They Only Look Dead: Why Progressives Will Dominate the Next Political Era*. New York: Simon and Schuster.

Ditton, P. M., and D. J. Wilson. 1999. *Truth in Sentencing in State Prisons*. Washington, DC: U.S. Department of Justice, Bureau of Justice Statistics.

Donziger, S. R. (Ed.). (1996). *The Real War on Crime: The Report of the National Criminal Justice Commission*. New York: Harper Perennial.

Federal Bureau of Investigation. 1999. *Crime in the United States: Uniform Crime Reports, 1998*. Washington, DC: U.S. Department of Justice.

Feld, B. C. 1998. "Juvenile and Criminal Justice Systems' Responses to Youth Violence." In M. Tonry and M. H. Moore (Eds.), *Crime and Justice: A Review of Research. Vol. 24: Youth Violence* (pp. 189–261). Chicago: University of Chicago Press.

Feld, B. C. 1999. "The Honest Politician's Guide to Juvenile Justice in the Twenty-First Century." *Annals of the American Academy of Political and Social Science* 564 (July):10–27.

Finckenauer, J. O., and P. W. Gavin. 1999. *Scared Straight: The Panacea Phenomenon Revisited*. Prospect Heights, IL: Waveland.

Finn, P. 1996. "No-Frills Prisons and Jails: A Movement in Flux." *Federal Probation* 60 (September):35–44.

Fox, J. A. 2000. "Demographics and U.S. Homicide." In A. Blumstein and J. Wallman (Eds.), *The Crime Drop in America* (pp. 288–317). Cambridge, UK: Cambridge University Press.

Frazier, C. E., D. M. Bishop, and L. Lanza-Kaduce. 1999. "Get-Tough Juvenile Justice Reforms: The Florida Experience." *Annals of the American Academy of Political and Social Science* 564 (July):167–84.

Gallagher, C. A. 1999. *Juvenile Offenders in Residential Placement, 1997*. Washington, DC: U.S. Department of Justice, Office of Juvenile Justice and Delinquency Prevention.

Garland, D. 1999. "The Commonplace and the Catastrophic: Interpretations of Crime in Late Modernity." *Theoretical Criminology* 3(3):353–64.

Gendreau, P. 1996. "The Principles of Effective Intervention with Offenders." In A. T. Harland (Ed.), *Choosing Correctional Interventions That Work: Defining the Demand and Evaluating the Supply* (pp. 117–30). Newbury Park, CA: Sage.

Gendreau, P., and C. Goggin. 2000. "Comments on Restorative Justice Programmes in New Zealand." Unpublished manuscript, Centre for Criminal Justice Studies, University of New Brunswick at Saint John.

Gendreau, P., C. Goggin, F. T. Cullen, and D. A. Andrews. 2000. "The Effects of Community Sanctions and Incarceration on Recidivism." *Forum on Corrections Research* 12 (May):10–13.

Gendreau, P., and R. R. Ross. 1979. "Effective Correctional Treatment: Bibliotherapy for Cynics." *Crime and Delinquency* 25 (October):463–89.

Gelsthorpe, L., and M. Fenwick. 1997. "Comparative Juvenile Justice: England and Wales." In J. A. Winterdyk (Ed.), *Juvenile Justice Systems: International Perspectives* (pp. 77–112). Toronto: Canadian Scholars' Press.

Gilliard, D. K., and A. J. Beck. 1998. *Prisoners in 1997*. Washington, DC: U.S. Department of Justice, Bureau of Justice Statistics.

Gordon, D. R. 1994. *The Return of the Dangerous Classes: Drug Prohibition and Policy Politics*. New York: W. W. Norton.

Greenwood, P. W., K. E. Model, C. P. Rydell, and J. Chiesa. 1996. *Diverting Children from a Life in Crime: Measuring Costs and Benefits*. Santa Monica, CA: RAND.

Griset, P. L. 1991. *Determinate Sentencing: The Promise and the Reality of Retributive Justice*. Albany, NY: State University of New York Press.

Hacker, A. 1992. *Two Nations: Black and White, Separate, Hostile, Unequal*. New York: Charles Scribner's Sons.

Henggeler, S. W. 1997. *Treating Serious Anti-Social Behavior in Youth: The MST Approach*. Washington, DC: U.S. Department of Justice, Office of Juvenile Justice and Delinquency Prevention.

Herrnstein, R. J., and C. Murray. 1994. *The Bell Curve: Intelligence and Class Structure in American Life*. New York: The Free Press.

Holden, G. A., and R. A. Kapler. 1995. "Deinstitutionalizing Status Offenders: A Record of Progress." *Juvenile Justice* 2 (2):3–10.

Hunt, M. 1997. *How Science Takes Stock: The Story of Meta-Analysis*. New York: Russell Sage Foundation.

Klein, M. (Ed.). 1984. *Western Systems of Juvenile Justice*. Beverly Hills, CA: Sage.

Kurki, Leena. 2000. "Restorative and Community Justice in the United States." In M. Tonry (Ed.), *Crime and Justice: A Review of Research, Vol. 27* (pp. 235–303). Chicago: University of Chicago Press.

Lacayo, R. 1995. "The Real Hard Cell: Lawmakers Are Stripping Inmates of Their Perks." *Time* (September 4):31–32.

Langan, P. A., and D. P. Farrington. 1998. *Crime and Justice in the United States and in England and Wales, 1981–96*. Washington, DC: U.S. Department of Justice, Bureau of Justice Statistics.

Langan, P. A., J. V. Fundis, L. A. Greenfeld, and V. W. Schneider. 1988. *Historical Statistics on Prisoners in State and Federal Institutions, Yearend 1925–86*. Washington, DC: U.S. Department of Justice, Bureau of Justice Statistics.

Latimer, J., C. Dowden, and D. Muise. 2001. *The Effectiveness of Restorative Justice Practices: A Meta-Analysis*. Ottawa, Canada: Research and Statistics Division, Department of Justice Canada.

Le Blanc, M., and Loeber, R. 1998. "Developmental Criminology Updated." In M. Tonry (Ed.), *Crime and Justice: A Review of Research, Vol. 23* (pp. 115–98). Chicago: University of Chicago Press.

Leschied, A. W., P. G. Jaffe, and W. Willis (Eds.). 1991. *The Young Offenders Act: A Revolution in Canadian Juvenile Justice*. Toronto: University of Toronto Press.

Levrant, S., F. T. Cullen, B. Fulton, and J. F. Wozniak. 1999. "Reconsidering Restorative Justice: The Corruption of Benevolence Revisited?" *Crime and Delinquency* 45 (January):3–27.

Lipset, S. M., and W. Schneider. 1983. *The Confidence Gap: Business, Labor, and Government in the Public Mind*. New York: The Free Press.

Lipsey, M. W. 1992. "Juvenile Delinquency Treatment: A Meta-Analytic Inquiry into the Variability of Effects." In T. D. Cook, H. Cooper, D. S. Cordray, H. Hartmann, L. V. Hedges, R. J. Light, T. A. Lewis, and F. Mosteller (Eds.), *Meta-Analysis for Explanation: A Casebook* (pp. 83–127). New York: Russell Sage.

Lipsey, M. W. 1999. "Can Intervention Rehabilitate Serious Delinquents?" *Annals of the American Academy of Political and Social Science* 564 (July):142–66.

Lipsey, M. W., and D. B. Wilson. 1998. "Effective Interventions for Serious Juvenile Offenders: A Synthesis of Research." In R. Loeber and D. P. Farrington (Eds.), *Serious and Violent Juvenile Offenders: Risk Factors and Successful Interventions* (pp. 313–66). Thousand Oaks, CA: Sage.

Lipton, D., R. Martinson, and J. Wilks. 1975. *The Effectiveness of Correctional Treatment: A Survey of Treatment Evaluation Studies*. New York: Praeger.

Losel, F. 1995. "The Efficacy of Correctional Treatment: A Review and Synthesis of Meta-Evaluations." In J. McGuire (Ed.), *What Works: Reducing Reoffending* (pp. 79–111). West Sussex, UK: John Wiley.

MacKenzie, D. L. 2000. "Evidence-Based Corrections: Identifying What Works." *Crime and Delinquency* 46 (October):457–71.

Mann, C. R. 1993. *Unequal Justice: A Question of Color*. Bloomington, IN: Indiana University Press.

Martinson, R. 1974. "What Works – Questions and Answers About Prison Reform." *The Public Interest* 35 (Spring):22–54.

Massey, D. S., and N. A. Denton. 1993. *American Apartheid: Segregation and the Making of the Underclass*. Cambridge, MA: Harvard University Press.

Matthews, R. 1999. *Doing Time: An Introduction to the Sociology of Imprisonment*. Hampshire, England: Macmillan.

Mauer, M. 1999. *Race to Incarcerate*. New York: The New Press.

Mehlbye, J., and L. Walgrave (Eds.). 1998. *Confronting Youth in Europe: Juvenile Crime and Juvenile Justice*. Copenhagen, Denmark: AKF Forlaget.

Merlo, A. 2000. "Juvenile Justice at the Crossroads: Presidential Address to the Academy of Criminal Justice Sciences." *Justice Quarterly* 17 (December): 639–61.

Miller, J. G. 1996. *Search and Destroy: African-American Males in the Criminal Justice System*. New York: Cambridge University Press.

Moon, M. M. 1996. "RECLAIM Ohio: An Innovative Initiative in Juvenile Corrections." Unpublished doctoral dissertation, University of Cincinnati.

Moon, M. M., J. L. Sundt, F. T. Cullen, and J. P. Wright. 1999. "Is Child Saving Dead? Public Support for Juvenile Rehabilitation." *Crime and Delinquency* 46 (January):38–60.

Moone, J. 1997a. *States at a Glance: Juvenile in Public Facilities, 1995.* Washington, DC: U.S. Department of Justice, Office of Juvenile Justice and Delinquency Prevention.

Moone, J. 1997b. *Juveniles in Private Facilities, 1991–1995.* Washington, DC: U.S. Department of Justice, Office of Juvenile Justice and Delinquency Prevention.

Nagin, D. S. 1998. "Criminal Deterrence Research at the Outset of the Twenty-First Century." In M. Tonry (Ed.), *Crime and Justice: A Review of Research,* Vol. 23 (pp. 1–42). Chicago: University of Chicago Press.

National Criminal Justice Association. 1997. *Juvenile Justice Reform Initiatives in the States: 1994–1996.* Washington, DC: U.S. Department of Justice, Office of Juvenile Justice and Delinquency Prevention.

Palmer, T. 1975. "Martinson Revisited." *Journal of Research in Crime and Delinquency* 12(July):133–52.

Parent, D., T. Dunworth, D. McDonald, and W. Rhodes. 1997. *Key Legislative Issues in Criminal Justice: Transferring Serious Juvenile Offenders to Adult Court.* Washington, DC: U.S. Department of Justice, National Institute of Justice.

Pileggi, N. 1977. "Inside the Juvenile-Justice System: How Fifteen-Year-Olds Get Away with Murder." *New York Magazine* 10 (June 13):36–44.

Piven, F. F., and R. A. Cloward. 1971. *Regulating the Poor: The Functions of Public Welfare.* New York: Pantheon.

Platt, A. M. 1969. *The Child Savers: The Invention of Delinquency.* Chicago: University of Chicago Press.

Redondo, S., J. Sanchez-Meca, and V. Garrido. 1999. "The Influence of Treatment Programmes on the Recidivism of Juvenile and Adult Offenders: An European Meta-Analytic Review." *Psychology, Crime and Law* 5(3):251–78.

Roberts, J. V., and L. J. Stalans. 1997. *Public Opinion, Crime, and Criminal Justice.* Boulder, CO: Westview.

Rosenthal, R. 1991. *Meta-Analytic Procedures for Social Research.* Newbury Park, CA: Sage.

Rothman, D. J. 1980. *Conscience and Convenience: The Asylum and Its Alternatives in Progressive America.* Boston: Little, Brown.

Sabol, W. J., and J. P. Lynch. 2000. *Crime Policy Report: Did Getting Tough on Crime Pay?* Washington, DC: Urban Institute.

Schiff, M. F. 1999. "The Impact of Restorative Interventions on Juvenile Offenders." In G. Bazemore and L. Walgrave (Eds.), *Restorative Juvenile Justice: Repairing the Harm of Youth Crime* (pp. 327–56). Monsey, NY: Willow Tree Press.

Schur, E. M. (1973). *Radical Non-Intervention: Rethinking the Delinquency Problem.* Englewood Cliffs, NJ: Prentice-Hall.

Schwartz, I., N. A. Weiner, and G. Enosh. 1999. "Myopic Justice? The Juvenile Court and Child Welfare Systems." *Annals of the American Academy of Political and Social Science,* 564 (July):126–41.

Sherman, L. W., H. Strang, and D. J. Woods. 2000. *Recidivism Patterns in the Canberra Reintegrative Shaming Experiments (RISE)*. Canberra, Australia: Centre for Restorative Justice, Research School of Social Sciences, Australian National University.

Shichor, D., and D. Sechrest (Eds.). (1996). *Three Strikes and You're Out: Vengeance as Public Policy*. Thousand Oaks, CA: Sage.

Sickmund, M., H. N. Snyder, and E. Poe-Yamagata. 1997. *Juvenile Offenders and Victims: 1997 Update on Violence*. Washington, DC: U.S. Department of Justice, Office of Juvenile Justice and Delinquency Prevention.

Snyder, H. N. 1998. *Juvenile Arrests 1997*. Washington, DC: U.S. Department of Justice, Office of Juvenile Justice and Delinquency Prevention.

Snyder, H. N., and M. Sickmund. 1999a. *Juvenile Offenders and Victims: 1999 National Report*. Washington, DC: U.S. Department of Justice, Office of Juvenile Justice and Delinquency Prevention.

Snyder, H. N., and M. Sickmund. 1999b. *Minorities in the Juvenile Justice System: 1999 National Report Series – Juvenile Justice Bulletin*. Washington, DC: U.S. Department of Justice, Office of Juvenile Justice and Delinquency Prevention.

Snyder, H. N., M. Sickmund, E. Poe-Yamagata. 1996. *Juvenile Offenders and Victims: 1996 Update on Violence*. Washington, DC: U.S. Department of Justice, Office of Juvenile Justice and Delinquency Prevention.

Snyder, H. N., M. Sickmund, E. Poe-Yamagata. 2000. *Juvenile Transfers to Criminal Court in the 1990's: Lessons Learned from Four Studies*. Washington, DC: U.S. Department of Justice, Office of Juvenile Justice and Delinquency Prevention.

Sparks, R. 1994. "Can Prisons Be Legitimate?" *British Journal of Criminology* 34 (Special Issue):14–28.

Spelman, W. 2000. "What Recent Studies Do (and Don't) Tell Us About Imprisonment and Crime." In M. Tonry (Ed.), *Crime and Justice: A Review of Research, Vol. 27* (pp. 419–94). Chicago: University of Chicago Press.

Stahl, A. L. 1999. *Offenders in Juvenile Court, 1996*. Washington, DC: U.S. Department of Justice, Office of Juvenile Justice and Delinquency Prevention.

Tonry, M. 1994. "Racial Disproportion in U.S. Prisons." *British Journal of Criminology* 34 (Special Issue):97–115.

Tonry, M. 1995. *Malign Neglect: Race, Crime, and Punishment in America*. New York: Oxford University Press.

Tonry, M. 1996. *Sentencing Matters*. New York: Oxford University Press.

Torbet, P. M. 1996. *Juvenile Probation: The Workhorse of the Juvenile Justice System*. Washington, DC: U. S. Department of Justice, Office of Juvenile Justice and Delinquency Prevention.

Torbet, P, and L. Szymanski.1998. *State Legislative Responses to Violent Juvenile Crime: 1996–97 Update*. Washington, DC: U.S. Department of Justice.

Tracy, P. E., M. E. Wolfgang, and R. M. Figlio. 1985. *Delinquency in Two Birth Cohorts: Executive Summary*. Washington, DC: U.S. Department of Justice.

Van Ness, D. W., and K. H. Strong. 1997. *Restoring Justice*. Cincinnati: Anderson.

Walgrave, L., and J. Mehlbye. 1998. "An Overview: Comparative Comments on Juvenile Offending and Its Treatment in Europe." In J. Mehlbye and

L. Walgrave (Eds.), *Confronting Youth in Europe: Juvenile Crime and Juvenile Justice* (pp. 21–53). Copenhagen, Denmark: AKF Forlaget.

Wilson, J. Q. 1975. *Thinking About Crime*. New York: Vintage.

Wilson, W. J. 1987. *The Truly Disadvantaged: The Inner City, the Underclass, and Public Policy*. Chicago: University of Chicago Press.

Weitekamp, G. M., H.-J. Kerner, and S. M. Herberger, S. M. 1998. "Germany." In J. Mehlbye and L. Walgrave (Eds.), *Confronting Youth in Europe: Juvenile Crime and Juvenile Justice* (pp. 251–304). Copenhagen, Denmark: AKF Forlaget.

Winterdyk, J. A. (Ed.). 1997. *Juvenile Justice Systems: International Perspectives*. Toronto: Canadian Scholars' Press.

Zimring, F. E., and G. Hawkins. 1995. *Incapacitation: Penal Confinement and the Restraint of Crime*. New York: Oxford University Press.

Zimring, F. E., and G. Hawkins. 1997. *Crime Is Not the Problem: Lethal Violence in America*. New York: Oxford University Press.

5

Adolescent Health Care in the United States: Implications and Projections for the New Millennium

Elizabeth M. Ozer, Tracy Macdonald, and Charles E. Irwin, Jr.

Adolescence is a unique developmental stage distinct from both childhood and adulthood. The second decade of life offers unique strengths, including greater access to life's opportunities resulting from self-discovery and emerging independence. It also has special vulnerabilities, health concerns, and barriers for accessing health care. In the new millennium, it is timely to consider the conditions of adolescents today and how current and future trends are likely to affect the health of adolescents in the 21st century. Maximizing adolescent health is particularly important in light of increasing recognition that the health of adolescents is crucial to their well-being as adults.

Most adolescents are considered healthy when assessed by traditional medical markers. However, an increasing number of adolescents are exposed to deleterious environmental conditions and engage in risky behaviors that threaten their current and future health. Thus, the

The major support for this document was provided by two national policy centers funded by the Maternal and Child Health Bureau – The National Adolescent Health Information Center & The Policy Information Center for Middle Childhood and Adolescence (4H06 00002, 6U93 MC0023 and 2 T71 MC00003). The Centers are located in the Division of Adolescent Medicine, Department of Pediatrics, and the Institute for Health Policy Studies, School of Medicine at the University of California, San Francisco. Additional support was provided by the Society for Research on Adolescence, and The California Wellness Foundation.

The authors thank Claire D. Brindis, Linda Rieder Gardner, and Mark Thompson for their contributions and insights. Thanks also to Michael Berlin, Scott Burg, Anne Claiborne, Jane Park, Pat Rosenbaum, and David Silverberg, of the University of California, San Francisco, Division of Adolescent Medicine for their administrative, research, and editorial support.

health threats for adolescents are primarily social and behavioral (Ozer, Brindis, Millstein, Knopf, & Irwin, 1998; U.S. Preventive Services Task Force, 1996).

Over the past decade there has been an unprecedented focus on the nation's youth. Several federal reports have focused on adolescents, with perhaps the most critical being the series developed by the former Office of Technology Assessment (OTA) in 1991: *Adolescent Health: Volumes I–III*, which served as an expansive assessment of the state of adolescent health as we entered the 1990s. Two of the documents' major recommendations focused on improving the environmental context of adolescents' lives and assuring access to health care for all youth. OTA and other major reports emphasized that adolescent health is embedded within a broad social and environmental context (e.g., National Research Council, 1993). Reducing adolescent morbidity and mortality requires strategies that enlist the support of the many individuals and institutions that affect the lives of adolescents. Multiple approaches delivered through a variety of settings (including schools, the mass media, communities, families, and health care settings) are most likely to be effective.

In this chapter, we explore how the health care system is responding to the changing nature and health needs of adolescents. We discuss the implications of current and projected trends in health policy and delivery of health care services for the well-being of adolescents. Since adolescent health should be considered within social and environmental contexts, the first section briefly reviews current and projected demographic and socio economic trends. The second section presents a health profile of adolescents. The third section provides an overview of policies that affect adolescent health services and financing. The fourth section presents an overview of adolescents' access to and utilization of health care services. The fifth section discusses trends in the provision of preventive health services, and the sixth section discusses the health implications of recent advances in information and medical technology. Finally, the seventh section provides an overview of implications and projections in adolescent health care for the new millennium.

SOCIAL AND ENVIRONMENTAL CONTEXT OF YOUTH TODAY

Significant changes in society's norms and structure suggest that adolescents in the next millennium will live in an environment that differs significantly from that typical for adolescents during the past 30 years.

The nature of these demographic and socioeconomic changes has implications for adolescents' health status and the appropriate role of the health care system. This section describes these transformed social and environmental contexts.

Highlights of Adolescent Population Trends

The number of adolescents in the United States is increasing rapidly, accompanied by important changes in the demographic composition of the population. The population of adolescents ages 10 to 19 is expected to increase from 38.8 million in 1998 to 50 million by the year 2040. However, adolescents will comprise a smaller percentage of the U.S. population in coming years due in part to delayed childbearing among "baby boomers" and an influx of young immigrants in their reproductive years (Day, 1996; U.S. Census Bureau, 2000). This decrease in the percentage of the adolescent population is consistent with trends in most developed regions of the world (Johns Hopkins School of Public Health, 1995).

In the coming decades, a greater proportion of adolescents will be youth of color. Key trends indicate that the non-Hispanic White population is decreasing in proportion, with a simultaneous increase in all other racial/ethnic groups. Hispanic adolescents are expected to outnumber Blacks as the largest minority group under age 18. It is projected that one in five children in the United States will be of Hispanic origin by the year 2020 – an increase of 70% from 1996 (Brindis & Wolfe, 1997). White adolescents will decline to less than 50% by the year 2040 (U.S. Census Bureau, 2000). Although ethnic heterogeneity does not in itself imply health problems, such diversity needs to be recognized by policymakers, researchers, and health professionals who serve adolescents.

Highlights of Socioeconomic Status and Family Structure

Changes in the socioeconomic status of youth are characterized by an increasing gap between the very rich and the poor. In 1999, the richest 2.7 million Americans (top 1%) had as much disposable income as the bottom 100 million (Congressional Budget Office, 1999). A greater percentage of adolescents are being raised in impoverished families than in previous generations, with 4 out of 10 Hispanic and Black children now being raised in poverty. The chances that a child will experience poverty is strongly influenced by his or her family structure. The percent of children living in two-parent households has fallen sharply in the last two decades, with children of color being less likely than their White peers to live in a two-parent household. Children and adolescents ages 6 to 17 living in households with only their mother present are 5 times as likely to be living in poverty than those living in two-parent households (Dalaker, 1998). Family income continues to be the strongest predictor of adolescent health status (Coiro, Zill, & Bloom, 1994; Ozer et al., 1998).

HEALTH PROFILE OF YOUTH

The health status of populations is typically assessed using traditional morbidity and mortality indicators. For the adolescent population there is often a focus on risky behaviors, as the majority of adolescent mortality and morbidity can be attributed to preventable risk factors. However, these data alone do not provide a comprehensive profile of the health of adolescents.

Adolescence has often been characterized as a period of psychosocial turmoil; however most adolescents successfully negotiate the important transitions of this period (Bandura, 1997; Petersen, 1988; Rutter, Graham, Chadwick, & Yule, 1976). Although the passage through adolescence to adulthood has become riskier than it was in the past, most theories of human behavior greatly overpredict the incidence of pathology under adversity. To focus only on risk fails to explain this resilience to adversity; one must also look to sources of enablement (Bandura, 1997). For example, in the National Longitudinal Study on Adolescent Health, Resnick and colleagues (1997) focus on the identification of protective factors that may reduce the likelihood of negative health and social outcomes. Their findings support the importance of family and school contexts, most notably a sense of parent-family connectedness and school connectedness, in protecting adolescents against risky health behavior (Resnick, Bearman, Blum, Bauman, Harris, Jones, Tabor, Buehring, Sieving, Shew, Ireland, Bearinger, & Udry, 1997).

A complete picture of the health of adolescents would provide data that focus on adolescent strengths, as well as the influence of important social contexts in reducing health risk behavior (Brindis, Ozer, Handley, Knopf, Millstein, & Irwin, 1997). At this time, the majority of national data sets reflect traditional mortality and morbidity indicators, with a more recent emphasis on health risk behavior. This section briefly describes the current status of adolescent health according to these indicators.

Mortality

The majority of adolescent mortality is preventable. In 1997, 73% of deaths among adolescents and young adults ages 10 to 24 resulted from injury and violence. At present, the leading causes of death are accidents and other unintentional injuries (43% of deaths in 1997), with motor vehicle accidents the leading cause of death for both males and females. Homicide (18%) is the second leading cause of death, and suicide (12%) is the third (CDC, 2000). Although motor vehicle related accidents are also the leading cause of death in most of Western Europe, Israel, Australia, Canada, and New Zealand for persons ages 15 to 24 years (Fingerhut, Cox, & Warner, 1998), rates of injury mortality are significantly lower than in the United States (Morrison & Stone, 2000).

Overall mortality rates for adolescents and young adults in the United States have declined 28% since 1980 and are now at or near all time lows. The overall decline in mortality reflects a decrease in motor vehicle deaths and other injuries as well as decreases in homicide rates among all groups of adolescents. Since peaking in the early 1990s, suicide rates have fallen sharply for most adolescents (CDC, 2000; Hoyert, Kochanek, & Murphy, 1999).

As adolescents grow older, their risk of death increases dramatically: Twenty- to 24-year-olds are over 3 times more likely to die than those 10 to 14 years of age. Mortality rates for males in all age categories are also higher than for females (CDC, 2000). There are also striking racial and ethnic disparities in mortality rates among adolescents. Within all age groups, the mortality rate for Black adolescents – both male and female – is much higher than rates for all other racial/ethnic groups. Homicide is the leading cause of death for Black adolescents ages 15 to 24, accounting for almost half of all deaths in 1997. Homicide is also largely responsible for higher Hispanic mortality rates, whereas high suicide rates among American Indian/Alaska Natives are responsible for much of the higher mortality for that group (Hoyert et al., 1999). (See Figure 5.1.)

Health Status/Morbidity

The majority of adolescents are healthy when assessed by traditional medical indicators such as disease patterns and health care utilization. Relatively few adolescents and young adults are hospitalized, and most adolescents depend on ambulatory care for their medical care. By both parent and adolescent self-report, the majority of adolescents are in good

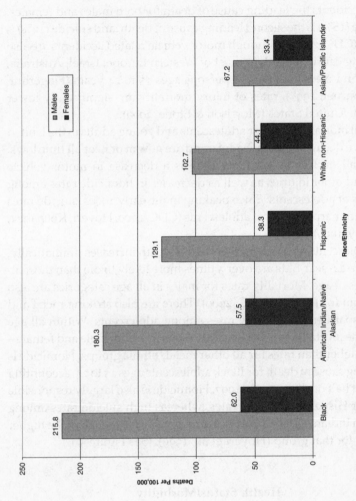

FIGURE 5.1. Mortality by gender and race/Ethnicity, ages 15–24, 1997. *Source:* Hoyert, D. L., Kochanek, K. D., & Murphy, S. L. (1999). Deaths: Final data for 1997. *National Vital Statistics Reports Vol. 47, No. 10.* Hyattsville: MD National Center for Health Statistics.

or excellent health (Klein, Wilson, McNulty, Kapphahn, & Collins, 1999; Newacheck, Brindis, Cart, Marchi, & Irwin, 1999).

However, some adolescents face multiple and complex health challenges. Adolescents with special health care needs are defined as "those who have or are at increased risk for a chronic, physical, developmental, behavioral, or emotional condition and who also require health and related services of a type or amount beyond that required by adolescents generally" (McPherson, Arango, Fox, Lauver, McManus, Newacheck, Perrin, Shonkoff, & Strickland, 1998). Children and youth living in poverty are almost twice as likely to have a chronic condition or to be in fair or poor health than their non-poor peers (Coiro et al., 1994).

Although a significant number of adolescents suffer from a physical disability, the leading single cause of disability among adolescents is mental health disorders (Gans, McManus, & Newacheck, 1991). The recently published Surgeon General's Report on Mental Health (Department of Health and Human Services [DHHS], 1999) provides a much needed focus on the mental health of young people. Utilizing data from the Methodology for Epidemiology of Mental Disorders in Children and Adolescents (MECA Study), the report estimates that almost 21% of youth, ages 9 to 17, have a diagnosable mental or addictive disorder associated with at least minimum impairment; about half of these youth (4 million) have a disorder that results in significant impairment (Shaffer, Fisher, Dulcan, Davies, Piancentini, Schwab-Stone, Lahey, Bourdon, Jensen, Bird, Canino, & Regier, 1996, cited in DHHS, 1999).

Rates of mental health disorder increase from late childhood through mid- to late-adolescence, with the major risk for onset of mental health disorder before the age of 18 (Newman, Moffitt, Caspi, Magdol, Silva, & Stanton, 1996). There is a sharp increase in reports of depression from childhood to adolescence (Kazdin, 1993) with evidence suggesting that increases in depression are greater for girls (Petersen, Compas, Brooks-Gunn, Stemmler, Ey, & Grant, 1993; Schoen, Davis, Scott-Collins, Greenberg, Des Roches, & Abrams, 1997). Other psychological disorders that emerge or increase in prevalence during adolescence include anxiety disorders, schizophrenia, eating disorders, and substance use disorders (Kazdin, 1993; Newacheck, 1989).

These data suggest that prevention and intervention efforts should target children and adolescents. Yet previous studies have shown that although many adolescents suffer from mental health problems, few receive mental health diagnoses, and fewer still receive the mental health services they need (Leaf, Alegria, Cohen, Goodman, Horwitz, Hoven,

Narrow, Vaden-Kiernan, & Regier, 1996; Lewinsohn, Rohde, & Seeley, 1998).

Health-Risk Behaviors. Risky health behaviors are important determinants of adolescent health status. Behaviors such as substance use and abuse, unsafe sexual practices, and risky vehicle use are increasingly responsible for the majority of deaths and disabling conditions through the fourth decade of life, and most of these behaviors are initiated during adolescence (Ozer et al., 1998).

Adolescents who engage in one health-damaging behavior are more likely to participate in others (Irwin, Igra, Eyre, & Millstein, 1997; Lindberg, Boggess, Porter, & Williams, 2000): Adolescents who use one type of substance tend to use other substances (Yamaguchi & Kandel, 1985); and there is considerable research establishing links between adolescents' substance use and sexual behavior (e.g., Mott & Haurin, 1988), as well as substance use and injury (reviewed in Elliott, 1993). Further, the prevalence of multiple risk behaviors increases with age (Brener & Collins, 1998).

Although the risky behavior of adolescents dominates the discussion of adolescent health, an overview reveals some positive trends. First, substance use among adolescents in the United States and many developed countries has been falling (World Health Organization, 1996). In general, European teenagers are still more likely to smoke cigarettes and drink alcohol than U.S. teenagers, whereas U.S. adolescents are far more likely to use marijuana and other drugs (Hibell, Andersson, Ahlstrom, O Balakireva, Bjarnason, Kokkevi, & Morgan, 2001).

In the United States, from 1975 until the early 1990s, there were fairly consistent declines in use of alcohol, drugs, and tobacco among high school seniors (Johnston, O'Malley, & Bachman, 1998). While the first half of the 1990s showed increases in adolescent drug use, recent data suggest that the use of most illicit drugs by adolescents has begun to level off (Substance Abuse and Mental Health Services Administration, 1999).

Still, rates of substance use are alarmingly high. In 1998, more than half of adolescents reported having used alcohol during the past 30 days, one quarter of adolescents reported using marijuana, and about 18% were cigarette smokers. Data also indicate a gradual increase in the proportion of students who report heavy or binge drinking, an increase in younger smokers over the past several years, as well as a rise in the use of "designer" drugs, such as MDMA (ecstasy) (Johnston et al., 1998; Substance Abuse and Mental Health Services Administration, 1999).

Second, most trends in the area of sexual behavior are positive. For the first time in two decades, fewer adolescents are having sexual intercourse. Contraceptive use among adolescents has also increased, with more than half of all adolescents now using some form of contraceptive at first intercourse (Abma, Chandra, Mosher, Peterson, & Piccinino, 1997; Sonnenstein, Ku, Duberstein-Lindberg, Turner, & Pleck, 1998). In what appears to be a consequence of these first two trends, adolescent birth rates across all racial and ethnic groups have been declining since 1991 (Ventura, Mosher, Curtin, Abma, & Henshaw, 2000).

In spite of the good news, data suggest the need for on-going preventive focus in this area. Adolescents in the United States have higher STD rates, birth rates, and abortion rates than adolescents in almost all other developed nations (Panchaud, Singh, Feivelson & Darroch, 2000; Singh & Darroch, 2000). Racial/ethnic disparities in adolescent birth rates persist: The birth rate for Hispanic adolescents is more than twice the rate for Whites. Adolescents also have the highest age-specific rates for most sexually-transmitted infections (STIs), with rates of infection especially high among Black adolescents (Division of STD Prevention, CDC, 1999). Although the number of actual AIDS cases among adolescents has been low, the high rate of STIs among adolescents indicates that this population is especially vulnerable to HIV infection. The incubation time between contracting the infection and the onset of AIDS is close to 10 years; thus many young adults were infected with HIV during adolescence.

The positive trends suggest that societal prevention messages have had an impact. However other data indicating the initiation of risky health behaviors at younger ages (Kann, Kinchen, Williams, Ross, Lowry, Grunbaum, & Kolbe, 2000), an increase in the proportion of overweight adolescents (Troiano, Flegal, Kuczmarkski, Campbell, & Johnson, 1995), and still prevalent use of alcohol and adoption of newer substances, suggest that prevention efforts must continue and include a focus on targeting even younger adolescents. In addition, most of the data on health behavior focuses on one risk area, rather than the co-variation of behaviors. Despite the decrease in adolescents' engagement in any single risk behavior, the percentage of adolescents (20–25%) who engage in multiple risky behaviors has remained relatively stable (Lindberg et al., 2000).

The clustering of risky behavior also raises questions about the best way to deliver health care to adolescents (Dougherty, 1999). For example, can preventing one behavior (e.g., alcohol use) prevent other problems from occurring? What is the primary problem on which to focus treatment? As described later in the chapter, numerous professional organizations have recommended that clinicians screen adolescents for a wide variety of health behaviors. However, given limited time in clinical encounters, comprehensive screening and delivery of services is a challenging task.

ADOLESCENT HEALTH POLICY

During the 1990s, there was an increase in the number of federal, state, and private efforts devoted to understanding and improving adolescent health. There are now more national institutions that focus on adolescent health issues than existed in previous decades, and the federal government has increased its financial commitment to adolescents and adolescent health. For example, in 1995, the Maternal and Child Health Bureau (MCHB) established an Office of Adolescent Health (OAH), which has been active in formulating policy for adolescent health issues and making grants to public, professional, and private organizations that focus on adolescent health.

There have also been several commissions, conferences, and reports dedicated to adolescent health, and there is currently an effort to improve the quality of adolescent health data. Limitations in available data sources have made it difficult to accurately assess adolescent health; thus additional adolescent-focused surveys and surveillance systems have been developed. These include: The National Longitudinal Survey on Adolescent Health (Add Health Study), a school-based study of health behaviors in adolescents in grades 7 through 12; and the Youth Risk Behavior Surveillance System (YRBSS), a national and state probability sample of high school students, conducted by the Centers for Disease Control.

Concurrently, there has begun to be a shift toward emphasizing prevention and fostering positive health behaviors, rather than solely addressing health care problems and illness. For example, the Centers for Disease Control and Prevention's Division of Adolescent and School Health (CDC-DASH) has led efforts to improve adolescent health in conjunction with the U.S. Office of Disease Prevention and Health Promotion's (ODPHP) Healthy People 2000 and 2010 initiative to improve the health of all Americans through prevention.

Over the past decade, there has also been a major devolution in the locus of responsibility and decision making for health policy from the federal government to state and local levels. Many health programs that were previously administered by federal agencies are now being combined and "block granted" to state and local agencies, which have greater decision-making authority over allocation of these funds. Concurrent with this shift, more states and counties have taken an increased interest in adolescent health, developing their own efforts to promote it globally or to target specific areas. Policy organizations such as the National Conference of State Legislatures support a Division of Adolescent and School Health which monitors health care legislation that affects adolescents; and the National Governors' Association has played a major role in helping states to design and implement their child health insurance programs (CHIP).

The Legal Context

Adolescents are greatly affected by the legal environment and its shifting constraints and protections. During adolescence, young people begin to seek increased autonomy and to take more responsibility for their own health and well-being. Research suggests that adolescents are capable of giving informed consent between 12 and 15 years of age and, depending upon the circumstances, generally arrive at the same health care decisions as adults (McCabe, 1996; Weithorn & Campbell, 1982). The ability to access some types of health care independently may encourage teens to seek services they might not otherwise receive, and it may increase their sense of competence for navigating the health care system and keeping themselves healthy.

The fear that confidentiality may be breached is an important reason why adolescents do not seek health care, and some would forgo health care if they thought their parents might find out (Cheng & Klein, 1995; Ford, Millstein, Halpern-Felsher, & Irwin, 1997). Because of confidentiality concerns, some adolescents delay seeking help for a variety of sensitive problems, such as sexually transmitted infections, physical or sexual abuse, pregnancy, substance abuse, and mental health concerns (English & Knopf, 1999).

In general, adolescents who are 18 years of age or younger must have the consent of a parent or legal guardian to receive medical care. However, to encourage early detection and treatment of sensitive health problems, all U.S. states have established at least some minor consent and/or minor emancipation statutes that allow minors to consent to their own care in a specific range of circumstances. For example, approximately half of all states have enacted statutes authorizing minors to give consent for pregnancy-related care, and almost every state allows minors to receive STI care without parental consent. Some states also include mental health counseling and/or substance abuse treatment in their consent statutes. Many federal health programs incorporate specific confidentiality protections for adolescents. At this time, family planning programs that receive federal funding under Title X of the Public Health Service Act are required to provide confidential family planning services to adolescents (English & Simmons, 1999).

There have been significant challenges waged against adolescents obtaining reproductive and sexuality-related health care – particularly abortion – on an independent and confidential basis. Persistent efforts to restrict access to reproductive care have been made in both the Congress and state legislatures, as well as in the courts. Most of these efforts have been unsuccessful, except for those related to parental notification for abortion services. Parental consent and notification laws are based on the assumption that adolescents lack the cognitive capacity to make rational abortion decisions (Wilcox, 1999). Despite lack of evidence for that assumption (e.g., Gittler, Quigley-Rick, & Saks, 1990; Melton, 1986), 39 states enacted statutes requiring either parental consent or parental notification for minors seeking abortion services in the 10 years between 1989 and 1999 (English & Simmons, 1999).

ACCESS TO CARE AND HEALTH CARE UTILIZATION

Access to Care

Adolescents require a range of preventive, diagnostic, and treatment services to respond to their diverse medical and psychosocial health needs. Yet, adolescents are the least likely of any age group to seek care through traditional office-based settings (Klein, 1994; Newacheck et al., 1999). Close to 1 in 5 adolescents report incidences of forgone health care, in which they thought that they should seek medical care, but did not do so (Ford, Bearman, Peter, & Moody, 1999). Barriers to access for adolescents include transportation/inconvenient hours; the costs of copayments and deductibles; a fragmented, disconnected system; concerns about confidentiality; the need for parental consent to obtain care; language/cultural barriers; and a shortage of providers trained in adolescent health (Brindis, VanLandeghem, Kirkpatrick, Macdonald, & Lee, 1999). Health insurance, however, is the primary determinant of whether adolescents will receive the health care services that they need.

Health Insurance

In most industrialized countries, governments play a central role in the delivery and financing of health care. However, in the United States, this role is primarily in the hands of the private sector (World Health Organization, 2000). For certain health risk behaviors, the structure of the U.S. health system may provide barriers to care. The effect of different health care systems in the United States, France, Germany, and the Netherlands were examined with regard to negative health outcomes associated with adolescent sexual behavior (Berne & Huberman, 1999). The authors conclude that the national health care system in Europe – which covers the costs of contraception, abortion, counseling services, physical exams, screenings, and treatment – is related to adolescents taking greater responsibility for their behavior, and the subsequent lower rates of STDs, abortions, and teenage births, as compared with the United States.

Beyond the area of sexual behavior, health insurance has important implications as uninsured adolescents use fewer health care services, have longer intervals between visits, and return for fewer follow-up appointments than their insured peers (Newacheck, Hughes, & Cisternas, 1995). Uninsured adolescents are also almost 3 times more likely than their insured counterparts to use an emergency room or urgent care center as their usual source of care (Newacheck et al., 1999).

As children grow older, they are less likely to have health insurance. Adolescents and young adults are among those with the lowest rates of insurance coverage. In 1995, 14.1% of adolescents ages 10 to 18 (4.2 million adolescents) were not covered by any form of health insurance (Newacheck et al., 1999). This is in large part due to federal and state Medicaid policies that have more generous income eligibility requirements for younger children than for adolescents. This decline in public health insurance coverage between childhood and early adolescence has not been matched by an increase in private coverage. In addition, many public and employer-sponsored health insurance programs establish eligibility cutoffs for children at age 18 or younger. This is of concern because adolescence and young adulthood are important times for establishing positive, independent health care relationships.

Uninsured adolescents are concentrated among poor and near-poor working families; the majority (80%) of uninsured adolescents live in families where at least one parent is employed full-time or part-time year round (Klein, Slap, & Elster, 1992). Because poverty is associated with increased risk of chronic health conditions, and because adolescents with low family incomes are less likely to have health insurance, these uninsured adolescents tend to have significant unmet health needs (Newacheck, McManus, & Brindis, 1990).

Hispanic adolescents are more than 2 times as likely as Blacks and 3 times more likely than their White peers to be without health insurance; nearly 1 in 3 Hispanic adolescents was uninsured in 1995. Ethnic differentials persist even after controlling for family income, employment, and family composition (Newacheck et al., 1999). In addition, recent changes in Medicaid coverage in response to welfare reform and changes in immigration policy have decreased insurance coverage for both non-citizen children and citizen children with non-citizen parents: Forty-three percent of non-citizen children and 27% of citizen children whose parents are non-citizens are uninsured (Brown, Wyn, & Ojeda, 1999). This trend is disconcerting because Hispanic/Latino and other immigrant youth are rapidly increasing as a percentage of the adolescent population. Such projections portend that a greater number of young people of color will be uninsured and unable to utilize primary care and preventive health care services.

Trends in Health Insurance.   Over the past several years, the number and proportion of adolescents covered by private, employer-based health insurance has declined, while public insurance coverage has increased. The decline in private insurance appears to result from market and economic factors: As health care premiums continue to rise, more employers are requesting higher employee payments for dependent coverage, with others eliminating dependent coverage entirely. Low-wage, part-time, temporary, or contractual jobs rarely provide coverage for workers, let alone their dependents. At the same time, public health insurance coverage for lower income adolescents has generally been increasing – rising 49% between 1989 and 1995 – with the vast majority of this coverage provided through the federal/state Medicaid program (Newacheck et al., 1999).

In 1997, the U.S. Congress took a major step to encourage the development and expansion of state-based health insurance programs for children and youth. The State Children's Health Insurance Program (CHIP) represents the first significant initiative to expand health insurance coverage for low-income adolescents since the creation of Medicaid in 1965. Approximately $40 billion in federal funding over the next 10 years has been allocated to CHIP, established as Title XXI of the Social Security Act. Title XXI encourages states to expand their Medicaid programs to cover uninsured children and adolescents up to age 19 at higher income levels than in the past by increasing the federal matching rate available to states for this program. States also have the option to use Title XXI to expand or create other (non-Medicaid) health insurance programs for children and adolescents (Brindis et al., 1999).

The State Children's Health Insurance Program represents an important opportunity for meeting the complex health care needs faced by low-income, uninsured adolescents. Virtually all states and territories have implemented CHIP programs, enrolling 1.3 million children and adolescents by June 1999 (English, Morreale, & Stinnett, 1999). An evaluation of the effect of receiving health insurance through a Children's Health Insurance Program indicates that the lower utilization rates of adolescents compared to younger children disappears when all age groups are covered by health insurance (Keane, Lave, Ricci, & LaVallee, 1999). These findings suggest that CHIP is an important step towards improving adolescents' access to care.

Since the 1980s, health care services for adolescents – as for all Americans – have increasingly been delivered through managed care arrangements; this is true for both public systems (such as Medicaid) and private ones (such as Blue Cross). In 1998, 85% of Americans and their dependents that had employer-based insurance were enrolled in a managed care plan (Levitt, Lundy, & Srinivasan, 1998), and 54% of all Medicaid enrollees received coverage through managed care in 1998, up from 14% in 1993 (HCFA, 1998).

Experts disagree about whether managed care has more positive or negative implications for adolescents. Certainly, the core principles that managed care has traditionally embraced – including prevention, wellness, population-based planning, and health promotion – are principles that, if operationalized, stand to serve adolescents well (Klein, 1994). The use of primary care providers can create a medical home for adolescents who might not otherwise identify with any particular provider or clinic. This might enhance continuity of care, as well as offer the increased potential for case management and coordination, as well as appropriate referrals to specialists when needed (American Academy of Pediatrics, 1992). This could benefit adolescents whose care is often fragmented. In addition, some managed care organizations offer better coverage for preventive services than do fee-for-service plans (English, Kapphahn, Perkins, & Wibbelsman, 1998).

On the other hand, some studies suggest that managed care plans impose restrictions on care that threaten adolescents' access to needed services, and that these barriers are even greater for those with special needs. For example, gatekeeper-type arrangements are designed to ensure that members do not overutilize health care services. Yet most health professionals agree that adolescents are at greater risk of underutilizing care, and need encouragement – not hurdles – to seek care.

There have been managed care reform efforts introduced at both the federal and state levels. The U.S. Congress has already passed several bills which limit the ability of managed care plans to deny coverage to individuals with preexisting conditions, and more legislation is pending. Specifically, there has been a great deal of attention to "patients' rights legislation" and the right to sue health plans. States are also considering laws and regulations related to quality assurance, rate-setting, and financial solvency. Although these reforms are not focused on adolescents, they are likely to have an impact on a large number of adolescents.

Health Care Utilization

Since adolescents are generally healthy, the question arises as to when and where adolescents seek care. Second, when adolescents do use the health care system, are they utilizing the most appropriate health services? Based on 1994 data from the National Ambulatory Medical Care Survey, it is estimated that 61.8% of the 90.1 million annual visits adolescents make to health care providers are to office-based physicians; an additional 16.3% are to hospital emergency departments; 8% are to hospital outpatient departments; 5.7% are to family planning clinics; and 1.8% are to school-based health centers (Ziv, Boulet, & Slap, 1999).

Ambulatory Care Physician Visits. The majority (73%) of adolescents ages 10 to 18 report that they have had at least one doctor contact in the past year (Newacheck et al., 1999). While early adolescents are most likely to visit pediatricians, middle adolescents and late adolescent males are most likely to visit general and/or family physicians, and late adolescent females are most likely to visit obstetricians/gynecologists (Ziv et al., 1999).

All age groups of adolescents are underrepresented in office-based physician visits relative to their proportion of the population (Ziv et al., 1999). However, there are striking disparities in utilization across gender and ethnic groups: Whites are overrepresented relative to their population proportion; Black and Hispanic adolescents are underrepresented; and females have significantly more visits than males starting in middle adolescence (ages 15–17) and continuing through older adolescence (ages 18–21). This gender differential is the result of increased female visits for reproductive health issues such as pregnancy and sexually transmitted infections. The racial differences in utilization persist after controlling for health insurance and socioeconomic factors (Newacheck et al., 1999).

The average adolescent office visit is 16 minutes and does not differ by age or sex. The leading reasons for both male and female visits are respiratory (19.4%), dermatological (10%), and musculoskeletal (9.7%). A similar profile was found for middle- and late-adolescent males. For middle- and late-adolescent females, the leading reason for visits was special obstetrical-gynecological examination (12.1% and 21.1%), and the leading diagnosis resulting from visits was pregnancy (9.5% and 20.4%) (Ziv et al., 1999).

Emergency Care. Adolescents rely heavily on emergency services for their primary care needs. In 1994, adolescents aged 11 to 21 years made an estimated 14.8 million visits to emergency departments. Emergency room use was more common among older adolescents ages 18 to 21 years versus younger adolescents ages 11 to 14; Black adolescents in all age groups were over-represented in emergency department use; as were adolescents without health insurance. In fact, the majority (53%) of adolescents utilizing emergency departments had public health insurance or were uninsured. Across all age groups and both sexes, approximately half of the visits were for non-urgent causes and few (3–5%) resulted in hospitalizations (Ziv, Boulet, & Slap, 1998).

Nationwide, injury is the leading reason for adolescent visits to emergency rooms in almost all age and gender subgroups. After injury, the most common reasons adolescents use emergency services are for musculoskeletal, respiratory, and digestive problems. For adolescent females over 15 years, pregnancy-related diagnoses account for a growing proportion of emergency department visits (Ziv et al., 1999). The low rate of hospitalization among adolescent emergency department patients, and the similarity of the diagnoses with those seen in adolescent office visits, suggest that many adolescents use emergency departments for their primary health care.

Inpatient Care. In 1997, only about 4% of all inpatient stays in the United States were for adolescents between the ages of 10 and 18 years ([National Center for Health Statistics] NCHS, 1999). Children and adolescents with lower family incomes average more hospital days than those from higher-income families (Department of Health and Human Services, 1998), supporting the notion that disadvantaged adolescents, with less access to outpatient care, are at increased risk for more serious medical problems.

The leading causes of hospitalization differ between younger and older adolescents. Among younger adolescents ages 10 to 14, the leading cause of hospitalization in 1996 was mental health disorders (61,000 discharges), followed by respiratory and digestive disease (60,000 and 59,000 discharges, respectively) and injury (48,000 discharges). Among older adolescents ages 15 to 19, pregnancy and childbirth (576,000 discharges) was the leading cause of hospitalization, followed by mental health disorders (130,000) and injury (97,000). Among young women ages 15 to 21, pregnancy and childbirth accounted for 69% of hospital discharges (Department of Health and Human Services, 1998).

In summary, the majority of adolescents receive care from a physician at least once a year. Most of these visits take place in outpatient offices, although a significant number of adolescents appear to use emergency rooms for their primary care. New insurance programs such as The State Children's Health Insurance Program may allow more adolescents to receive appropriate care through outpatient visits. In addition, utilization trends suggest that adolescents and their families need further education about how to appropriately access the health care system. Gender and racial disparity in use of outpatient care suggests the need for focused outreach.

Adolescents with Special Health Care Needs. Services provided to youth with special health care needs account for an estimated 25 to 50% of all child health expenditures (King, 1999). Adolescents with disabilities use more health care services than the rest of the adolescent population. They average 3 times more physician visits per year, are 5 times more likely to be hospitalized, and spend 10 times as many days in the hospital (Newacheck & McManus, 1989; Department of Health and Human Services, 1998). In addition to the primary and preventive services that all adolescents need, those with special health care needs require access to a range of services that consider their overall growth and development, such as pediatric specialty care, family support services, nutritional counseling, special education, and related rehabilitative services. The challenge for families of adolescents with special health care needs lies in accessing an often fragmented system of care, where specialty services are not coordinated with primary care, and often coverage for services is not comprehensive (Brown, 1999).

TRENDS IN THE PROVISION OF ADOLESCENT HEALTH SERVICES

The ability of an adolescent to access the health care system is the first step towards receiving effective health care. The content and quality of the health care interaction then becomes fundamental. Is an adolescent visit to a primary care provider utilized most effectively? Since most adolescents visit a physician each year, there is an opportunity to integrate prevention into clinical encounters. Guidelines specifically targeting the delivery of adolescent clinical preventive services have been developed by several national consensus groups.[1]

These guidelines suggest a fundamental change in the emphasis of adolescent services, whereby a greater number of services are directed at primary and secondary prevention of the major health threats facing youth. In general, the guidelines recommend that all adolescents have an annual, confidential visit during which primary care providers should screen, educate, and counsel adolescent patients in a number of biomedical and sociobehavioral areas. In addition, it is recommended that health guidance be given to parents of adolescents to help them respond appropriately to the health needs of their child. This includes providing information about normative adolescent development; the signs and symptoms of disease and emotional distress; parenting behaviors that promote healthy adolescent adjustment; and methods (e.g., monitoring) to help adolescents avoid potentially harmful behaviors.

To complement the development of practice guidelines, there is increasing interest in measures and systems that monitor the care provided to adolescents. For example, the National Committee for Quality Assurance (NCQA) includes a strong focus on prevention in its health plan accreditation process and the most recent version of the Health Plan Employer Data and Information Set (HEDIS). HEDIS – a set of quality indicators used to rank the performance of clinicians and health

---

[1] The Maternal and Child Health Bureau's Bright Futures: Guidelines for Health Supervision of Infants, Children, and Adolescents (Green & Palfrey, 2000), the American Medical Association's Guidelines for Adolescent Preventive Services (GAPS) (Elster & Kuznets, 1994), the U.S. Preventive Services Task Force's Guide to Clinical Preventive Services (1996), and the American Academy of Pediatrics' Health Supervision Guidelines (Stein, 1997).

plans – tracks preventive measures for adolescents such as an annual preventive service visit, substance abuse counseling, and chlamydia screening (NCQA, 1997).

In addition to working toward definable prevention objectives with expected health benefits, prevention has also been seen as a means to reduce health care expenditures. Projections of clinical cost and resource savings suggest that even limited success in risk identification, behavioral change, and morbidity reduction would have significant effects on adolescent health and health care costs (Downs & Klein, 1995; Gans, Alexander, Chu, & Elster, 1995). The ascendance of managed care, with a focus on wellness and population-based health, may have the potential to complement prevention efforts.

The Implementation of Adolescent Clinical Preventive Services

With the linking of adolescent preventive screening and counseling to quality performance measures, substantial attention has focused on the integration of these services into adolescent health care. Yet despite evidence that adolescents trust health providers and are interested and willing to talk with them about topics outlined in the guidelines (Blum, Beuhring, Wunderlich, & Resnick, 1996; Joffe, Radius, & Gall, M., 1988; Steiner & Gest, 1996), delivery of preventive services to adolescents is below recommended levels. This is the case in private practice and community based settings (Franzgrote, Ellen, Millstein, & Irwin, 1997; Igra & Millstein, 1993), as well as in managed care organizations (Halpern-Felsher, Ozer, Millstein, Wibbelsman, Fuster, Elster, & Irwin, 2000). Although primary care providers often screen adolescents for some risky behavior, there is inconsistency in screening across different risk areas (Halpern-Felsher et al., 2000).

It is clear that under most circumstances, parental expectations, satisfaction, and collaboration are critical to the provision of good medical services for children and have been linked to better health outcomes (e.g., Auslander, Thompson, Dreitzer, Santiago, 1997; Lewis, Pantell, & Sharp, 1991). Further, the findings of the National Longitudinal Study on Adolescent Health support recommendations that health guidance be given to parents of adolescents. For example, parental disapproval of early sexual debut was associated with later onset of sexual intercourse (Resnick et al., 1997).

However, the amount and content of the guidance and counseling provided to parents has received little attention: With few exceptions

(Fisher, 1992), there is little data on what type of health guidance parents expect and would like to receive from their child's provider. It is also unclear how much and what kind of health guidance parents currently receive from their adolescent's primary care provider. This area deserves further study.

A number of factors determine whether providers will adhere to preventive care and other guidelines. In a recent systematic review of the literature on barriers to guideline adherence, general categories of barriers were identified (Cabana, Rand, Powe, Wu, Wilson, Abboud, & Rubin, 1999). These include physician knowledge (lack of awareness or familiarity), physician attitudes (lack of agreement or self-efficacy), and external factors (time limitations, reimbursement, lack of a reminder system).

Physician factors, such as knowledge and attitudes, may be linked to training: For example, almost half (45%) of primary care physicians who see adolescent patients cited insufficient training as the most significant barrier to their delivery of health care to adolescents (Blum & Bearinger, 1990). Medical training and continuing medical education should focus on improving clinicians' knowledge and skills in conducting adolescent preventive interventions (Klein, Portilla, Goldstein, & Leininger, 1995). Yet even with adequate knowledge and attitudes, external barriers, such as lack of time and other system resources, can affect a physician's ability to execute recommendations. Thus, both physician and external/system barriers need to be overcome in order to effectively provide preventive care to adolescents.

In an attempt to overcome these barriers, The American Medical Association's Department of Adolescent Health has developed a provider training program and materials to assist in the implementation of preventive services in a variety of health care settings. Likewise, some health plans have developed their own training sessions, questionnaires, and charting forms to help facilitate the implementation of guidelines. It is still not clear how to bring all the necessary pieces together to best implement comprehensive preventive services in an efficient and effective manner (Fisher, 1999) or whether comprehensive preventive services are even feasible in the current health care system. With this in mind, studies to evaluate models for implementing adolescent clinical preventive services are currently being conducted in a variety of health care settings (Lustig, Ozer, Adams, Wibbelsman, Fuster, Bonar, & Irwin, 2001; Klein, Allan, Elster, Stevens, Cox, Hedberg, & Goodman, 2001; Ozer, Adams, Lustig, Millstein, Comfield, El-Diwany, Volpe & Irwin, 2001).

Do Preventive Services Make a Difference?

Beyond the question of how to effectively implement preventive services is the question of whether clinical preventive services result in improved health status for adolescents. Despite the current trend towards emphasizing prevention, we lack data on the efficacy of clinical preventive services on adolescent health (Hedberg, Klein, & Andresen, 1998; Rosen, Elster, Hedberg, & Paperny, 1997).

Decisions about whether to provide specific clinical services are increasingly made based on the perceived cost-effectiveness of the services to achieve measurable improvements in health outcomes (Hedberg et al., 1998). Because managed care plans continuously experience member turnover the initial fiscal burden of implementing preventive services for adolescents may outweigh the long-term benefits. This is especially the case since the short-term costs are incurred by purchasers, employers, and insurers, whereas the long-term costs may be accrued by other insurers, families, and the greater society. At the same time, the notion of longer-term health payoffs and the continuity of health services has become a more established theme in health care, and an espoused commitment of managed care. Just as immunizations and mammograms have become accepted standards of care, consumer and purchaser expectations may come to support comprehensive annual adolescent visits with a focus on risky behaviors.

It may also be productive and necessary to view investment in preventive services from a broader perspective (Ozer, 2000). Most preventive guidelines focus on specific topic areas, with evaluation of the efficacy of those guidelines focusing on behavior/health change in a specific area. Structuring prevention and risk reduction interventions in ways that promote self-regulation has been shown to be effective. This involves helping people develop skills for regulating their own motivation and behavior through self-monitoring, setting short-term attainable goals to motivate and direct their efforts, and positive incentives and social supports to support and sustain their efforts (Bandura, 1997). Once empowered with skills and a belief in their capabilities, people are better able to adopt health-promoting behavior. As such, an adolescent preventive services intervention should focus not only on the content of screening areas, but on the process of enhancing adolescents' perceived control and responsibility over their own health and well-being (Ozer et al., 2001).

INFORMATION AND MEDICAL TECHNOLOGY

Over the past several decades, advances in information and medical technology have affected adolescent behavior and health, as well as the delivery of health care services to adolescents. As these advances accelerate in the 21st century, their impact is likely to grow. This section of the chapter discusses the impact of the media on adolescent health as well as how technological changes affect health services delivered to adolescents.

How the Media Shape Adolescent Health

Existing research indicates that the media have an effect on adolescents' health, including violent behavior and attitudes about drinking, smoking, and body image (Brown & Witherspoon, 1998). The media help to shape adolescents' perception of the world and are an important source of information about health and risky behaviors. For example, more than half of adolescents report that they learned about pregnancy and birth control from television and movies, and more than half of all adolescent girls report that they have learned about sex from magazines (Kaiser Family Foundation, 1996).

Over the past decade, the media appear to have recognized the vast and growing audience that adolescents represent, with income and entertainment time at their disposal. As a consequence, more media outlets – including radio, magazines, and movies – appear to be targeted primarily or exclusively to adolescents. Observers of media and popular culture note an increase in the number of television programs and movies that feature adolescents as their central characters, often more intelligent and mature than their parents or teachers, and thus suggesting that the adult world is almost trivial, with frivolous rules that are made to be broken. On the other hand, several television shows and movies have attempted to portray more responsibly the consequences of risky behaviors such as substance use and unsafe sex, normalized the psychosocial problems that many adolescents experience, offered resources for problems such as eating disorders and depression, and/or tried to promote positive social change in such areas as race relations and academic achievement.

Relatively recent developments in media such as digital cable and the World Wide Web have expanded the number of media options available and have given adolescents more control over when and where they will use them.

Information Technology

There is no question that the new millennium will continue to be an "information age" characterized by massive shifts in the amount and type of data that are generated and disseminated. Perhaps more than any other group, adolescents are affected by the new technologies. A large and growing percentage of America's adolescents use a personal computer, either at home or at school. Between 1993 and 1999, the percentage of schools with access to the Internet increased from 35 to 95% (Department of Education, 2000). Adolescents are increasingly sophisticated in using these new technologies (Anderson, this volume).

The Internet. In theory, the widespread use of computers and the Internet by both adolescents and health care providers should improve access to the newest information about health care conditions, diagnostic methods, and forms of treatment. These technologies have the potential to disseminate the newest information in "real time" thus eliminating the time lag that sometimes occurs between discovery, publication, and review. In reality, however, many providers have no more time or inclination to regularly review medical updates over the Internet than they did to read professional journals. Some face the additional constraints of not having the right equipment and/or skills to use it; still others may find themselves overwhelmed by the prospect of too much information, and reject it all in reaction. At the same time, it has become increasingly difficult to discern which health information resources are accurate or appropriate for various users (Kim & Eng, 1999).

It may be providers' adolescent patients who are more likely to follow advancements in health and medical science. Given their greater familiarity with computers, their relative newness to the health care system, and potential discomfort with talking to providers about some sensitive issues, adolescents may be more likely to turn to the Web as a source for health advice or information.

In some cases, this is clearly a positive trend. A number of health-promoting Websites have been created by organizations such as Planned Parenthood, Advocates for Youth, and the American Social Health Association. These sites provide accurate health information to young people on a variety of topics, from the risks of tobacco use and HIV prevention to healthy diets and how to communicate with parents. Some adolescents use the Internet as a safe place to ask questions and obtain information about personal health concerns (Brown & Witherspoon, in press). More than three quarters of 7th to 12th graders say that they would rather research information online than use a book or a magazine (Henry, 1997). This trend potentially empowers young people to take greater ownership and responsibility for their own health.

At the same time, there are risks inherent to Internet use by adolescents. For example, some alcohol and tobacco companies have created Websites that are attractive to teenagers. There is also a risk that medical advice dispensed online will replace the more thorough examination of a trained health care provider. This would run counter to the goal of most health professionals to encourage adolescents to have more regular health care visits.

For both adolescents and health care providers, a final risk relates to the inability of regulatory mechanisms to keep up with advances in Internet technology. An article in the *New York Times* notes that the explosion of Websites devoted to health and medicine – some providing information and advice, others selling medications and other products – blurs the line between objective information and advertising, science and commercialism (Noble, 1999). Although federal and state governments have traditionally regulated medical practices fairly carefully, the use of the Internet to provide medical information has posed a yet-unresolved challenge to regulatory agencies. The Federal Trade Commission recommends that Websites require parental consent before they send information to a minor's e-mail or home address; however, even sites that choose to ask a user's age typically have no way to verify it. Similarly, parents, schools, and libraries that prevent access to certain Websites by installing filtering software may block Websites, such as Planned Parenthood's, that include the words "sex" or "reproduction" but that provide medically accurate, health-promoting information. Nineteen percent of U.S. adolescents report that their online activities are limited by filtering software versus less than 4% in France, Italy, Sweden, and the Netherlands (Angus Reid Group, 2000). The ability of adolescents to access health information, while simultaneously restricting inappropriate content, will be an important challenge in the ongoing development of Internet regulation.

E-mail and instant messaging, over a standard computer or a wireless device, are popular means of communication among adolescents, and present an additional method for teens to communicate with health care providers (NUA Internet Surveys, 2000). In one study of the utilization of e-mail with patients at university and college health centers, researchers found that 63.6% of schools surveyed used some form of electronic communication with patients. Possible types of communication in this setting included medical advice, laboratory results, appointments, administrative information or health education (Neinstein, 2000). Physicians outside the university or college health center setting are more reluctant to use e-mail with patients. Approximately 10 to 20% of physicians e-mail their patients, but many are reluctant to do so until security concerns and liability and reimbursement issues are resolved (Wiebe, 2000).

Electronic Medical Records. A related innovation is the electronic medical record. Based on sophisticated databases, computerized medical records allow users to review medical information in a variety of useful formats without the ambiguity of provider handwriting and reams of forms. These systems also allow providers to create "ticklers" which may be especially useful for adolescents – for example, prompting them to provide a second Hepatitis B vaccination or follow-up counseling for identified risky behaviors.

Many health care organizations are implementing new health features that depend on electronic medical records. For example, one HMO recently began to allow members to make an appointment, ask nurses for advice, and/or refill prescriptions online. Soon, the HMO expects its online service to relay patients' laboratory test results via special e-mail accounts. Another HMO reviews patient records to find candidates for its disease management programs, which offer special services for patients with chronic conditions.

Although the advantages of such a system are obvious, they also raise questions about confidentiality and access to confidential information. Until protocols are established and electronic security systems are improved, there are inherent risks to network-based systems.

Trends in Information and Medical Technology

Medical Technology. There have been some important medical advances in recent years, with clear implications for adolescents and young adults. Immunizations for Varicella (chicken pox) and Hepatitis A and B have become available and commonly recommended for adolescents in a variety of circumstances. Therapeutic treatments for asthma and a variety of mental health disorders are more refined; there are also innovations in treatments for chronic health problems such as leukemia and diabetes.

There have also been a number of innovations in reproductive health technologies, including the development of new hormonal birth control methods, many of which are appealing to adolescents. Single-dose antibiotic therapy has made the treatment of bacterial STIs easier for infected adolescents and their partners. Finally, the advent of accurate urine-based screening for chlamydia and gonorrhea may replace the need for invasive pelvic exams and urethral swabs. According to one study, this advance in STI screening, because of its ease of use, cost-effectiveness, and relative acceptability by adolescents, will allow a greater number of young people to be tested and treated for STIs earlier, averting more significant health problems (Shafer, Pantell, & Schachter, 1999).

Computerized Risk Assessment. At least one HMO has developed an interactive risk assessment tool that helps to screen adolescents for a variety of risky behaviors and potential health problems. Adolescents sit at a workstation, answering a variety of questions about their lifestyles and health; this information is used to create a personal health profile for the adolescent. A counselor or health educator then reviews this profile in conjunction with the adolescent to identify areas of risk, possibilities for change, and areas that need to be handled clinically. During pilot testing, adolescents stated that they were more comfortable answering personal questions by computer than they would be with their doctor, suggesting that more accurate information might be obtained this way, thus allowing health care systems to more effectively meet adolescents' needs (Paperny & Hedberg, 1999). However, methods such as these also raise questions about the most appropriate role of the physician and/or primary care provider in establishing a relationship with the adolescent and directly providing care.

Telemedicine and Telehealth. With modems and cables that allow providers and patients to exchange increasing amounts of complex information in "real time" (i.e., with little or no delay between transmission and receipt), technology promotes the use of remote systems for diagnosing, triaging, and even treating illness and injury that previously required face-to-face visits. The use of telecommunications technology for a wide variety of health-related activities has proliferated in recent years. With the ability to exchange high resolution images, sounds, live video, and other patient records over long distances electronically, telemedicine and telehealth have the potential to greatly improve access to medical care for underserved populations, including adolescents (Collen, 2000). Although much of the current focus is on specialty services such as radiology, cardiology, and orthopedics, other applications such as management of chronic illness, emergency/triage, and mental health care are becoming increasingly common. For example, providers can now monitor symptoms and vital statistics without disrupting their patients' home or school lives. Such systems have the potential to improve the management and care for adolescents with chronic or sub-acute health problems. The success of advanced technology in improving adolescent health will depend on achieving an appropriate balance between technical innovations and traditional provider interactions.

IMPLICATIONS AND PROJECTIONS FOR THE 21ST CENTURY

The final section of this chapter seeks to project key trends in adolescent demographics, health policy, financing and health care delivery, and research into the next decade and beyond. Implications of these trends for the health and well-being of America's adolescents are discussed.

Demographics

As America's Adolescents Become More Culturally and Socioeconomically Diverse, Health Disparities Will Grow. Demographic trends indicate growing numbers of adolescents of color, immigrants to the United States, and adolescents who live in single-parent families – the very young people who face the greatest health risks. As the socioeconomic divide grows, so too will the health status of America's adolescents. Because factors such as family income, parental education and race/ethnicity are the strongest predictors of health status and health care utilization, these shifts portend a decrease in the health status of adolescents and an increase in their prevention, medical, and mental health needs.

Health Policy and Law

The Pattern of Devolution from the Federal Government to States Will Continue. The shift in federally funded programs from federal mandates to state-driven and locally driven programs with broad federal guidance is unlikely to wane in the years ahead. Most law- and policy-makers across the political spectrum appear to support devolved responsibility and accountability for health care and social service programs. Although arguments in favor of devolution are appealing (i.e., greater local control allows for better targeting of local needs; smaller federal bureaucracy reduces administrative costs), this strategy also presents the risk that state and local governments will neglect the needs of certain populations, such as adolescents. In the absence of stringent federal rules to support state block grants, for example, services for adolescents are likely to vary substantially by geographic region, thus perpetuating many of the inequities that federal programs were designed to reduce. The increased discretion given to states will be reflected in their Children's Health Insurance Programs (CHIP), among other state-level initiatives and policies.

Greater Accountability Will be Manifest at Various Levels. At the state level, Title V Maternal and Child Health programs report their progress on national and state performance measures, and have recently begun to document health status indicators. In future years, federal block grant funding may be linked to states' performance in these areas. For example, as a component of the welfare reform initiative, the U.S. Department of Health and Human Services allocates generous "bonuses" with their welfare block grants to the 3 states that achieve the greatest reductions in out-of-wedlock births (that are over and above general declines and do not accompany increases in abortions).

Greater accountability will also be seen among health plans and health care providers: as purchasers and the tools available to them become more sophisticated, these groups will be held more responsible for meeting the needs of adolescents. Health plan "report cards" and performance measures will support this accountability. Although these systems have not traditionally included a large number of adolescent-specific indicators, progress is being made in this area.

Policies Will Reflect the Tension Between Differing Perspectives on Adolescence. Policies, laws, and regulations are often led by a particular perspective on adolescence, rather than empirical findings (William T. Grant Foundation, 1999): If adolescents' immaturity is emphasized, then restrictive approaches may be proposed. As described earlier, there have been multiple efforts by states and the federal government to restrict adolescents' access to various types of confidential health care services.

Preventive policies have also been implemented both to protect adolescents and the community. For example, several states have begun to restrict drivers' licenses for young people under the age of 18, whether by raising the age at which minors can drive alone or establishing a curfew after which adolescents cannot operate a vehicle.

On the other hand, if the emphasis is on fostering competence and independence, then granting adolescents adult rights and responsibilities may be indicated. Sometimes the same perspective may be used to different ends. For example, advocates for adolescents have long promoted allowing adolescents to access certain health services independent of their family members, arguing that adolescents are competent to act reasonably and give their own consent in some situations. However, building on this same notion of adolescent competence, a movement has surfaced to begin sentencing juvenile offenders as if they were adults – increasing criminal penalties, reducing confidentiality protections, and incarcerating offenders in local or state correctional facilities rather than in special youth facilities. A statewide ballot proposition on juvenile crime passed in California in March 2000 that included all of these provisions.

This debate over the appropriate view of adolescent maturity and competence will continue to influence political and legal debate (Cullen & Wright, this volume).

States Will Continue to Enact Restrictive Immigration Laws. Although the federal government recently interpreted immigration laws to allow immigrants more access to publicly funded health programs, many states are enacting laws that seek to restrict this access. With immigration issues increasingly the subject of intense political debate, sound public policy is unlikely to be the basis for eligibility determinations. In light of current immigration trends, this situation is likely to leave a large and growing segment of children and adolescents especially vulnerable to the physical and economic consequences of illness.

Health Insurance/Financing

The Shift from Private to Public Health Insurance Will Continue. As current demographic trends continue, more adolescents will become eligible for existing entitlement programs such as Medicaid; in addition, new public programs, such as CHIP, will continue to emerge at the state and federal levels. At the same time, private health insurance coverage for adolescents is unlikely to expand. Without significant incentives from the federal government (in the form of tax breaks and/or regulatory requirements), it is unlikely that U.S. businesses will reverse the trend toward declining health insurance coverage for workers and their dependents. As premiums for health insurance continue to rise, more firms are likely to drop this coverage. Other trends in employment – for example, toward smaller firms and more temporary and contract-based work – will only exacerbate this effect and its impact on adolescents.

Both Public and Private Grantmaking Will Emphasize Collaboration, Interdisciplinary Models, and Community Involvement. Private foundations often require that grants awarded for youth-serving programs include community leadership and the involvement of multiple stakeholders. This model is now being followed by more public agencies: for example, the new Safe Schools, Healthy Students initiative is an interagency partnership between the U.S. Departments of Education, Justice, and Health and Human Services. Grantees are required to create a partnership that includes the local educational agency, public mental health authority, law enforcement, students, families, and juvenile justice officials.

Programs/Service Delivery

More Adolescents Will be Covered by Managed Care Arrangements. Managed care is likely to remain a permanent fixture in the adolescent health care delivery system. Given this reality, more research is needed to determine the specific features of managed care that benefit adolescents; methods to promote adolescent health under managed care; and ways to ensure that managed care is not limiting access for at-risk adolescents. With the focus on legislation that addresses patients' rights in managed care, there may be more flexibility in certain managed care provisions, for example, greater choice of providers or easier access to specialists. However, as competitive pressures continue to rise, there is a risk that reimbursement levels will fall so low that there will be an incentive for managed care organizations to either enroll only the healthiest adolescents, or to limit the range of covered adolescent health services. It will therefore be critical for policymakers and program administrators to balance the desire to hold down costs with appropriate incentives for providing high-quality, accessible care to eligible adolescents.

Services Will Become More Integrated and Interdisciplinary. There are indications that the fragmented orientation of adolescent service delivery will gradually be replaced with more comprehensive systems of care. In several counties across California, public agencies, providers and community-based organizations are forming integrated partnerships for delivering a comprehensive continuum of care to high-risk adolescents. Greater coordination among the agencies that serve youth, together with incentives that reward efficiency and performance, will hopefully result in improved health outcomes for adolescents as well as reduce the overall costs of providing the care.

The growth in managed care may also help to support the trend toward greater integration. In exchange for a capitated monthly rate, managed care organizations and providers appear to be taking on functions once left to the public health system (e.g., adolescent pregnancy prevention, violence prevention, health education). In order to attract members and meet regulatory requirements, health plans will expand their benefit packages for adolescents. In a corresponding movement, the federal government is requiring greater parity of coverage for physical and mental health services under health insurance benefit packages. This trend provides a precedent for more comprehensive coverage for all Americans.

Non-physicians – including nurses, health educators, social workers, and other types of behavioral specialists – may play a growing role in the care of young people. Utilizing non-physician and lower paid providers is driven by cost containment, and at times, may raise questions of clinical appropriateness. However, this trend also reflects some recognition of the psychosocial health needs of adolescents and suggests the possibility that a wider variety of adolescent health needs can be met by expanding the provider base.

The Current Emphasis on Preventive Services for Adolescents Will Continue. As described above, there has been a major movement to provide preventive services to adolescents in clinical settings. The development of adolescent preventive guidelines has placed a greater focus on what primary care clinicians can do to improve the health of adolescents. Recommendations for yearly visits, reinforced with health plan report cards and quality assurance measures, have turned attention to a group that has traditionally under-utilized health care services. There remains little knowledge about the feasibility of incorporating preventive services into primary care or the efficacy of comprehensive preventive care visits. The challenge lies in providing that data.

As managed care programs grow, provider incentives will be more linked to keeping people healthy than to treating illness and injury. The managed care system holds promise that adolescents will have access to comprehensive primary and preventive services because managed care plans have built-in incentives for cost containment (Brindis, 1998). Recent data do, in fact, suggest that pediatricians in one major managed care organization are delivering preventive services to their adolescent patients at higher rates than pediatricians practicing in other settings (Halpern-Felsher et al., 2000).

More Programs Will be Targeted Toward Adolescent Males. Adolescent males, who experience the highest negative health outcomes in terms of morbidity and mortality rates, are the lowest utilizers of outpatient health services (Klein et al., 1999; Ziv et al., 1999). Many adolescent health services have been targeted towards girls, especially those that address reproductive health. There is currently a focus on increasing the use of appropriate health care services by adolescent males as well as actively involving males in family planning. For example, the California Department of Health Services, Office of Family Planning has developed the "TeenSMART" program to lower the incidence of pregnancy and sexually transmitted infections among adolescents. The program guidelines have a strong emphasis on involving male adolescents and participants' partners in the counseling (Office of Family Planning, 1996).

Research

Adolescent Health Data Sources Will Continue to Improve. Despite recent improvements in national adolescent health data efforts, there remain numerous limitations. The most significant problem is that adolescents are often not considered as a separate group. In many national surveys, adolescents are classified in age groups with children (e.g., under age 18) or with young adults (e.g., ages 15–24). Trends pertaining to adolescents can often not be separated from those pertaining to children or young adults. The most meaningful data sources are those that separate adolescents into two periods: early adolescence (ages 10–14) and late adolescence (ages 15–19).

An additional problem in assessing trends within the adolescent population is the lack of information on non-Black minority groups.

Historically, national data were collected only by the categories White, Black, and "Other." More recently, Hispanic, Asian/Pacific Islander and American Indian/Alaskan Native categories have been added to a number of national data sets; however, there continues to be significant diversity within many ethnic groups. For example, the Hispanic category includes Cubans, Puerto Ricans, Mexicans, and other South Americans and Central Americans. The socioeconomic status and cultures of these populations may differ dramatically, masking important health trends. In addition, few data sets separately assess socioeconomic status (SES), thereby confounding these variables, and attributing some health risks to race/ethnicity that might be more accurately linked to class. In the future, more accurate SES measures will be needed to supplement these variables.

A limitation of the adolescent health utilization data is that it relies primarily on the report of parents or other adults for information on adolescents. For example, the National Health Interview Survey (NHIS) asks the adult respondent in a given household about the health of adolescents living in that household, as well as their health insurance status and use of various health care services. Although this methodology may result in accurate, reliable information in some cases, it is likely to understate health problems and service utilization in others (e.g., use of reproductive or other sensitive services), resulting in skewed data that fail to illuminate the real health and service use patterns of America's adolescents. A California component of the National Health Interview Survey (CHIS) has recently been developed that includes a large random sample of adolescents as respondents (UCLA, 2000).

Finally, most of the national data sets are cross-sectional, making it difficult to identify trajectories of health status, use of health services, and the initiation and cessation of both health damaging and protective behaviors. Typically, mental health issues are treated as distinct from physical health, and monitored through separate surveys or data collection systems. Although some epidemiological studies have examined the co-morbidity of various adolescent risk behaviors, there is a general shortage of national data that reflect the relationship(s) between various risky behaviors and mental and physical health problems.

Future data collection strategies that improve on these limitations will be critical in our efforts to understand, monitor, and improve adolescent health.

The Demand for Measurable Health Outcomes Will Increase. Efforts to monitor the health of adolescents and other populations have often relied on process measures such as information about the receipt of health care services that are believed to have an impact on health status. There is now a greater demand to justify health services with measurable health outcomes. This has led to a focus on health services research that carefully tracks health and cost outcomes, as well as an emphasis on translating conceptually based research into clinical practice. For example, the Agency for Healthcare Research and Quality (AHRQ) has funded demonstration projects which focus on evaluating strategies for translating research into practice through the development of partnerships between researchers and health care systems. Improvements in information technology and quality assurance instruments by managed care plans are likely to support this emphasis on health outcomes.

More Research Will Focus on the Biological Basis of Adolescent Behavior and Adolescent Problems. In the past, research on adolescent health has been largely behavioral. There is now a greater focus on the biological aspects of adolescent health. For example, recent neurological research has uncovered developmental differences between adolescent and adult brains. With the advent of new technologies such as magnetic resonance imaging, scientists have discovered that the adolescent brain is far less "mature" than they had originally believed (Thompson, Giedd, Woods, MacDonald, Evans, & Toga, 2000). Simultaneously, other research on the levels of various neurotransmitters and nervous system development may help to explain increases in risk-taking behavior in adolescence, as well as increases in aggressiveness and irritability seen at adolescence. Research on adolescent sleep patterns has also gained attention, with several investigators releasing studies that identify important physiological changes in sleep that occur at puberty and throughout adolescence (National Sleep Foundation Sleep and Teens Task Force, 1999).

In response to the growth of neurological and pharmacological research, as well as financial incentives for pharmaceutical companies to include children and adolescents in clinical trials, there will be an increase in medications developed for adolescents. As a result, more providers will be utilizing these tools in treating mental health problems. The challenge will be to balance the appeal of these generic, inexpensive methods – which may be highly effective in some circumstances – with those that delve more deeply into the psychosocial causes of many adolescents' problems.

The Movement to Shift the Focus from Pathology to Health Will Continue. There is increased attention on the mental health of adolescents. The peak in adolescent suicide rates in the early- to mid-1990s, along with vivid media coverage of violent, suicidal adolescents, has likely contributed to the focus on adolescent mental health. Although mental illness is a serious problem that deserves attention, the health of adolescents should be construed in a broader context than disease or pathology. Partially in response to the public and the media's negative portrayal of adolescents, researchers, advocates, and policymakers are now promoting models that emphasize adolescent health and wellness. An example is the "youth development movement," promoted by groups such as the Search Institute (2000) and the William T. Grant Foundation (1999), and supported by data from The National Longitudinal Survey on Adolescent Health. The focus is on fostering positive behavior and ways to help adolescents contribute to society, such as peer relationships and "connectedness" to family, school, and community rather than concentrating primarily on the problems of young people.

Adolescent Health Status: The Next Steps

As we begin the 21st century, many of the health trends among adolescents have been positive. Specifically, mortality rates are down among adolescents; drug use is decreasing once again; the proportion of teenagers who report having sex has recently declined; sexually transmitted diseases and pregnancy rates are down; and condom use has gone up.

The question is whether we can sustain current improvements given the projected demographics of the adolescent population. Traditionally, resources have been targeted toward problems, rather than areas that show improvement. Yet in reviewing longitudinal data from the 1990s, it is clear that trends can shift over the course of a few years. As the nation begins to take for granted improvement in a given risk area, we often see a shift in adolescents' attitudes and beliefs about that risky behavior. For example, in 1992, after a downward trend in the use of drugs, the proportion of teenagers who reported that they perceived drug use to be very risky, as well as those who said that they disapproved of drug use, began to decline. After 1992, the use of illicit drugs rose sharply among high school students (Johnston et al., 1998).

To cite another example, the encouraging trends in reproductive and sexual health behavior, noted earlier, are largely attributed to a multi-prong approach to improvement at national, state, and local levels. Resources have been directed toward family planning and abstinence education programs, schools, community partnerships, and media campaigns such as those conducted by the National Campaign to Prevent Teen Pregnancy. For federal fiscal year 1996, it is estimated that the federal government invested 138.1 million dollars to prevent teenage pregnancy. (It is important to note, however, that the federal government expended over $38 billion – 275 times more money – to provide services and support to families that began with a birth to a teen.) (Feijoo, 1999).

Lessons learned from other health trends suggest that efforts at multiple levels must continue or even increase in order to sustain current gains. For example, the projected increase in the number of adolescents alone will result in greater numbers of adolescent mothers unless we deploy significantly more resources to prevent adolescent pregnancy. The shifting composition of ethnic/racial groups within the adolescent population also indicates the need to tailor the next generation of prevention efforts to the needs of ethnically diverse adolescents (Brindis, Peterson, & Brown, 1997).

Investing in the health of adolescents can make a difference. Yet, adolescents represent a smaller proportion of the population than the elderly, potentially placing them in competition for health care resources. As the drive to contain health expenditures continues, it is important to continue to increase the investment in the healthy development of adolescents, a time in which lifelong health patterns begin. One age group does not have to be pitted against another: At least one study suggests that Americans would be willing to pay more in health insurance premiums, alcohol/tobacco taxes, and other subsidies to fund more prevention and community-based health efforts (Bodenhorn & Kemper, 1997). Although health care resources have traditionally been allocated using categorical approaches and programs devoted to a specific problem (e.g., adolescent pregnancy), supporting the healthy development of adolescents to help them become both economically and socially productive stands to benefit all in society (William T. Grant Foundation, 1999). This chapter has focused on the health care system. Health care providers alone, however, will have minimal impact on adolescent health promotion and prevention in the absence of efforts from other sectors of the adolescent's environment (Irwin, 1993). The 21st century needs to be a time in which each system that interacts with adolescents assumes responsibility for the health of our youth.

References

Abma, J., Chandra, A., Mosher, W., Peterson, L., & Piccinino, L. (1997). Fertility, family planning, and women's health: New data from the 1995 National Survey of Family Growth. *Vital and Health Statistics, 23* (DHHS Publication No. PHS 97-1995). Hyattsville, MD: National Center for Health Statistics.

American Academy of Pediatrics. (1992). The medical home. *Pediatrics, 90*(5), 774.

Angus Reid Group. (2000, September 11). The face of the Web: Youth, the latest multi-country survey of more than 10,000 youth aged 12 to 24. Internet invaluable to students worldwide. Retrieved from the World Wide Web: http://www.Ipsos-Reid.com/media/content/ Displaypr.cfm? id_to_view=1073

Auslander, W. F., Thompson, S. J., Dreitzer, D., & Santiago, J. V. (1997). Mother's satisfaction with medical care: Perceptions of racism, family stress and medical outcomes in children with diabetes. *Health and Social Work, 22*(3), 190–199.

Bandura, A. (1997). *Self-Efficacy: The Exercise of Control.* New York: W.H. Freeman & Company.

Berne, L., & Huberman, B. (1999). *European Approaches to Adolescent Sexual Behavior and Responsibility.* Washington, D.C.: Advocates for Youth.

Blum, R. W., & Bearinger, L. H. (1990). Knowledge and attitudes of health professionals toward adolescent health care. *Journal of Adolescent Health Care, 11*(4), 289–294.

Blum, R. W., Beuhring, T., Wunderlich, M., & Resnick, M. D. (1996). Don't ask, they won't tell: The quality of adolescent health screening in five practice settings. *American Journal of Public Health, 86*(12), 1767–1772.

Bodenhorn, K. A., & Kemper, L. D. (1997). Spending for health: Californians speak out about priorities for health spending. Sacramento, CA: California Center for Health Improvement.

Brener, N., & Collins, J. (1998). Co-occurrence of health-risk behaviors among adolescents in the United States. *Journal of Adolescent Health, 22*(3), 209–213.

Brindis, C. D. (1998). Financing adolescent health services. In S. B. Friedman, K. Schonberg, & E. M. Alderman (Eds.), *Comprehensive Adolescent Health Care* (2nd ed., pp. 114–118). St. Louis, MO: Mosby-Year Book, Inc.

Brindis, C. D., Ozer, E. M., Handley, M., Knopf, D. K., Millstein, S. G., & Irwin, C. E., Jr. (1997). Improving adolescent health: An analysis and synthesis of health policy recommendations. San Francisco: University of California, National Adolescent Health Information Center.

Brindis, C. D., Peterson, S. A., & Brown, S. (1997). Complex terrain: Charting a course of action to prevent adolescent pregnancy: An analysis of

California's policy landscape. San Francisco: University of California, Institute for Health Policy Studies, Center for Reproductive Health Policy Research.

Brindis, C. D., VanLandeghem, K., Kirkpatrick, R., Macdonald, T., & Lee, S. (1999). Adolescents and the State Children's Health Insurance Program (CHIP): Healthy options for meeting the needs of adolescents. Washington, DC: Association of Maternal and Child Health Programs, & San Francisco: University of California, Policy Information and Analysis Center for Middle Childhood and Adolescence, National Adolescent Health Information Center.

Brindis, C., & Wolfe, A. (1997). Adolescent population growth in California and in the U.S., 1995–2005. San Francisco: University of California, National Center for Reproductive Health Policy.

Brown, E. R., Wyn, R., & Ojeda, V. D. (1999). Access to health insurance and health care for children in immigrant families. Los Angeles: University of California, Center for Health Policy Research.

Brown, J. D., & Witherspoon, E. M. (2002, in press). The mass media and American adolescents' health. *Journal of Adolescent Health*.

Brown, T. (1999, January). The impact of the State Child Health Insurance Program (SCHIP) on Title V children with special health care needs programs (Issue Brief). Washington, DC: Association of Maternal and Child Health Programs.

Cabana, M. D., Rand, C. S., Powe, N. R., Wu, A. W., Wilson, M. H., Abboud, P. A., & Rubin, H. R. (1999). Why don't physicians follow clinical practice guidelines? A framework for improvement. *Journal of the American Medical Association, 282*(15), 1458–1465.

Centers for Disease Control and Prevention. (2000, January). CDC Wonder online database, Mortality data set (compressed). Atlanta, GA: Author. Retrieved January 2000, from World Wide Web: http://www.wonder.cdc.gov/mortsql.shtml

Cheng, T. L., & Klein, J. D. (1995). The adolescent viewpoint: Implications for access and prevention. *Journal of the American Medical Association, 273*(24), 1957–1958.

Coiro, M. J., Zill, N., & Bloom, B. (1994). Health of our nation's children. *Vital and Health Statistics, 10*(191), 1–61 (DHHS Publication No. PHS 95-1519). Hyattsville, MD: National Center for Health Statistics.

Collen, M. F. (2000). Historical evolution of preventive medical information in the U.S.A. *Methods of Information in Medicine, 39*(3), 204–207.

Congressional Budget Office (1999). Preliminary estimates of effective tax rates. Washington, DC: Author.

Dalaker, J. (1998). Poverty in the U.S., 1998. (U.S. Census Bureau Current Population Reports, Series P60-207). Washington DC: U.S. Government Printing Office.

Day, J. C. (1996). Population projections of the United States by age, sex, race, and Hispanic Origin, 1995 to 2050 (U.S. Bureau of the Census, Current Population Reports Nos. P25-1130). Washington, DC: U.S. Government Printing Office.

Department of Education, Office of Educational Technology. (2000). Progress report on educational technology: State-by-state profiles. Retrieved November, 2000, from the World Wide Web: http://www.ed.gov/Technology/index.html

Department of Health and Human Services. (2000). Healthy people 2010 (Conference Edition, in Two Volumes). Washington, DC: Author.

Department of Health & Human Services, Health Resources & Services Administration & Maternal and Child Health Bureau. (1998). Child health U.S.A., 1998. Washington, DC: U.S. Government Printing Office.

Department of Health and Human Services. (1999). Mental health: A report of the surgeon general: Executive summary. Rockville, MD: National Institute of Mental Health.

Division of STD Prevention, Department of Health and Human Services. (1999). Sexually transmitted disease surveillance, 1998. Atlanta: Centers for Disease Control and Prevention.

Dougherty, D. M. (1999). Health care for adolescent girls. In N. G. Johnson, M. C. Roberts, & J. Worell (Eds.). *Beyond Appearance: A New Look at Adolescent Girls* (pp. 301–325). Washington, D.C.: American Psychological Association.

Downs, S. M., & Klein, J. D. (1995). Clinical preventive services efficacy and adolescents' risky behaviors. *Archives of Pediatrics and Adolescent Medicine, 149*(4), 374–379.

Elliott, D. S. (1993). Health enhancing and health-compromising lifestyles. In S. G. Millstein, A. C. Petersen, & E. O. Nightingale (Eds.), *Promoting the Health of Adolescents* (pp. 119–145). New York: Oxford University Press.

Elster, A. B., & Kuznets, N. J. (1994). *AMA Guidelines for Adolescent Preventive Services (GAPS): Recommendations and Rationale.* Chicago, IL: American Medical Association.

English, A., Kapphahn, C., Perkins, J., & Wibbelsman, C. J. (1998). Meeting the health care needs of adolescents in managed care: A background paper. *Journal of Adolescent Health, 22*(4), 278–292.

English, A., & Knopf, D. (1999). Adolescents and confidentiality: A brief guide for managed care. Chapel Hill, NC: Center for Adolescent Health and the Law, & San Francisco: University of California, National Adolescent Health Information Center.

English, A., Morreale, M., & Stinnett, A. (1999). Adolescents in public health insurance program: Medicaid and CHIP. Chapel Hill, NC: Center for Adolescent Health & the Law.

English, A., & Simmons, P. S. (1999). Legal issues in reproductive health care for adolescents. *Adolescent Medicine: State of the Art Reviews, 10*(2), 181–194.

Feijoo, A. N. (1999). Teenage pregnancy: The case for prevention: An updated analysis of recent trends and federal expenditures associated with teenage pregnancy. Washington, DC: Advocates for Youth.

Fingerhut, L. A., Cox, C. S., Warner, M. (1998). International comparative analysis of injury mortality: Findings from the ICE on injury statistics (Advance data from Vital and Health Statistics, No. 303). Hyattsville, MD: National Center for Health Statistics.

Fisher, M. (1992). Parents' views of adolescent health issues. *Pediatrics, 90*(3), 335–341.

Fisher, M. (1999). Adolescent health: Assessment and promotion in office and school settings. *Adolescent Medicine: State of the Art Reviews, 10*(1), 71–86.

Ford, C. A., Bearman, P. S., Peter, S., & Moody, J. (1999). Foregone health care among adolescents. *Journal of the American Medical Association, 282*(23) 2227–2234.

Ford, C. A., Millstein, S. G., Halpern-Felsher, B. L., & Irwin, C. E., Jr. (1997). Influence of physician confidentiality assurances on adolescents' willingness to disclose information and seek future health care. *Journal of the American Medical Association, 278*(12), 1029–1034.

Franzgrote, M., Ellen, J. M., Millstein, S. G., & Irwin, C. E., Jr. (1997). Screening for adolescent smoking among primary care physicians in California. *American Journal of Public Health, 87*(8), 1341–1345.

Gans, J. E., Alexander, B., Chu, R., & Elster, A. B. (1995). The cost of comprehensive preventive medical services for adolescents. *Archives of Pediatrics and Adolescent Medicine, 149*(11), 1226–1234.

Gans, J. E., McManus, M. A., & Newacheck, P. W. (1991). Adolescent health care: Use, cost, and problems of access. *American Medical Association Profiles of Adolescent Health Series, 2*, Chicago, IL: American Medical Association.

Gittler, J., Quigley-Rick, M., & Saks, M. (1990). Adolescent health care decision making: The law and public policy. Washington DC: Carnegie Council on Adolescent Development.

Green, M. E., & Palfrey, J. S. (2000). Bright futures: Guidelines for health supervision of infants, children, and adolescents (2nd ed.). Arlington, VA: National Center for Education in Maternal and Child Health.

Halpern-Felsher, B. L., Ozer, E. M., Millstein, S. G., Wibbelsman, C. J., Fuster, C. D., Elster, A. B., & Irwin, C. E., Jr. (2000). Preventive services in a health maintenance organization: How well do pediatricians screen and educate their adolescent patients? *Archives of Pediatrics and Adolescent Medicine, 154*(2), 173–179.

Hedberg, V. A., Klein, J. D., & Andresen, E. (1998). Health counseling in adolescent preventive visits: Effectiveness, current practices, and quality measurements. *Journal of Adolescent Health, 23*(6), 344–353.

Henry, T. (1997, April 23). Techno-kids can't live without their computers. *USA Today*, p. A1.

Hibell, B., Andersson, B., Ahlstrom, S., Balakireva, O., Bjarnason, T., Kokkevi, A., & Morgan, M. (2001, February). The 1999 ESPAD Report: Alcohol and other drug use among students in 30 European countries. Paper presented at the meeting of the WHO European Ministerial Conference on Young People and Alcohol Conference, Stockholm, Sweden.

Hoyert, D. L., Kochanek, K. D., & Murphy, S. L. (1999). Deaths: Final data for 1997. *National Vital Statistics Reports Vol. 47 No. 10*. Hyattsville, MD: National Center for Health Statistics.

Igra, V., & Millstein, S. G. (1993). Current status and approaches to improving preventive services for adolescents. *Journal of the American Medical Association, 269*(11), 1408–1412.

Irwin, C. E., Jr. (1993). The adolescent, health, and society: From the perspective of the physician. In S. G. Millstein, A. C. Petersen, & E. O. Nightingale (Eds.), *Promoting the Health of Adolescents: New Directions for the Twenty-First Century* (pp. 146–150). NY: Oxford University Press.

Irwin, C. E., Jr., Igra, V., Eyre, S., & Millstein, S. (1997). Risk-taking behavior in adolescents: The paradigm. In M. J. Jacobson, J. M. Rees, M. H. Golden, & C. E. Irwin, Jr. (Eds.), *Adolescent Nutritional Disorders: Prevention and Treatment*. NY: The New York Academy of Sciences.

Joffe, A., Radius, S., & Gall, M. (1988). Health counseling for adolescents: What they want, what they get, and who gives it. *Pediatrics, 82*(3, Pt. 2), 481–485.

Johns Hopkins School of Public Health. (1995, October). Population Reports (Series J, No. 41, Table 1, p. 4). Retrieved January 19, 2001, from UNESCO database (Table 1, Adolescents in the World Population) on the World Wide Web: http://www.unescobkk.org/Infores/rechpec/handbk1/sec1.htm

Johnston, J. D., O'Malley, P. M., & Bachman, J. G. (1998). National survey results on drug use from the monitoring the future study, 1975–1997. Rockville, MD: Department of Health and Human Services, Public Health Service.

Kaiser Family Foundation. (1996). The Kaiser Family Foundation survey on teens and sex: What they say teens today need to know and who they listen to. Menlo Park, CA: Author.

Kann, L., Kinchen, S. A., Williams, B. I., Ross, J. G., Lowry, R., Grunbaum, J. A., & Kolbe, L. (2000). Youth risk behavior surveillance-United States, 1999. Atlanta, GA: Centers for Disease Control and Prevention, Department of Health and Human Services.

Kazdin, A. E. (1993). Adolescent mental health: Prevention and treatment programs. *American Psychologist 48*(2), 127–141.

Keane, C. R., Lave, J. R., Ricci, E. M., & LaVallee, C. P. (1999). The impact of a children's health insurance program by age. *Pediatrics, 104*(5, Pt. 1), 1051–1058.

Kim, P., & Eng, T. R. (1999). Review of published criteria for evaluating health-related Websites. *Western Journal of Medicine, 170*, 329–332.

King, M. P. (1999). Insuring more kids: Options for lawmakers. Denver, CO: National Conference for State Legislatures.

Klein, J. D. (1994). Adolescents, the health care delivery system, and health care reform. In C. E. Irwin, Jr., C. Brindis, K. Langlykke, & K. Holt (Eds.), *Health Care Reform: Opportunities for Improving Adolescent Health* (pp. 17–28). Washington, DC: Maternal and Child Health Bureau.

Klein, J. D., Allan, M. J., Elster, A. B., Stevens, D., Cox, C., Hedberg, V. A., and Goodman, R. A. (2001). Improving adolescent preventive care in community health centers. *Pediatrics, 107*(2), 318–327.

Klein, J. D., Portilla, M., Goldstein, A., & Leininger, L. (1995). Training pediatric residents to prevent tobacco use. *Pediatrics, 96*(2, Pt. 1), 326–330.

Klein, J. D., Slap, G. B., & Elster, A. B. (1992). Access to health care for adolescents: A position paper for the Society of Adolescent Medicine. *Journal of Adolescent Health, 13*(2), 162–170.

Klein, J. D., Wilson, K. M., McNulty, M., Kapphahn, C., & Collins, K. S. (1999). Access to medical care for adolescents: Results for the 1997 Commonwealth

Fund survey of the health of adolescent girls. *Journal of Adolescent Health, 25*(2), 120–130.

Leaf, P. J., Alegria, M., Cohen, P., Goodman, S. H., Horwitz, S. M., Hoven, C. W., Narrow, W. E., Vaden-Kiernan, M., & Regier, D. L. (1996). Mental health service use in the community and schools: Results from the four-community MECA study. *Journal of the American Academy of Child and Adolescent Psychiatry, 35*(7), 889–897.

Levitt, L., Lundy, J., & Srinivasan, S. (1998). Wall Street's love affair with health care. *Health Affairs, 17*(4), 126–131.

Lewinsohn, P. M., Rohde, P., & Seeley, J. R. (1998). Major depressive disorder in older adolescents: Prevalence, risk factors, and clinical implications. *Clinical Psychology Review, 18*(7), 765–794.

Lewis, C., Pantell, R., & Sharp, L. (1991). Increasing patient knowledge, satisfaction and involvement. *Pediatrics, 88*(2), 351–358.

Lindberg, L. D., Boggess, S., Porter, L., & Williams, S. (2000). Teen risk taking: A statistical report. Washington DC: Urban Institute.

Lustig, J. L., Ozer, E. M., Adams, S. H., Wibbelsman, C. J., Fuster, C. D., Bonar, R. W., & Irwin, C. E., Jr. (2001). Improving the delivery of adolescent clinical preventive services through skills-based training. *Pediatrics, 107*(5), 1100–1107.

McCabe, M. A. (1996). Involving children and adolescents in medical decision making: Developmental and clinical considerations. *Journal of Pediatric Psychology, 21*(4), 505–516.

McPherson, M., Arango, P., Fox, H., Lauver, C., McManus, M., Newacheck, P., Perrin, J., Shonkoff, J., & Strickland, B. (1998). A new definition of children with special health care needs. *Pediatrics, 102*(1, Pt. 1), 137–140.

Melton, G. B. (Ed.). (1986). *Adolescent Abortion Psychological and Legal Perspectives.* Lincoln: University of Nebraska Press.

Morrison, A., & Stone, D. (2000). Trends in injury mortality among young people in the European Union: A report from the EURORISC Working Group. *Journal of Adolescent Health, 27*(2), 130–135.

Mott, F. L., & Haurin, R. J. (1988). Linkages between sexual activity and alcohol and drug use among American adolescents. *Family Planning Perspectives, 20*(3), 128–136.

National Center for Health Statistics. (1999). National hospital discharge survey, 1997. Atlanta, GA: Centers for Disease Control and Prevention.

National Committee for Quality Assurance. (1997). HEDIS 3.0. Washington, DC: Author.

National Research Council. (1993). *Losing Generations: Adolescents in High-Risk Settings.* Washington, DC: National Academy Press.

National Sleep Foundation, Sleep and Teens Task Force. (1999). Adolescent sleep needs and patterns. Washington, DC: Author.

Neinstein, L. (2000). Utilization of electronic communication (E-mail) with patients at university and college health centers. *Journal of Adolescent Health, 27*(1), 6–11.

Newacheck, P. W. (1989). Adolescents with special health needs: Prevalence, severity, and access to health services. *Pediatrics, 84*(5), 872–881.

Newacheck, P. W., Brindis, C. D., Cart, C. U., Marchi, K., & Irwin, C. E., Jr. (1999). Adolescent health insurance coverage: Recent changes and access to care. *Pediatrics, 104*(2, Pt. 1), 195–202.

Newacheck, P. W., Hughes, D., & Cisternas, M. (1995, Spring). Children and health insurance: An overview of recent trends. *Health Affairs, 14*(1), 244–254.

Newacheck, P. W., & McManus, M. A. (1989). Health insurance status of adolescents in the United States. *Pediatrics, 84*(4), 699–708.

Newacheck, P. W., McManus, M. A., & Brindis, C. D. (1990). Financing health care for adolescents: Problems, prospects, and proposals. *Journal of Adolescent Health Care, 11*(5), 398–403.

Newman, D. L., Moffitt, T. E., Caspi, A., Magdol, L., Silva, P. A., & Stanton, W. R. (1996). Psychiatric disorder in a birth cohort of young adolescents: Prevalence, comorbidity, clinical significance, and new case incidence from ages 11 to 21. *Journal of Consulting and Clinical Psychology, 64*(3), 552–562.

Noble, H. B. (1999, September 5). Hailed as a surgeon general, Koop is faulted on Web ethics. *New York Times*, pp. 1, 18.

NUA Internet Surveys. (2000, December 21). Cahners in-stat group: Adolescents propel U.S. wireless market growth. *NUA Internet Surveys By Category*. Retrieved January 31, 2001, from the World Wide Web: http://www.mua.ie/surveys/?f=VS&art_id=905356271&rel=true

Office of Family Planning, State of California Department of Health Services. (1996, June). TeenSMART: Enhanced counseling guidelines. Sacramento, CA: Pronto Productions.

Office of Technology Assessment. (1991). Adolescent health: Vol. I–III (Publication No. OTA-H-466,-467,-468). Washington, DC: U.S. Government Printing Office.

Ozer, M. N. (Ed.). (2000). *Management of Persons with Chronic Neurological Illness*. Woburn, MA: Butterworth-Heinemann.

Ozer, E. M., Adams, S. H., Lustig, J. S., Millstein, S. G., Camfield, K., El-Diwany, S., Volpe, S., & Irwin, C. E., Jr. (2001). Can it be done? Implementing adolescent clinical preventive services, *Health Services Research, 36*(6, Pt. 2), 150–165.

Ozer, E. M., Brindis, C. D., Millstein, S. G., Knopf, D. K., & Irwin, C. E., Jr. (1998). America's adolescents: Are they healthy? San Francisco: University of California, National Adolescent Health Information Center.

Panchaud, C., Singh, S., Feivelson, D., & Darroch, J. E. (2000). Sexually transmitted diseases among adolescents in developed countries. *Family Planning Perspectives, 32*(1), 24–32, 45.

Paperny, D. M., & Hedberg, V. A. (1999). Computer-assisted health counselor visits: A low-cost model for comprehensive adolescent preventive services. *Archives of Pediatrics and Adolescent Medicine, 153*(1), 63–67.

Petersen, A .C. (1988). Adolescent development. In M. R. Rosenzweig, & L. W. Porter (Eds.), *Annual Review of Psychology* (pp. 583–607). Palo Alto, CA: Annual Reviews.

Petersen, A. C., Compas, B. E., Brooks-Gunn, J., Stemmler, M., Ey, S., & Grant, K. E.(1993). Depression in adolescence. *American Psychologist, 48*(2), 155–168.

Resnick, M. D., Bearman, P. S., Blum, R. W., Bauman, K. E., Harris, K. M., Jones, J., Tabor, J., Buehring, T., Sieving, R. E., Shew, M., Ireland, M., Bearinger, L. H., & Udry, J. R. (1997). Protecting adolescents from harm: Findings from the National Longitudinal Study on Adolescent Health. *Journal of the American Medical Association, 278*(10), 823–832.

Rosen, D. S., Elster, A., Hedberg, V., & Paperny, D. (1997). Clinical preventive services for adolescents: Position paper of the Society for Adolescent Medicine. *Journal of Adolescent Health, 21*(3), 203–214.

Rutter, M., Graham, P., Chadwick, O. F., & Yule, W. (1976). Adolescent turmoil: Fact or fiction. *Journal of Child Psychology and Psychiatry, 17*(1), 35–56.

Ryan, S. A., Millstein, S. G., Greene, B., & Irwin, C. E., Jr. (1996). Utilization of ambulatory health services by urban adolescents. *Journal of Adolescent Health, 18*, 192–202.

Schoen, C., Davis, K., Scott-Collins, K., Greenberg, L., Des Roches, C., & Abrams, M. (1997). The Commonwealth Fund survey of adolescent girls. NY: The Commonwealth Fund.

Search Institute. (2000). Levels of assets among young people. Retrieved May 23, 2000, from the World Wide Web: http:\\www.search-institute.org/research/assets/assetlevels.html

Shafer, M. A., Pantell, R. H., & Schachter, J. (1999). Is the routine pelvic examination needed with the advent of urine-based screening for sexually-transmitted diseases? *Archives of Pediatrics and Adolescent Medicine, 153*(2), 119–125.

Shaffer, D., Fisher, P., Dulcan, M. K., Davies, M., Piancentini, J., Schwab-Stone, M. E., Lahey, B. B., Bourdon, K., Jensen, P. S., Bird, H. R., Canino, G., & Regier, D. A. (1996). The NIMH Diagnostic Interview Schedule for Children Version 2.3 (DISC-2.3). Description, acceptability, prevalence rates, and performance in the MECA Study. Methods for the epidemiology of child and adolescent mental disorders study. *Journal of the American Academy of Child and Adolescent Psychiatry, 35*(7), 865–877.

Singh, S., & Darroch, J. E. (2000). Adolescent pregnancy and childbearing: Levels and trends in developed countries. *Family Planning Perspectives, 32*(1), 14–23.

Sonnenstein, F. L., Ku, L., Duberstein-Lindberg, L., Turner, C. F., & Pleck, J. H. (1998). New data on sexual behavior of teenage males: sexual activity declines, contraceptive use increases from 1988 to 1995. Washington, DC: The Urban Institute.

Stein, M. E. (1997). *Health Supervision Guidelines* (3rd ed.). Elk Grove Village, IL: American Academy of Pediatrics.

Steiner, B. D., & Gest, K. L. (1996). Do adolescents want to hear preventive counseling messages in outpatient settings? *Journal of Family Practice, 43*(4), 375–81.

Substance Abuse and Mental Health Services Administration. (1999). 1998 National Household Survey on Drug Abuse. Rockville, MD: Department of Health and Human Services.

Thompson, P. M., Giedd, J. N., Woods, R. P., MacDonald, D., Evans, A. C., & Toga, A. W. (2000). Growth patterns in the developing brain detected by using continuum mechanical tensor maps. *Nature, 404*(6774), 190–193.

Troiano, R. P., Flegal, K. M., Kuczmarski, R. J., Campbell, S. M., & Johnson, C. L. (1995). Overweight prevalence and trends for children and adolescents: The national health and nutrition examination survey, 1963–1991. *Archives of Pediatric and Adolescent Medicine, 149*(10), 1085–1091.

UCLA Center for Health Policy Research. (2000, June 15). California Health Interview Survey. Los Angeles, CA. Retrieved June 15, 2000, from the World Wide Web: http://www.healthpolicy.ucla.edu/chis

U.S. Census Bureau, Population Divisions Branch. (2000, January). Population projections, online data set. Washington, DC: Author. Retrieved January 2000, from database on the World Wide Web: http://www.census.gov

U.S. Preventive Services Task Force. (1996). Guide to clinical preventive services (2nd ed.). Alexandria, VA: International Medical Publishing.

Ventura, S. J., Mosher, W. D., Curtin, S. C., Abma, J. C., & Henshaw, S. (2000). Trends in pregnancies and pregnancy rates by outcome: Estimates for the United States, 1976–1996 *Vital Health Statistics, 21*(56), 1–47. Washington DC: National Center for Health Statistics.

Weithorn, L. A., & Campbell, S. B. (1982). The competency of children and adolescents to make informed treatment decisions. *Child Development, 53*(6), 1589–1599.

Wiebe, C. (2000). More doctors hit 'reply' to patients' e-mail queries. *Medscape Money & Medicine,* 1–7. Hillsboro, OR: Author. Retrieved January 31, 2001, from the World Wide Web: www.medscape.com/medscape/MoneyMedicine/journal/2000/v02.n05/mm1002.wiebe/mm1002. Wiebe. html

Wilcox, B. L. (1999). Sexual obsessions: Public policy and adolescent girls. In N. G. Johnson, M. C. Roberts, & J. Worell (Eds.), *Beyond Appearance, A New Look at Adolescent Girls* (pp. 333–354). Washington, DC: American Psychological Association.

William T. Grant Foundation (1999). Helping the nation value young people [Brochure]. New York: Author.

World Health Organization. (2000). Health systems: Improving performance. *World Health Report, 2000.* Geneva, Switzerland: Author. Retrieved January 5, 2001, from the World Wide Web: http://www.who.int/whr/2000/en/report.htm

World Health Organization. (1996, August). Trends in substance use and associated health problems. Fact Sheet (N 127). Retrieved January 5, 2001, from the World Wide Web: http://www.who.int/inf-fs/en/fact127.html

Yamaguchi, K., & Kandel, D. (1985). Drug use and other determinants of premarital pregnancy and its outcome: A dynamic analysis of competing life events. *Journal of Marriage and the Family, 49*(2), 257–270.

Ziv, A., Boulet, J. R., & Slap, G. B. (1998). Emergency department utilization by adolescents in the United States. *Pediatrics, 101*(6), 987–994.

Ziv, A., Boulet, J. R., & Slap, G. B. (1999). Utilization of physician offices by adolescents in the United States. *Pediatrics, 104*(1, Pt. 1), 35–42.

6

Youth and Information Technology

Ronald E. Anderson

Economists around the world acknowledge rapid movement toward a global, knowledge-oriented economy, although this transformation is labeled different things such as "information society," "global economy," and the "new economy." Although they do not agree on projections for the speed of this transition, policy decision makers in numerous countries have adopted the rhetoric of the information society and the inevitability of rapid social change. For instance, a UNESCO study group on Learning Without Frontiers released a report on Information and Communications Technology (ICT) (Blurton, 1999), as did the World Bank (1998) Consultative Group on International Agricultural Research. Both reports projected major social changes from the global information economy and both recommended special attention to developing new mechanisms for lifelong learning using information technology.

This chapter analyzes how these global and societal changes have influenced the lives of adolescents and how they are likely to affect them in the future. For contemporary youth, the most immediate consequences of the growing information infrastructure are the technologies that help them interact with friends and family. With personal computers and hand held mobiles, more and different forms of interpersonal communication have become possible. New forms of leisure, shopping, and working also have become possible. Perhaps most noteworthy is the rapid access to new forms and types of knowledge.

All of these new opportunities, made possible by rapidly evolving information technology, are forcing young users of this technology to confront new ethical and legal issues. New opportunities for cheating, plagiarism, and access to private, personal information are attractive to children, and unless new educational strategies and materials emerge, the life styles of the younger generations may subvert the ethics and values of past generations.

Adolescents inevitably are attracted to adult entertainment, and the Internet greatly simplifies access to adult pastimes such as gambling and sexual interaction. The genre of computer and Internet games tends to be dominated by violent content. Neither family nor educational institutions are prepared to adequately restrict access of youth to such adult-oriented materials that many find objectionable, particularly without adult supervision. For these reasons, socializing children in responsible use of technology is an important challenge for social policy.

Socializing youth in responsible behavior with technology is critical to society from the standpoint of reducing the potential damage that they can create by releasing computer viruses or by disrupting information systems in other ways. While there have been few young people who commit computer crime, in some cases the damage has been very costly and painful. In the future, as computer networking becomes dramatically more powerful and people more dependent on it, the risks will be far greater and the damages more devastating for social institutions. The biological, cell-based computing devices of the more distance future will magnify such potential destruction many fold. New forms of both technical and social control for criminal deterrence will be needed to curtail devastating consequences of irresponsible behavior with technology.

In this chapter, after defining some basic terms related to technology, the implications of the emerging knowledge economy are noted. Then, the latest data on technology access by youth are summarized for some 25 countries in which surveys have been conducted. Following these statistical data is a summary of the academic research on the social impact of technology. Finally, the discussion moves to the present, specifically those technologies emerging at the beginning of the 21st century, with speculations about the decades ahead.

TERMINOLOGY

In the past decade, many communities (both academic and general) increasingly have been using the terms "technology" or "information technology" (IT) rather than "computer" to discuss computers and their applications. People often use the terms technology and computers synonymously even though technology can be understood to refer to a wide range of other tools in addition to the computer. Most of the non-American world tends to refer to information technology as ICT, which stands for Information and Communication Technologies. Despite the minor distinctions that some might assign to these various terms, in this chapter the labels IT, ICT, technology, and computers will refer to the same thing. Other jargon within this field will be defined when used.

The term "technologically advanced" is used in this chapter to refer to those countries with a relatively high concentration of IT. There is a fairly high correlation between economic wealth and the concentration of IT across countries (Anderson & Lundmark, 1996). But neither wealth nor technology should be taken as a sign of being culturally advanced. It is also the case that many countries like South Africa or China, which are not technologically advanced overall, contain social sectors that are very technologically advanced.

THE EMERGING KNOWLEDGE SOCIETY

Social analysts around the world acknowledge rapid evolution toward a global, knowledge-oriented economy, and many use the concepts of the "knowledge society" and the "information society" as well as the "global economy," and the "new economy." Although they do not agree on projections for the speed of this transition, policy decision makers in numerous countries have adopted the rhetoric of the information society and note the inevitability of rapid social change.

The Group of Eight (G8) on July 24, 2000, issued the "Okinawa Charter on Global Information Society" (http://www.library.utoronto.ca/g7/g20/), which is arguably the highest political statement yet on the need for IT and lifelong learning. A more in-depth analysis of "Information Society" issues appeared in a report by Kling and associates, *Learning from Social Informatics* (2000).All these reports projected major social changes from the global information economy and recommend special attention to the implications this trend has for developing new mechanisms for lifelong learning using information technology.

The implications of the global knowledge society derive from two major forces, greater inter-cultural interaction and an economic system that treats knowledge as a commodity. Underlying the new role of knowledge in society is, on the one hand an explosion of information and what people think is knowledge, and on the other hand, a greatly increased

TABLE 6.1. *Implications of the demands of the global knowledge economy for youth in terms of required skills and learning strategies*

Demands of Society	Required Skills	Learning Strategies
Knowledge as commodity	Knowledge construction	Inquiry, project learning, constructivism
Rapid change, renewal	Adaptability	Learning to re-learn, on-demand learning
Information explosion	Finding, organizing, retrieving	Multi-database browsing exercises
Poorly organized information	Information management	Database construction
Poorly evaluated information	Critical thinking	Evaluation problem solving
Collective knowledge	Teamwork	Collaborative learning

value for knowledge that helps people get what they most want. Table 6.1 shows the major implications of the global knowledge economy for the skills and learning strategies of young people, particularly those entering the work force. For instance, making knowledge a commodity means that youth must learn skills in constructing new knowledge such as working on projects.

Another characteristic of the knowledge society is a much faster pace of change in what is known and what is institutionalized. The second line in Table 6.1 notes that young people need to learn adaptation skills and to use on-demand information systems. They can expect that it may be necessary to be highly mobile occupationally, switching among jobs, if not careers. It is no longer possible to keep up with all the knowledge in a field, and employers are more preoccupied with how well a prospective worker is able to learn than how much he or she knows already. The explosion of knowledge implies using systems that require new skills for accessing, organizing, and retrieving knowledge. The knowledge is poorly organized and poorly evaluated, which means that there is a premium on the ability to manage information and critically evaluate it. Furthermore, because knowledge is increasingly collective it is necessary to learn collaboration skills and to spend more time working in teams.

DATA ON YOUTH AND TECHNOLOGY ACCESS

Because technology is such a global phenomenon, cross-national data are needed to understand its growth and impact. Although almost all the research on technology use is done at national or local levels, a major exception is the IEA Second International Technology in Education Study (SITES). Key findings are summarized here with technical details of the sample and study methodology given in Appendix A. Further details are available at http://www.mscp.edte.utwente.nl/sitesm1 and in Pelgrum and Anderson (1999). While the United States did not officially participate in the study, comparable statistics are available on some indicators from a survey conducted in the United States about the same time. Relevant results of that study, Teaching, Learning, and Computing, 1998, which the author and Henry Becker co-directed, are summarized in Anderson and Ronnkvist (1999) and in other reports at the same Web site.

Technology and Schools

School-based technology data is particularly useful because the school is the only place where many young people get experience with computers and the Internet. In addition, those adolescents with access to ICT at home typically also spend time with it at school. This section characterizes the nature of school ICT access, emphasizing how it varies across countries.

First, we report the student-computer ratio, because it is the most common indicator of opportunity for student access. The best measure of this ratio is simply the total number of students in a given category of schools divided by the total number of computers devoted primarily for instruction in those schools. Note that the higher the ratio the lower the computer density and vice versa. The SITES data are shown in Figure 6.1 where the first bar for each country shows the number of students per computer for 1995, as found by the IEA TIMSS study, and the second bar shows the number of students per computer for 1998 from the IEA SITES study. United States statistics are not included in the charts because the United States did not officially participate in SITES. However, the U.S. ratios and percentages are nearly identical to the Canadian's.

At the lower secondary level the majority of countries had student-computer ratios in the range of 10 to 40. However, Canada and 4 other countries had fewer than 10 students per computer in 1998, and the bar chart (Figure 6.1) shows that these countries with a high density of computers dropped their ratios by about 50%, which means doubling the computer density. In the United States the number of computers in

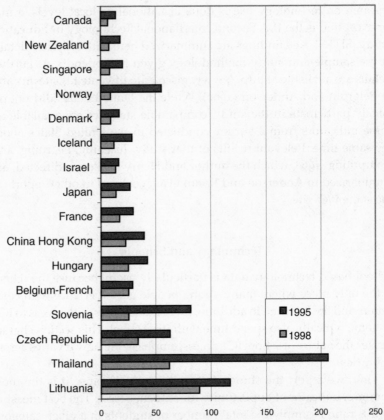

FIGURE 6.1. Change between 1995 and 1998 in students per computer in lower secondary schools. *Source*: Data from IEA TIMSS and SITES

schools has increased at a rate of about 15% per year (Anderson and Ronnkvist, 1999). Although some of the smaller countries have been able to expand their infrastructure at much faster rates in specific years, overall the pattern of growth in ICT has been surprisingly similar. However, there were a few exceptional countries, namely Norway, Slovenia, and Thailand, where the concentration of computers actually tripled, due largely to national policy initiatives.

Multimedia. An increasingly popular indicator of whether or not the ICT is adequate for contemporary applications is the percentage of school computers that are multimedia-ready. This generally means that at a minimum the computer has a CD-ROM drive and a sound card. Essentially, all of the computers targeted to the home market have this

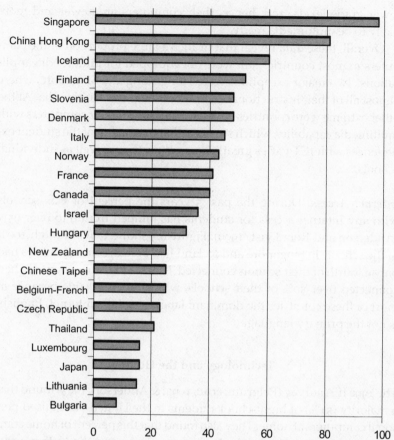

FIGURE 6.2. Average percent of multimedia-ready computers in lower secondary schools, 1998 IEA SITES

capability, but many of the computers in schools were acquired some years ago and do not have it. Figure 6.2 shows the average percent of instructional computers equipped for multimedia in each country for lower secondary schools.

The differences between primary and secondary schools in multimedia-ready computers is interesting but not shown in Figure 6.2. At the primary school level the averages range between 50% and 75%, whereas at the secondary level they range between 25% and 50%. This pattern of favoring the lower grade levels with a greater concentration of multimedia computers probably results from a historical policy trend. Most countries introduced computers into the higher grades in earlier years. In recent years "catch-up" programs have targeted ICT for the lower grade levels, and, hence, their computers are newer and more likely to be multimedia ready.

Overall, these data reveal that in 1998 a large proportion of the computers in most countries still were not equipped for multimedia applications. Two major exceptions were Hong Kong and Singapore, where almost all of their instructional computers could use multimedia. At the other extreme were countries with less than 20% of their computers with multimedia capability, which suggests that the quality of the student experiences with ICT varies greatly across countries as well as individual schools.

Internet Access. During the past 5 years the percent of U.S. schools with any Internet access for students has jumped from 0 to over 95% (Anderson and Ronnkvist, 1999). Figure 6.3 shows that although 100% of the schools in Singapore and Iceland had access, some countries had only a fourth of their schools connected. Most of the other countries had connected over 50% of their schools, which is remarkable because in most of these countries the dominant language of the Internet, English, is not the primary language.

Technology and the Home

The 1992 IEA survey (Pelgrum, et al., 1993; & Anderson, 1993) found that a majority (51%) of high school students in the United States used personal computers at home. They also found that this percent of home computer use was even higher in Austria, Germany, and the Netherlands. Comparable cross-national statistics are not available for recent years, but a U.S. study (NPR [National Public Radio], 2000) in December 1999 found that 78% of youth ages 10 to 17 had a computer at home, and 98% of them said they used it. In fact a majority said they used it "almost every day." Of those with a computer at home, 73% said they used their home computer for Internet access or e-mail. Eighty-one percent said they had access to the Internet at school, and one-third of them said they used it at school "almost every day." These findings are in general agreement with other surveys conducted about the same time including the UCLA Internet Project (Cole, 2000), Online Victimization Survey (Finkehor et al., 2000), and Jupiter Media Metrix (2001). Appendix B of this chapter summarizes these surveys.

These data indicate that computer access, especially Internet access, has been increasing very rapidly, and this is true for young people both

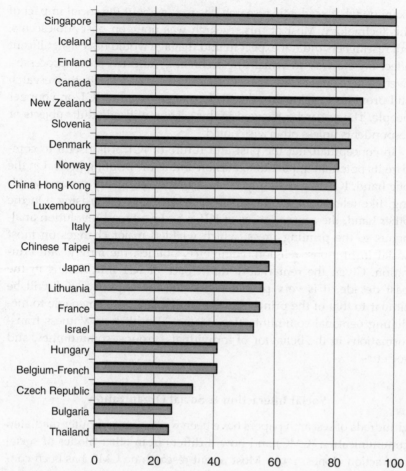

FIGURE 6.3. Average percent of lower secondary schools with internet access, 1998 IEA SITES

at home and school. Tremendous variation in access was found across countries, and in some countries the access is highly stratified by social groups (Anderson and Ronnkvist, 1999). Such findings have generated recent attention to the so-called digital divides by policy makers at many levels of education and government.

RESEARCH ON SOCIAL IMPACT OF TECHNOLOGY

With the forgoing data as a background profile of the general exposure of young people to information technology at home and school, we examine what academic research has to say about the social impact of this technology. Most of this research was done on post-adolescents, but researchers did not expect to find that age would have a significant effect on the way in which the technology affected social processes. Even though adolescents were not always used as subjects, this research still provides insights into the likely consequences of ICT on younger people. The research reviewed in this section utilized adult subjects or respondents unless otherwise noted.

In conceptualizing the past and future of ICT, it is useful to compare its potential impact to television and to the printing press. On the one hand, ICT might simply be a narrow evolutionary process yielding, like television, another form of leisure and advertising. On the other hand, the consequences of ICT may be a broad revolution analogous to the printing press, which wielded major changes on most social institutions: religion, commerce, politics, the family, and education. Given the remarkably rapid pace of ICT innovations in the past decade, it is very plausible that the net impact of ICT will be similar to that of the printing press. In that ICT is so amenable to mediating personal communication, we are also likely to witness transformations in the behavior of individuals, groups, communities, and societies.

Social Interaction & Social Organization

Hundreds of research papers have been written on computer mediated communication (CMC) and how it differs from other modes of social interaction (Jones, 1995). Most recent research on CMC has been concentrating on the compositional, linguistic, and communication patterns rather than the social aspects. However, a large number of researchers examine social factors along with other dimensions of communication (Kiesler, 1985; Sproull and Kiesler, 1993; Walther, 1992; Wellman, et al., 1996).

The early experimental research found that groups using CMC, compared with face to face groups, took longer to reach consensus, participated more equally, showed more openness to alternative approaches, and displayed more uninhibited verbal behavior, which is often called flaming (Kling, 1996). Recent studies have found that electronic mail and forums tend to have distinctly different social properties, for example, lower level or more peripheral persons in organizations may have more influence and visibility (Sproull & Kiesler, 1995).

A large segment of the social research on Internet interaction is concerned primarily with small groups and their decision-making processes (McGrath and Hollingshead, 1994). This line of research has found that basic group processes including leadership patterns, level of member participation, consensus requirements, member satisfaction, and productivity may sometimes be different in an online context as compared with a face to face structure.

The contemporary mainstream of research on social interaction using the Internet is represented by Gotcher and Kanervo (1997), who surveyed e-mail users on their perceptions of their patterns of e-mail communication. They concluded that many e-mail users need training in the areas of confidentiality and the expression of anger. Many e-mail users violated expectations to preserve the confidentiality of e-mail messages received and to control their expression of anger in e-mails sent. This might well be less of a problem for youth now as many started communicating by e-mail as pre-teens.

Self-Concept

In her latest book, Turkle (1995) developed the notion of the virtual self and claimed that Internet interaction has yielded changes in our sense of self. Kilger (1996) elaborated on this concept of the virtual self and examined how individuals use digital channels to form multiple social selves. Both authors have noted the tendency toward attribution of human characteristics to machines and software, especially among children. Laboratory experiments by Orcutt and Anderson (1974), Matheson and Zanna (1990), and Matheson (1991) found that many adults also attribute human characteristics to computer systems. And even more important, they found that subjects were more aggressive and less empathic when interacting with a machine-controlled machine as compared with a machine they thought had a person behind it. Research has not confirmed that such effects have long-term consequences for one's self-concept.

"Chat," which is the collegial term for synchronous communication among two or more persons online, is a new form of social interaction with unique demands. The prerequisite and highly valued skills are rapid expression of thoughts via keyboard and the use of commands to express emotions. In a 1997 ethnographic study of chat, particularly in online communities structured within MOO (Multi-user Object-Oriented) online interaction environments, Markam (1998) investigated the sense of self and reality of heavy users, and found that most heavy users of chat preferred online communication because of a greater control of their presentation of themselves. But ironically their belief in limitless agency online may have made them even more vulnerable to the influence of others, as they sometimes let down their guard against deception.

Markam concluded that the expression "eloquence makes me beautiful online" represents the motivation of many of those skilled and active in chats. Indeed, escape from negative feelings of one's physical appearance or social self, seems to drive many into chat. But although Markam found many online people with complex, multiple selves, she did not find widespread evidence of negative effects on the lives or personalities of chat users. Online technology has the capacity to facilitate obsessions and escapes, so it may be unhealthy for some. From the research done to date it appears that for the large mass of people, both young and old, participating in chat, the effects tend to mirror those of in-person communication.

Sexual Interaction and Victimization

Media polls in the year 2000 found that between 25% and 30% of Internet users visited an "adult entertainment site" each month (Weiss, 2001), but some visits may be fleeting or even unintentional. As of this writing, research is scarce on regular users of "hard core" pornography and explicit sexual Internet interaction. An important exception is that of Markam (1998), who, among other situations, described online sharing of masturbation where friends cheer at one's climax. Impersonal group sex is not new, but the virtual world of the Internet with private chat rooms provides an unusually safe social context for persons of all ages including youth.

The best data on adolescent exposure to sexual matters on the Internet can be found in the 1999 "Online Victimization" study by Finkehor, Mitchell, and Wolak (2000). Appendix B of this chapter provides the methodology for this national survey of American youth from ages 10 to 17 who were regular Internet users, which was defined as someone using the Internet at least once a month for the past six months. Some highlights of the findings were:

- One in 4 youth (about 6 million) during the past year had been subjected to an unwanted sexual exposure, defined as unexpected pictures of naked people or people having sex.

- One in 5 youth (about 4.5 million) had received a sexual solicitation, defined as a request for sex or sexual information.
- One in 17 youth (about 1.4 million) had been harassed online, defined as "feeling worried or threatened" because they were being bothered, harassed, or embarrassed online.
- One third of those harassed online (about 500,000) felt very upset or afraid as a result.
- Three percent of the regular Internet-using youth (about 700,000) reported an "aggressive solicitation," which was defined as offline (mail, phone, or in-person) attempt for sexual contact.

The pattern in these incidences by age of the victim was especially intriguing and deserving of further research. All 5 types of victimization peaked at age 14 and 15. Very few 10- and 11-year-olds reported incidents, and the rates declined for 16- and 17-year-olds. Although the decline after age 15 may have resulted from a period effect, it would seem more likely that it was produced by an age effect, specifically that the older youth had learned techniques and strategies for avoiding unwanted exposure and solicitation.

All together these findings confirm that sexual exploitation of youth is a non-trivial problem. While 85% of parents claimed that they discussed issues of the Internet and sex with their children, the importance of more explicit and repeated discussions is underscored by these findings. The study also found that both youth and parents need more knowledge about sources for help in reporting and dealing with exploitive actions on the Internet.

Lifestyles

To what extent does the Internet or IT in general actually change the lifestyles of young people? We know from the UCLA survey and other polls that Internet use among adults is associated with heavier use of almost all media but especially the use of books, recorded music, and radio. But that may largely reflect the demographic makeup of Internet users. The NPR (2000) "Kids and Technology" survey asked youth if their computer use led them to watch more or less television and nearly half said "less" and nearly half said "no difference." Robinson and Godbey (1997) found from a 1995 *Times-Mirror* survey that, contrary to what one might expect, computer and Internet technology users had not displaced time spent with traditional mass media. In fact heavier ICT use was associated with greater use of print media, even after a variety of controls were applied (Robinson, Barth, and Kohut, 1997). What is not yet clear from the research is whether these discrepancies in findings arise from methodological differences among the studies, population differences, or the change over time in the amount and quality of appealing material and activity on the Internet.

A number of studies have found evidence that heavy use of e-mail does indeed replace some share of time spent in face-to-face communication. In the NPR survey, 40% of the young people said they thought that computers have led them to spend *less* time with families and friends and 50% said "not much difference." But while face-to-face time may have been replaced, survey responses in the NPR and other surveys as well indicate that, in general, neither adolescents nor adults believe this change has reduced the quality of their interpersonal relationships. In fact, heavy e-mail users tend to see their electronic communications as enhancing their ability to maintain relationships with friends.

The Pew Internet Project (Pew, 2001) found that over 50% of the adult Internet users in 2000 said that they had gone online to obtain hobby or medical information, get news, buy products, and browse for fun. Two other major draws of the Internet are religion and sex (Weiss, 2001). Although less than half of Internet users in the United States go to the Internet for religious purposes or sex, the percentages are well over 20%. Religious pursuits and sexual exploration are more common on the Internet than trading stocks or searching for financial information.

The generalizability of these data are somewhat limited and the findings must be interpreted with great caution. Some of these surveys did not disaggregate the results by age group, and thus the findings can not be attributed to an adolescent cohort. Furthermore, the Internet utilization patterns are very volatile, changing very rapidly. This should be taken into account in speculating about cultural changes in future years.

Community and Collective Actions

Rheingold (1993) popularized the notion of the Internet as a virtual community. More academic discussions such as Baym (1995) and Jones (1995) continue to explore the sociological implications of communities that are electronically based. Most of the interesting questions remain unanswered. Research is needed on such questions as the prevalence and consequences of virtual communities. To what extent do adolescent members of these communities consider them a substitute for face-to-face communities? And if they perceive them as a substantial substitute, under what conditions do they do so? The longer-term question is: To what extent will highly interpersonal, face-to-face community life be replaced by less personal relationships among various types of young people?

Much of the writing on Cyberspace communities is action-oriented. Activists promote local and regional networks for community planning and development. Their function is not only communication and improved democratization but also collection of important policy data and influence over the policy process. These types of communities may have major implications in terms of changes in participation and diversity, opportunities to access government, and changes in centralized or decentralized control. By the time today's youth reach middle age, the relationship between government and their citizenries may be quite different.

Many questions, especially on privacy and intellectual property, remain unanswered by either empirical research or public policy. A major dilemma exists in that even the technological experts disagree on such questions as whether or not there are technological solutions like encryption that could adequately protect the communications and privacy of people. Questions such as to what extent should a citizen's (or an employee's) e-mail files be protected from monitoring by others can only be answered by public policy; however, empirical research could contribute to the process by providing both factual and opinion data regarding existing patterns and trends. Another case in point is the question of the seriousness of violations of software copyrights, such as making backup copies or pirating software. These issues cross national and cultural boundaries, making them particularly challenging but important with many ramifications for the future.

Unequal Access

Research and policy on the digital divide has concentrated in two areas: gender and socio-economic (SES) status, although unequal access by racial or disability lines is also of concern (Anderson, et al., 1994). While the gender gap has been decreasing during the past decade, the SES gap has been increasing in the United States (U.S. Department of Commerce, 1999). Teenagers in high-income families were many times more likely to have a computer at home than those in very low income families. The U.S. Department of Commerce (1999) study found that low-income and minority groups were more likely to use libraries and other public access sites for computer access, but there was evidence that the gaps in the quality of Internet utilization continued to widen.

In the year just before and after Y2K, some rapid demographic changes appeared to take place among Americans accessing the Internet (Weiss, 2001). For the first time, women exceeded men among those online to the Internet, and the percent of persons with low income accessing the Internet also made a sharp rise. The digital divide became more cultural than structural in that access appeared to be equalizing but big differences in the type and quality of access remained (Weiss, 2001). Lower-income persons were found to be more likely to use the Internet for gambling than those with higher income. Blacks were much more likely than other racial groups to use the Internet for listening to music. The Jupiter Consumer Survey (http://us.mediametrix.com/data/teensconcept.pdf) in 2000 found that teenage girls were much more likely than boys to use the Internet for sending greetings, reading online magazines, and for doing homework, whereas the boys were much more likely to play games, download software, and use online auctions. Although the digital divide may be lessening on the surface, it is too early to determine whether or not current trends will reduce the inequity among different social groups in their ability to utilize information technology for success in school and work.

EMERGING TECHNOLOGIES

Now we shift from social research to the technology itself. In this section, contemporary ICT trends are identified with an eye toward those most likely to impact adolescents. These technology trends include both hardware devices and software technologies. Although some of these technologies are experienced by only a few young people at the time of this writing, it is expected that they will become part of the daily lives of most youth in technologically advanced countries in the near future.

Computers

Special-purpose microprocessors are embedded in every electronic or digital device and in this sense are ubiquitous in every technologically advanced country. General-purpose microprocessors, which we call computers, can be programmed by the user, and in most cases provide a variety of software applications. At the smallest end of the scale are personal digital assistants (PDA), which are popular as personal organizers. While tiny, hand-held computers are widely available, most families have desktop or laptop computers because of their versatility. As noted in Appendix B of this chapter, over three-fourths of adolescents in most technologically advanced countries have access to a computer at home. An even larger share use them in school, and computer work is an essential part of the jobs of many young people. In the last few years the principal function of many personal computers has become to access and process information from the Internet.

Networks

Almost every organization in technologically advanced nations has its own local area network (LAN) or networks, but the Internet, on which the World Wide Web (WWW or Web) is based, is the most commonly used network. Home networks are just beginning to be popular but will soon be commonplace as they can help to manage appliances, utilities, home security, and entertainment units. Such functions can be performed not only from home but also from accessing a Web site anywhere. As noted by Chon (2001) and Waldo (2001), in the near future many more such machine devices will be linked to the Internet than the number of people linked to the Internet. This will make it possible for many youth products like pieces of clothing and books to have embedded electronic processors that interact with each other and supply practical information to their owners.

The NRP (2000) survey revealed that e-mail is the most common way that adolescents use the Internet, and they use it for regular interaction with friends, family, and other associates. Personal Web site construction has become popular among many youth on the Web. Children find that they can use it to promote things, express themselves, and share their experiences and creations.

The potential of the Internet, and the Web in particular, for rapid search of diverse information is well known, and the technology for effective browsing and searching is improving very rapidly. For instance, in the late 1990s, meta-searching (e.g., www.metacrawler.com) was invented whereby the results of a range of different search engines are quickly pooled and summarized. Even more important search technologies are expected in the near future as the ability to identify, search, and link specialized databases continues to expand and allow for more individualization.

Wireless Telephones

The use of wireless phones (also called cell phones or mobiles) are increasing exponentially among both children and adults in advanced countries. Despite the cost of heavy use of some wireless services, the convenience of talking to friends and parents has made this technology very attractive to young people. By the start of the decade about 30% of teens in the United States were using cell phones, but 70% of teens in the U.K. were using them (Barnes, 2000). That degree of concentration among youth was not projected until after 2005 (Barnes, 2000). Apparently adolescents in many European and Asian countries are more likely to use mobile phones than in the United States because wireless is relatively inexpensive compared with fixed-line service and because teens can get "pay-as-you-go" service requiring no credit checks or parental approval. In Finland most adolescents carry one with them every day. They are routinely used not only for voice calls, but purchasing and ordering Internet services and for Short Message Service (SMS), which provides for simultaneous text-based e-mail.

Digital Video

High-quality video conferencing is still rather expensive, but the development of color video screens for mobiles and the ability of many personal computers to store and edit large video files point toward a near-term future in which video and computing technologies will offer new lifestyles. As a supplement to audio phone calling, video offers new privacy issues as well as additional modes of expression and communication. Interactive, digital home cinema using DVD and later technologies may influence how and where families spend recreational time. Children growing up with online video cams as well as personal video production, made possible with digital video technology, will have skills and expectations not possible in previous generations.

Digital Audio

The popular sound compression technology called MP3 led to the popularization of tiny personal music players that store audio files downloaded from computers and the Internet. Part of their attraction to adolescents is the ability to listen unobtrusively to their favorite music within a variety of social settings. Digital audio, combined with other digital technologies, yields a variety of new applications with major social consequences.

Electronic Navigation

Personal and automotive devices for electronic navigation employ a satellite-linked global positioning system (GPS) to identify the precise coordinates of the device. This not only provides an electronic map showing where you are at all times in case you get lost, but it offers a way for someone to track you down. Another type of navigation device fixes the distance between one's vehicle and the one just in front. It is anticipated that once most cars and trucks have such devices that traffic conditions may be more orderly, but additional risks are also likely.

Digital Implants

Electronic medical devices have been successful in narrow roles, for example, automatic heart stimulators, but broader roles such as monitoring location and body temperature are expected. Devices implanted just under the skin with GPS technology and additional intelligence would make it possible to monitor a child's location and medical conditions anywhere in the world. Probably the most popular implant for parents will be a tiny chip that combines a GPS locator with sensors that constantly transmit vitals like temperature, pulse, blood pressure, and white blood count to parents or a designated security agency. Such chips could be implanted in random body locations so that a kidnapper would find them difficult to remove.

Similar devices may become common for electronic monitoring of offenders and juvenile delinquents. Electronic monitoring has been used in the correctional system for almost a decade, but its use has not become widespread for three reasons. One is the implication for principles of civil liberty; another is the potential liability to law enforcement officials of having information without appropriately responding to it; and the third is the inability of computer systems to handle the huge volume of information simultaneously transmitted by numerous electronic bracelets. The latter problem will be solved in a matter of time, and the civil liberty issues seem to be dissipating in the wake of apparent increases in crime rates and public fear of crime. Both of these changes are likely to result in solutions to the liability threat also.

Video Eye Glasses

Eyeglasses with video screens in part of the lens are now available for watching your favorite video or movie. They also play an important role in VR (virtual reality) applications and many computer games. Ultimately they could become as common as earphones. Combined with a video cam implant or a video database implant, they could become very compelling as memory tools.

Language Recognition

Speech recognition and translation software have been under development for 25 years, but only in the late 1990s did it become commercially viable. This technology still requires time for "training" the software to recognize each speaker's speech patterns, and the volume of errors in recognition are still too high for many applications. While it is impossible to know how accurate these systems may become, it is safe to anticipate major improvements. If the quality of the recognition becomes extremely high in these systems, we can anticipate that many computer interfaces will omit the keyboard, making it possible for those without typing skills to have a more equal footing in the computer world. Eventually earplug devices may have enough intelligence for you to carry on a conversation with someone who is speaking to you in a foreign language.

Personal Software Agents

Agents are program units with sufficient autonomy to carry out supportive tasks for users such as personalized searches, well-informed health consulting, and smart job counseling. It is expected that in the near future, clever agents that cruise the Internet for their owners will be widespread and popular, but not necessarily free. It is expected that there will be many classes or types of agents, and that some will be easily user-programmable. Agents that are customizable for the special needs or interests of youth are likely to be quite popular. For example, a student might send an agent out to look at the e-mail of all her classmates to see who was going to the class dance and what they would wear. Or an agent could be instructed to alert the owner whenever tickets for Madonna concerts within 200 miles went on sale.

E-recreation

Although recreation can take many forms, probably the most common forms using IT are chat systems and games. Chat systems are especially interesting sociologically because most of these systems are organized around special but common interests. Unlike e-mail, chat systems provide for synchronous communication. Multi-user games on the Internet also generally have a synchronous component. A moderately small number of adolescents spend a huge amount of time playing these games with others on the Internet. Many, if not most, of the games have a violent aspect to them, which was widely discussed after it was revealed that the boys responsible for the Littleton, Colorado, massacre were heavy players of these games.

E-commerce

The Internet has made new forms of trading and business possible. Electronic trading systems or auctions (e.g., www.ebay.com) are a case in point. These auctions, which began in the late 1990s, have become very popular among all ages and some traders spend many hours at them every week. It is expected that numerous variations on these trading systems will emerge, and local or regional systems may be the most popular.

E-education

The use of the Internet for learning is compelling for students of all ages. In addition to information searching and e-mail communication, the electronic field trip has become quite popular. Typically several classrooms around the world get regular e-mail and video transmissions for an expedition by one or more experts in a remote geographical area. Not only does this make it possible for students to inexpensively experience some of the excitement of discovery, it also makes it possible for students to have a chance to communicate with professionals and experts as they conduct their work. The Internet facilitates inter-connectiveness between students and knowledge resources in other ways (Collis, 1996). Combined with other digital technologies, the Internet gives a major boost to lifelong learning strategies and facilitates the home schooling movement as well.

SPECULATIONS ON THE FUTURE IMPACT OF TECHNOLOGY

The final section of this chapter moves from present reality to emphasizing guesses about the future. Although the previous section, Emerging Technology, may have implied a technological inevitability or even determinism, the earlier section, Research on Social Impacts of Technology, should have clarified that the adoption of technology by society is a process involving interplay between social processes and technological options. Stewart and Williams (1998) offer a useful framework for forecasting the future of new technologies. They recommend that any technological forecasting take into account not only the technical components but also the delivery systems and the human application processes of the technologies. In other words, the future trends of technology in society will shape how the new technologies are marketed and how people, both young and old, want to use them.

General Cultural Processes

Given the history of technology and society to date, it is reasonable to predict that the following general processes will continue in the foreseeable future: increases in cultural memory due to facilities such as archives that retain and retrieve more information and increases in new knowledge due to more rapid sharing of information, which yield more rapid formation of mutual social constructions. This faster intellectual pace may result in increases in the formation of collective movements, deviant subgroups, and cults, which may also be due to reduced cost of building new relationships and organizing diverse activities.

One implication of this is that those who are adolescents now will likely experience a faster intellectual pace as they reach adulthood and throughout their life course. Whether or not they take advantage of the greater potentials for sharing, for collective memory, and for collective action depends on many other factors. But those who seek to benefit from these new cultural processes are more likely to have opportunities to do so. Furthermore, this increased adolescent control, or sense of control, in the future might reduce the force of family and other social institutions.

Social Interaction

It is nearly certain that young people will depend more and more on electronic communicators in the form of wireless phones with computing power and Web access. In the same way that the telephone yielded a major restructuring of communication patterns in Western countries, an evolving restructuring of social interaction is likely. Some relationships will benefit greatly. For example, students attending boarding school or schools in other countries can speak or send e-mails every day with their parents and friends back home.

The existing ICT already fosters greater interaction across national and cultural boundaries. Electronic dating and mating research suggests that a much higher number of cross-cultural couplings will continue to occur within Internet contexts. But breakthroughs in automatic translation of text from one language to another could yield dramatic increases in inter-cultural interactions. And if that technology can be extended to audio files, there will be even greater increases in cross language exchanges.

The Digital Divide

Increased cross-cultural interaction, both within and between countries, will be partially offset by the concurrent widening of the digital divide along income and racial lines. Not only does the cost of ICT services present an obstacle for low-income and minority groups, lack of skills, especially language skills, hinder participation in ICT advantages. Furthermore, certain subcultures may lack the values that support broad or deep use of ICT activities. In ethnically diverse countries such as the United States, the widening of these sub-cultural gaps even more is bound to be a serious problem. Adolescents who are both poor and members of a racial minority group that is separated culturally from ICT will likely have difficulty participating in the work force where most jobs presume technological familiarity.

Sex

The increased use of various types of computer-mediated communication may result in less personal and less emotionally expressive forms of interaction. A byproduct of such a scenario might be a greater sense of isolation and a perceived loss of social support. A rise in the use of the Internet for sexual experiences may well result in perceptions of sex as less of an interpersonal process and more of an individual one.

It is safe to say that the effects of ICT on sexual behavior will be complex. The "voyeur dormitory" is a case in point. At least one college dormitory has been wired with video cameras, and the women residents get free tuition in return for allowing anyone who pays a subscription fee to view their lives anytime of day or night. This has led to serious questions of the nature of appropriate privacy, the boundaries between prostitution and private sex, and the distinction between commercial and personal sexual display. As they continue to emerge, such innovative institutions may not become part of mainstream culture, but they might still lead to changes in attitudes among youth about what is acceptable and desirable with respect to sexuality. It is likely that most young people will follow their elders and choose physical contacts with intimates, but those with disabilities and those with negative beliefs about their attractiveness may be more likely to follow these new patterns of gratification online.

Ethics and Values

In Finland, where nearly every high school student carries a mobile (wireless phone with Internet access and e-mail capabilities), students have been known to use their phones for sharing answers to questions during exams. In some instances teachers routinely collect all mobiles before administering a test. In the United States, the Internet appears to be fostering cheating by high school students by making it very easy to find pre-written essays and papers. The legal and educational systems have failed to clarify how the law and ethical principles apply to different uses of different types of information. Little and sporadic enforcement of existing laws yields the impression that violation of intellectual property norms is not a serious matter. With the larger society remaining confused and sympathetic to minor forms of intellectual property violations, it is difficult for teachers and school administrators to enforce rules on cheating. In this sense, the ethical ambiguity and chaos regarding use of resources on the Internet may be helping to lure many students into improper behaviors that are formally defined as cheating by the educational system and by older generations. As a caveat it should be noted that the legal system may rapidly change the legitimization of these activities, as the Napster court case over MP3 music copying attests.

Education

Within the last 5 years of the 20th century more than half of the classrooms in the United States became connected to the Internet (Anderson and Ronnkvist, 1999). The same rapid diffusion of this technology into classrooms has happened in at least a dozen other countries as well. For an institution that at times seems invincible, this change is suggestive of how rapidly the process of learning may change for adolescents. The new ICT already offers many new methods for acquiring and analyzing knowledge. As adolescents routinely carry wireless devices that link them to friends, family, and co-workers via the Web, systems will facilitate collaborative learning, to say nothing of improving their technology skills. With the help of new information technologies, home schooling may become very well organized and very popular. Such a movement will have a deep and broad impact on the family and the lifestyles of adolescents.

Mental Health

In another article in this volume, Kate Hellenga reviews the mental health issues of the Internet. I do not want to duplicate her rich discussion but merely to give a brief speculative comment. While there has been research (Kraut et al., 1998) that found that heavy use of the Internet reduced social involvement and increased chances of depression of some people, one remaining question is, how widespread or narrow might such an impact be? Another question is, what factors mediate this impact when it does occur? For what types of people, using which applications, and for how long might such effects be observable? Adolescents may be more vulnerable than adults for some of these negative consequences, but it is my speculation that it will still be a small minority that suffers seriously. The Finnish experience, with most youth using mobiles and e-mail, has not yet shown any major problems.

Inevitably due to lower costs of networking, we will continue to see scattered examples such as Heavens Gate Rancho Santa Fe, California and the Littleton, Colorado, massacre where the Internet and its variants play a prominent role. Nonetheless, the public at large, and adolescents in particular, will probably not be broadly affected in such dramatic ways. In this regard, a key question for speculation and research is how widespread such negative effects will be? Even if they are not widespread, there may be other unanticipated or gradual cultural changes.

A Longer-Term Projection

So far the analysis has taken a short-term perspective on the future, that is, the impact of technology has been examined from the viewpoint of the first 5 years of the 21st century. In this section we briefly consider the longer-term possibilities, specifically the next 30 years. Our projection perspective is 30 years because this is the time frame suggested by Joy (2000) in analyzing existing trends and their implications for the future. His analysis is supported by Chon (2001), Drexler (1992), Kurzweil (1999; 2000; 2001), Leslie (1996) and others.

In the past 20 years the growth of computer power in terms of processor speed has been doubling every 18 months, in accord with Moore's Law (Joy, 2000). This remarkable pace continues but the cost of producing physical devices that don't overheat is also rising rapidly. It is generally agreed among experts that the cost-effectiveness of this dramatic rise in computing power with silicon chip technology will end between 2010 and 2015 (Joy, 2000; Kurzweil, 2000). This realization has stimulated considerable attention to other forms of devices for microelectronics. The alternative getting the most attention is molecular electronics, a sub-field of nanotechnology (Drexler, 1992; Lampton, 1993; Reed and Tour, 2000). This new field uses live cells to build mechanisms for storing or controlling information.

As progress moves rapidly with molecular electronics, a number of scientists have noted the revolutionary implications of a convergence of molecular electronics with genetic engineering and robotics (Joy, 2000; Kurzweil, 1999). Not only does this trend imply the reality of live cell-based molecular processors, it also offers the concrete possibility of self-reproducing computers. Cells can reproduce themselves, which could yield a quantum leap in "computing power." Not only does this suggest radically new productive capabilities for information technologies, it also yields possibilities that may pose grave risks for human society (Leslie, 1996).

Self-reproducing systems may be much more difficult to control than existing computer chips. In the hands of criminal minds they could do great damage. In fact, Joy (2000) and others have speculated that this technology will provide the potential for the human race to either destroy or replace itself. The human species could theoretically be replaced by transfer of human cells to robots using molecular electronics, that, in turn, reproduce new varieties of cells based on their human input. Speculation also continues on the possibility of human-cell downloads to machines (Bell and Gray, 2001). Not only would this offer a way to clone one's self but perhaps a method of immortality. This seems to be an appropriate point to recall an ancient Chinese proverb: "When men speak of the future, the gods laugh."

Computing technology is only 70 years old, and many major communications technologies are less than 10 years old. In this historical perspective, most of our speculations about the short-term future are rather cautious. Our longer-term speculations are less cautious but plausible and most certainly sobering. Within the lifetime of our children, ICT will produce many dramatic new improvements in the quality of life, but it might also result in catastrophic consequences as well. Both analyses of the short and longer-term future of ICT point to the same conclusion. Human well-being, if not survival, will depend mostly on how well we educate youth to deal with the ethical, political, and sociological issues raised by ICT.

APPENDIX A: THE IEA SITES M1 STUDY AND DESIGN

Organization of the Study

The International Coordinating Center (ICC) of SITES M1 (Module-1) was located at the University of Twente, Center for Applied Educational Research (OCTO) in the Netherlands. The International Coordinator was Dr. W. J. Pelgrum, and the Chair of the International Steering Committee for the study was R. E. Anderson, University of Minnesota. The main funding for the international study was provided by the ministries of education of Japan, the Netherlands, and Norway. Each of the countries was represented by a National Research Coordinator who was responsible for collecting the survey data in her or his country following guidelines that had been agreed on by all participants.

Design and Development

Pilot studies were completed by June 1998, and the final questionnaires were completed by September 1998 so the survey data collection could be conducted in each country by December 1998. The national centers that participated in the study were required to submit national sampling plans that contained detailed proposals with regard to the definition of national populations and procedures for drawing the samples. The criteria for national sampling were: selection of schools with a probability proportional to the number of students from the desired target population; a response rate of at least 85% after one replacement; a minimum of 70% response rate if no replacements for non-responding schools were used or if the design was a complete enumeration. A minimum sample size of 200 computer-using schools per population level was required. The data reported here are limited to schools at the lower-secondary level, which was defined as schools containing the grade with the most 14-year-old students. Also included in the full study were primary schools and upper secondary schools. Further details can be found in Pelgrum and Anderson (1999).

APPENDIX B: METHODS OF YOUTH TECHNOLOGY SURVEYS

This appendix is a summary of the methodology of several recent surveys intended to investigate the technology-related experiences and opinions of American youth. These technology polls or surveys are summarized in Table 6.2.

Before describing each of these four surveys, some commonalities will be highlighted. It is not accidental that all deal with the Internet as the main area of concern, but the Internet topics differ as noted in the table. All reasearchers conducted their interviews during the year 2000, although the Online Victimization Survey was conducted in 1999 as well. Although the Jupiter Survey did not report details of its methodology,

TABLE 6.2. *Youth Technology Surveys*

	NPR Kids and Technology Survey	UCLA Internet Project	Online Victimization	Jupiter Media Metrix Survey
Internet topic	access, usage costs & benifits	opinions about the Internet	sexual solicitation, risks, harassment	consumer behaviour advertisement
Date of poll	December 2000	Spring 2000	Aug. 1999–Feb. 2000	August 2000
Respondent age range	10–17	12 and older	10–17	12–17
Sample size	625	2,096 including adults	1,501	1,520
Sample type	probability	probability	probability with screening	not reported
Response rate	not reported	not reported	82% of those eligible	not reported
Sampling error	+/−5%	not reported	+/−2%	not reported
Citation	NPR (2000)	Cole (2000)	Finkehor et. al. (2000)	Jupiter Media Metrix (2000)

presumably, all of the surveys used probability samples that allow for some degree of generalization to teens or young people in the United States ages 12 through 17. Actually, the NPR Survey included 10- and 11-year olds as well, and the Online Victimization Survey included the 10- and 11-year-olds and reported statistics separately by age.

It should be noted that during August 2000 the U.S. Census Bureau in their annual Current Population Survey included some questions on Internet and e-mail usage. The data from that study are not described here as their methodology is somewhat different. Specifically, one household member was selected to serve as a proxy or informant for all other members of the household. This technical summary of youth Internet surveys also does not include information about the Pew Internet Project Survey (Pew, 2001) because its sample consisted of adults 18 and older. The Pew Internet Project Survey included a large number of questions on media and technology usage; it is cited frequently as a source of information on Internet behavior.

NPR Kids and Technology Survey

This survey was sponsored by National Public Radio, the Kaiser Foundation, and the Kennedy School of Government. At about the same time, a survey of adults was conducted as well. Neither survey should be confused with the well-known survey, "Kids and Media," which was conducted in 1998 by the Kaiser Foundation (1999).

UCLA Internet Project

The UCLA Internet Project Survey was designed as a representative sample of American adults, but they interviewed a random sample of persons 12 and older. Thus, the young people can be analyzed separately and compared with older groups. A wide variety of Internet-related topics were included; however, few comparisons by age have yet been published.

Online Victimization

Although this survey was designed for the explicit purpose of investigating the incidence of several types of victimizations of young people on the Internet, some of the results do confirm the patterns of Internet utilization found in other studies. It was a carefully designed probability study, but the main youth questions were limited to households where at least one person ages 10 through 17 was a regular Internet user, defined as someone using the Internet at least once a month for the past six months. The survey interviewed the adolescent in each household who regularly used the Internet the most, and, thus, the incidence rates were slightly higher than would be found in a probability survey of all adolescents.

Jupiter Media Metrix Survey

The Jupiter Survey was conducted in the United States; however, some portions of it were replicated in other countries. This survey, and other research by Jupiter Media Metrix, is conducted for commercial purposes and is proprietary, for the most part. Thus, both the results and the methodological details are difficult to find, if not unavailable. The results that have been made available on the Web are generally consistent with findings from other surveys.

References

Anderson, R. E. (ed. 1993). *Computers in American Schools, 1992: An Overview, IEA Computers in Education Study*, Minneapolis, MN: University of Minnesota, Department of Sociology.

Anderson, R. E., and Lundmark, V. (1996). "Cross-national perspectives on inequity in computer education." In Plomp, T., Anderson, R. E., and Kontogiannopoulou-Polydorides, G. (eds.). *Cross National Policies and Practices on Computers in Education*. Dordrecht, Netherlands: Kluwer Academic Publishers.

Anderson, R. E., Lundmark, Vicki, Harris, Linda, and Magnan, Shon (1994). "Equity in computing." Pp. 352–385 in Huff, Charles and Fineholt, Tom (eds.). *Social Issues in Computing: Putting Computing in its Place*. New York: McGraw-Hill, Inc.

Anderson, R. E., and Ronnkvist, Amy. (1999). "Teaching, learning, and computing, 1998," University of California, Irvine. (http://www.crito.uci.edu/tlc/html/findings.html).

Barnes, Cecily. (2000). "Half of U.S. teens to own cell phones by 2004," CNET News (December 19). (http://news.cnet.com/news/).

Baym, N. K. (1995). "The emergence of community in computer-mediated communication." Pp. 138–163 in Jones, S. G. (ed.). *Cybersociety: Computer-Mediated Communication and Community*. Thousand Oaks, CA: Sage.

Bell, Gordon, and Gray, Jim (2001). "Digital immortality," *Communications of the ACM*, 44,3 (March):28–30.

Blurton, C. (1999). "New directions of ICT-use in education," UNESCO World Communication and Information Report, UNESCO, Paris, France.

Brummelhuis, A. C. A. (1999). "ICT-monitor 1997–1998," "*Voortgezet Onderwijs*. Enschede, the Netherlands: University of Twente, OCTO.

Chon, Kilnam (2001). "The future of the Internet digital divide," *Communications of the ACM*, 44,3 (March):116–117.

Cole, Jeffey (2000). "Surveying the digital future," The UCLA Internet Report, UCLA Center for Communication Policy, Los Angeles, CA. (http://www.ccp.ucla.edu/pages/internet-report.asp).

Collis, B., (1996). *Tele-Learning in a Digital World – The Future of Distance Learning*. London, UK: International Thomson Computer Press.

Drexler, K. Eric. (1992). *Nanosystems: Molecular Machinery, Manufacturing, and Computation*, New York: Wiley Interscience.

Finkelhor, David, Mitchell, Kimberly J., and Wolak, Janis. (2000). "Online victimization: A report on the nation's youth," National Center for Missing and Exploited Children. Alexandria, Virginia. (http://www.missingkids.com/download/nc62.pdf).

Gotcher, M., and Kanervo, E. (1997). "Perceptions and uses of electronic mail: A function of rhetorical style." *Social Science Computer Review*, 15,2:145–158.

Gurak, L. J. (1996). "The case of Lotus MarketPlace: Organization and ethos in a Net-based protest." In Herring, Susan (ed.). *Computer-Mediated Communication*. Amsterdam: John Benjamins.

Jones, S. G., (ed). (1995). *Cybersociety: Computer-Mediated Communication and Community*. Thousand Oaks, CA: Sage Publications.

Joy, Bill. (2000) "Why the future doesn't need us," *Wired*, 8,4 (April):1–11.

Jupiter Media Metrix. (2001). "Targeting teens is a gender game." (http://us.mediametrix.com/data/feature.jsp).

Kaiser Foundation. (1999). "Kids and media and the new millenium." A report of the Henry J. Kaiser Family Foundation. (http://www.kff.org/content/1999/1535/KidsReport%20FINAL.pdf).

Kiesler, S. (1985). "Affect in computer-mediated communication: An experiment in synchronous terminal-to-terminal discussion." *Human-Computer Interaction*, 1,1:77–104.

Kilger, M. (1996). "Emergence of the digital individual." Paper presented at the 1996 Conference on Computer for the Social Sciences, University of Minnesota, Minneapolis, MN, USA.

Kling, R. (ed.). (1996). *Computerization and Controversy*, 2nd edition, New York, NY: Academic Press.

Kling, Rob, and Associates. (2000). *Learning from Social Informatics*. Bloomington, Indiana: Center for Social Informatics, Indiana University.

Kraut, R. Patterson, M., Lundmark, V., Kiesler, S., Mukophadhyay, T., and Scherlis, W. (1998). "Internet paradox: A social technology that reduces social involvement and psychological well-being?" *American Psychologist*, 53,9:1017–1031.

Kurzweil, Ray. (1999). *The Age of Spiritual Machines, When Computers Exceed Human Intelligence*. New York: Viking/Penguin Books.

Kurzweil, Ray. (2000). "The future according to Ray Kurzweil," *BusinessWeek Online*. (http://www.businessweek.com/bwdaily/dnflash/june2000/nf00629i.htm).

Kurzweil, Ray. (2001). "Promise and peril – The deeply intertwined poles of 21st century technology," *Communications of the ACM*, 44,3 (March):88–91.

Lampton, C. (1993). *Nanotechnology Playhouse*. Devon, UK: Waite Group Press.

Leslie, John. (1996). *The End of the World: The Science and Ethics of Human Extinction*. New York, NY: Routledge.

Markham, A. N. (1998). *Life Online – Researching Real Experience in Virtual Space*. Walnut Creek, CA: AltaMira Press.

Matheson, K, and Zanna, M. P. (1990). "Computer-mediated communication: The focus is on me." *Social Science Computer Review*, 8,1:1–12.

Matheson, K. (1991). "Social cues in computer-mediated communication: Gender makes a difference." *Computers in Human Behavior*, 7,3:137–145.

McGrath, J. E., and Hollingshead, A. B. (1994). *Groups Interacting with Technology*. Thousand Oaks, CA: Sage.

NPR. (2000). "NPR/Kaiser/Kennedy School Kids and Technology Survey." (http://npr.org/programs/specials/poll/technology/technology. kids.html).

Orcutt, J., and Anderson, R. E. (1974). "Human-computer relationships: Interaction and attitudes," *Behavior Research Methods and Instrumentation*, 6,2 (March):219–222.

Pelgrum, W., and Anderson, R. E. (ed.). *ICT and the Emerging Paradigm for Life Long Learning: A Worldwide Educational Assessment of Infrastructure, Goals and Practices*. Amsterdam: International Association for the Evaluation of Educational Achievement, 1999.

Pelgrum, W. J., Janssen Reinen, I. A. J., and Plomp, T. (1993). Schools, Teachers, Students and Computers: A Cross-National Perspective. International Association for the Evaluation of Educational Achievement (IEA), Hague, Netherlands.

Pew. (2001). "Pew Internet Tracking Report." Pew Internet & American Life Project, Washington DC. (http://www.pewinternet.org/reports/pdfs/ PIP_Changing_Population.pdf).

Reed, Mark A., and Tour, J. M. (2000). "Computing with molecules," *Scientific American*, 282,6 (June):68–75.

Rheingold, H. (1993). *The Virtual Community; Homesteading on the Electronic Frontier*. Reading, PA: Addison-Wesley.

Robinson, J. P., and Godbey, G. (1997). *Time for Life*. University Park, PA: Pennsylvania State University Press.

Robinson, J. P., Barth, K., and Kohut, A. (1997). "Personal computers, mass media, and use of time," *Social Science Computer Review*, 15,1:65–82.

Silberman, S. (1999). "Just say Nokia." *Wired* 7, 9 September: 135–141.

Sproull, L., and Kiesler, S. (1993). "Computers, networks, and work. Global networks: Computers and international communication." Pp. 105–119 in Harasim, L. M. (ed.). Cambridge, MA: MIT.

Stewart, James, and Williams, Robin. (1998). "The coevolution of society and multimedia technology: Issues in predicting the future innovation and use of a ubiquitous technology," *Social Science Computer Review*, 16,3:268–282.

Turkle, S. (1995). *Life of the Screen: Identity in the Age of the Internet*. New York: Simon and Schuster.

U.S. Department of Commerce. (1999). "Falling through the Net: Defining the digital divide." (URL: http://www.ntia.doc.gov/ntiahome/fttn99/contents.html).

Waldo, Jim. (2001). "When the network is every think," *Communications of the ACM*, 44,3 (March):68–69.

Walther, J. B. (1992). "Interpersonal effects in computer-mediated interaction: A relational perspective, *Communication Research*, 19,1:52–90.

Weiss, Michael J. (2001). "Online America," *American Demographics* (March). (Available online at http://www.demographics.com/publications/ad/01_ad/0103_ad/ad010301.htm).

Wellman, Barry, Salaff, J., Dimitrova, D., Garton, L., Gulia, M., and Haythornthwaite, C. (1996). "Computer networks as social networks: Virtual community, computer supported cooperative work and telework," *Annual Review of Sociology* 22,1(February):213–238.

7

Social Space, the Final Frontier: Adolescents on the Internet

Kate Hellenga

The recent rapid growth of the Internet, with the advent and expansion of the World Wide Web (WWW), has engendered both optimism and concern about the potential impact of new communication technologies on our collective social future. Whence comes the vehemence with which pundits and social observers expound on the dangers of the Web or on its virtues? Computer-mediated communication (CMC) in all its forms is a new phenomenon, and its growth is so rapid that we cannot clearly imagine what forms it will take in the future. Those who imagine and predict the Internets' potential impact on our future rely on observations of earlier technological advances, such as telephones and television, and on projections of current trends in the Internets' availability, use, and effects. In spite of these common starting points, the resulting visions are remarkably polarized.

The most optimistic views of the Internet focus on the unique capabilities offered by the technology, in particular the capacity for rapid communication and collaboration across great distances. Social connectedness is a major theme. This reward-focused rhetoric emphasizes "a renewed sense of community . . . [in which] [C]omputer-mediated communication . . . will do by way of electronic pathways what cement roads were unable to do, namely, connect us rather than atomize us, put us at the controls of a 'vehicle' and yet not detach us from the rest of the world" (Jones, 1995, p. 11). Beyond this social benefit, Internet optimists point out the growth of new literary and artistic forms, especially interactive forms, which blur the boundary between the creator and the audience.

The democratization of information is another boundary shift made possible by the Internet and emphasized in the reward-focused view of this new medium (Cartlidge, 1998). In the near future, some say, Internet access will be so cheap as to become universal (Barlow, 1999). When that happens, previously disenfranchised individuals and communities will gain what has been denied them for so long, the powers of knowledge and widespread communication; the pedagogy of the oppressed can be made real in the virtual world. For adolescents, this positive vision might include increased self-esteem and a sense of "voice" for marginalized youth and communities, a stronger sense of global culture, a greater interest in worldwide politics and events, or a sharpened ability to see connections among superficially disparate issues (e.g., feminism and Green politics).

Internet optimists focus on the increased social connections made possible by online communication, while Internet pessimists attend more to the ways that online activity will dehumanize us, damaging or diminishing existing, offline social connections. Thus we are warned of the dangers of computer-mediated connections: the decrease in social skills and intimacy (Robson & Robson, 1998), the potential for misinformation and exploitation, and the possibilities of "Internet addiction" (Young, 1996). One author describes the World Wide Web as "a giant wanking machine . . . [that] offers an illusion of intimacy to disguise the isolated, addictive, desensitizing reality of the experience" (Aitkenhead, 1998, p. 13). Skeptics point out the ease with which one can adopt a false identity and with which government entities and corporations can follow the electronic tracks made by individuals who believe their Internet conversations and Web explorations are private. From this perspective, adolescents who spend too much time online run the risks of losing their friends, their mental health, or their social skills, being made prey to all manners of exploitation and falsehood, or even becoming online addicts or delinquents (e.g., 17-year-old hacker "Coolio" (CNN, 2000)).

Adolescents may be particularly likely to encounter the rewards and risks of Internet activity. Adolescence is a stage of life generally understood to represent a shift from immersion in the family to increasing connections with the larger social world, from parent-defined to self- and peer-influenced identity and values. Given the developmental task of negotiating a relationship with "the wider world," adolescents may be disproportionately affected by current and future changes in communication technologies, which make available increasing amounts and types of information and which increase contacts with a variety of cultures, personal styles, and values. Considering the current rate of growth of the Internet's infrastructure and the rapid changes in Internet technology (e.g., wireless, high-speed fiber, and satellite connections), many adolescents will soon have access to each other, and to vast quantities of information worldwide.

How accurate are the reward- and risk-focused assessments of the Internet's impact, and how will adolescents' experience of themselves and their world be affected by their online interactions? Much like teenagers' parents, we need to begin asking where they are going, what they are doing with whom and with what probable results. To begin answering these questions, we first need to know how adolescents use media in general, and how they use computers and the Internet in particular. In this chapter I review research that suggests adolescents are indeed making use of the Internet, especially those functions allowing for interpersonal connection and conversation. The social space created by the Internet has unique qualities which do, indeed, present both risks and rewards for adolescent users. I will address these aspects of Internet activity in the second section of the chapter, and I will close with a set of predictions about the likely directions that adolescents' Internet use, and its effects, will take in years to come.

ADOLESCENT INTERNET USE

Current trends in computer access and Internet growth suggest that many adolescents will have access to the Internet in the near future. However, rates of growth and access differ markedly across class and ethnicity within nations, and across nations and geographic regions worldwide. These inequities are larger for home computer use and Internet access than for public site and school access (Anderson, this volume). However, this paper will focus on adolescents' home computer use and Internet access, on the assumption that use at home is more likely to represent freely chosen activity types than school or public terminal use might. In school or at a library, Internet access may be restricted to certain sites or activities, and there may also be time requirements (e.g., minimum time in order to ensure adequate exposure to new technology in the schools, maximum time to allow equal access to numerous users in schools or libraries). Anderson (this volume) provides a more detailed discussion of Internet availability and impact in schools.

Observing current trends in adolescents' adoption and use of the Internet provides a focus for discussing future uses and their effects. However, reliable research on actual Internet use is somewhat scarce at this time, presumably because the field is relatively new and because Internet research presents numerous challenges to traditional research methodologies. Direct observation of individuals is likely to affect their activity choices; remote observation by logging accessed sites provides no guarantee of the user's identity and limits Internet observation to the World Wide Web, which is only one of many possible Internet uses (see Appendix A of this chapter for a discussion of possible online activities). Some studies ask participants to describe their online time each day, but respondents' reports tend to be somewhat inaccurate (Subrahmanyam et al., 2001) and tend to leave out those activities considered embarrassing or unacceptable. Online surveying is a relatively new study method, appealing for its availability to a wide audience of Internet users. The Internet does not have a universal "broadcast" mechanism, so these surveys are likely to reach only a select group of Internet users. For this reason, the generalizability of the resulting data is limited. In addition, online surveys are susceptible to repeat responses and false responses by users without adequate means of verifying respondents' identities.

In spite of numerous methodological difficulties, research on individuals' Internet activity does exist, although it focuses primarily on United States citizens. The following discussion presents relevant data from several Internet use studies. Variations in the dates, methods, and age-group aggregations of the studies referenced limit the validity of direct comparisons. However, in combination with information about young peoples' use of other media, the available data do begin to answer some basic questions about adolescents' Internet use and its relationship to other activities.

Adolescents use computers and prefer them to other media; young people are rapidly claiming the new technology as their own. In a study of 820 young people (Roberts et al., 1999), with respondents chosen to represent the U.S. population in terms of demographics, 8–13- and 14–18-year-olds identified computers as their most preferred medium (in comparison to six other types, such as books and magazines, television, CDs and tapes, etc.).[1] The standing of computers increases greatly

[1] Based on participants' choices from a list of media (radio, TV, CDs/tapes, etc.), in response to the following question: "If you were going to a desert island (OK, a desert

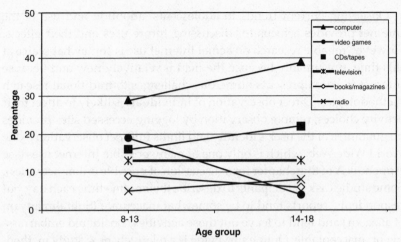

FIGURE 7.1. Media preferences by age group.
Source: Kaiser Family Foundation, 1999.

over that of other media for adolescents (see Figure 7.1), compared with younger children. Twenty-nine percent of 8–13-year-olds preferred the computer to any other medium, followed by 19% for video games. However, computers were the preferred medium for 39% of 14–18-year-olds, whereas only 4% identified video games as their most preferred medium. Adolescents' daily computer use does not appear to reflect their increased (i.e., more likely) preference for computers. Both children (8–13) and adolescents (14–18) reported using computers about 50 minutes daily, with 30 minutes (7% of both groups' total daily media time) devoted to recreational use (Roberts et al., 1999). Adolescents' current interest in computers is likely to drive the production and marketing of teen-oriented software, Web sites, and online activities, thus encouraging future generations of teens to further incorporate computers and Internet activity into their everyday lives.

When teens get online, they are likely to spend time "going places" on the Internet and "talking to people" via e-mail. This is congruent with the concept of adolescence as a time of exploring the world and social relationships. Although the amount of time spent with computers does not appear to change significantly from childhood to adolescence, the specific activities in which young people engage do shift with age. Of particular interest is the move toward online activities; adolescents

island with electricity), and you could take only one of the following things, which would you choose?" (Roberts et al., 1999)

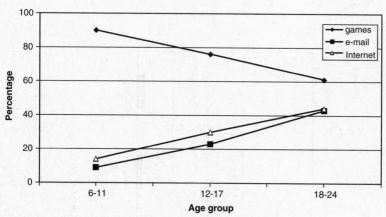

FIGURE 7.2. Use of home computer functions, by age group.
Source: U.S. Census Bureau, 1999 (data corrected by U.S. Census 3/20/00).
Note: Data are for all home computer users, rather than Internet users alone.

are more likely than their younger counterparts to use the computer for e-mail and Internet functions and less likely to use it for games. Figure 7.2 shows the percentages of respondents to a 1997 U.S. Census survey who reported using computer games, e-mail, and the Internet. The graph indicates a trend of increasing preference for online activity with development from childhood through emerging adulthood. Teens may like the Internet more as they develop online relationships and discover the "frontiers" of Internet content and capabilities.

A closer analysis of adolescents' online activities suggests that the Internet's social functions in particular are attractive to teenagers. Figure 7.3 provides a breakdown of the online activities of 12–17-year-old Internet users, again using data from the 1997 U.S. Census survey. Although the most popular choice was searching for information, the next two are social functions: e-mail and chat rooms. Notably, these data reveal that adolescents are more likely to visit chat rooms at some time than any other age group (40%, as opposed to 28% for younger children and an average of 25% for the 18–24 and 25–49 age groups) (U.S. Census Bureau, 1999). In a separate study, nearly 40% of 11–20-year-old respondents accessed chat groups *daily or weekly*. Of those "frequent" chat group users, the majority (60%) considered chat groups an indispensable Internet function (Georgia Tech Research Corporation, 1998). The respondents in the latter study were much less representative of the current U.S. population than the census respondents. According to the researchers, their respondents were recruited largely through

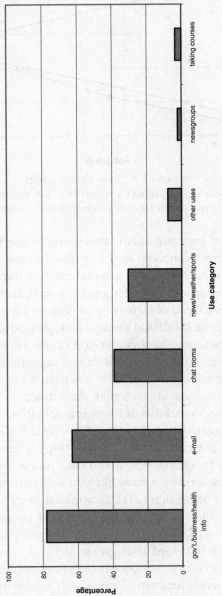

FIGURE 7.3. Internet uses by 12–17-year-olds.
Source: U.S. Census Bureau, 1999 (data corrected by U.S. Census 3/20/00).

online advertising and were much more active and knowledgeable computer users than the average American. Their strong involvement in chat rooms may be a harbinger of things to come as Internet access increases and adolescents familiarize themselves with this new territory. Teenagers may be especially drawn to chat rooms, which combine direct, immediate interaction with relative anonymity for users, allowing risk-free observation and practicing of social skills. These unique social conditions also hold great potential for changing the experience of adolescence, as I will argue in the next section of this chapter.

At first glance, the focus of adolescents' chat room activity also seems to indicate predominantly social interests. According to the Roberts et al. (1999) study, adolescents are most likely to visit chat rooms dealing with "relationships and lifestyles" (40% of respondents) followed by "entertainment" (33%) and "hobbies or groups" (17%). For Web sites, entertainment (60%), sports (30%), and search engines (22%) were the most likely categories for the same age group. Web sites dealing with relationships and lifestyles were less popular, receiving only 8% of reported hits. Without a clear idea of the relative availability of chat room and Web site types, these data are somewhat difficult to interpret. Research concerning stated preferences (as opposed to reported chat room or Web site visits), overall availability of different site types, and the amount of time users spend in each type would be an appropriate next step in understanding adolescents' online activities.

Although we don't know how long teenagers spend at particular sites, we do have information about how much time they are spending online. As noted earlier, average daily computer use for 14–18-year-olds totals approximately 50 minutes. Adolescent "computer users" (students who had used a computer the day before they responded to the survey), however, spend twice as much time (1 hour, 37 minutes) using the computer. Of those 97 minutes, 37 (38%) are spent online (Roberts et al., 1999). Figure 7.4 depicts 14–18-year-olds' time spent in various computer-related activities, including e-mail, chat rooms and the WWW.

Adolescents are clearly incorporating computers and the Internet into their daily lives, but they still use computers less than they watch television. American adolescents average about two hours of television viewing daily (Robinson & Bianchi, 1997, cited in Larson & Verma, 1999); this is more than twice as long as the average adolescent's daily use of computers, and about three times as long as recent computer users' daily time on the Internet. The discrepancy between television and online time is at least partly a result of greater home access to television than to computers. Nearly all (99%) 14–18-year-olds in the Roberts and

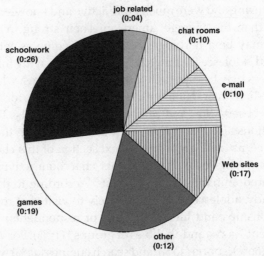

FIGURE 7.4. Computer use time (minutes per day), 14–18-year-old computer users.
Source: Kaiser Family Foundation, 1999.

colleagues (1999) study lived in a home with at least one television; only 79% had at least one home computer, and 54% had Internet access. Teenagers may also be less interested in computers and the Internet or less comfortable using them. The relatively Internet-savvy adolescents in the online Georgia Tech survey may provide a glimpse into the future, when access, interest, and comfort levels are likely to have increased. Thirty-three percent of Georgia Tech respondents reported using their WWW browsers between 10 and 20 hours a week, and another 34% reported spending 20 to 40 or more hours per week browsing the Web, far surpassing average adolescents' television, computer, or Internet use. The majority of adolescent Georgia Tech respondents (64%) reported using the Web instead of watching television on a daily basis. Indeed, nearly 90% of Georgia Tech respondents stated that among Internet capabilities, the WWW and e-mail are indispensable (Georgia Tech Research Corporation, 1998).

The Georgia Tech respondents, 11–20-year-olds who use the Internet frequently, consider it a crucial tool, and develop skills beyond just "pointing and clicking" (e.g., creating a Web page, customizing a browser startup page), may represent the first wave of teenagers' future on the Net. In other words, they perceive and use the Internet much the way the average American might use a telephone or electronic appliance. The Internet's current rapid growth suggests that using it will become commonplace, an unremarkable feature of everyday life, within the next few decades. That has already happened for a small segment of the U.S. population, represented in part by the Georgia Tech respondents. Thus we might predict that the average adolescent of the future will spend much more time online than is currently the case and may replace some daily activities with Internet use. Today's "average" adolescents use chat rooms and e-mail more than any other Internet function (excluding information searches), implying a specific attraction for the social-connections potential of the Internet. As social explorers seeking to develop their own identities and connect to a world beyond the family, adolescents will probably continue to seek new social experiences and information online. We can more fully grasp the impact, and the potential risks and rewards, of the interplay between adolescent development and Internet activity if we have some idea of what online life can be like.

THE INTERNET AS A UNIQUE SOCIAL SPACE

The Internet has evolved and has been conceptualized thus far as a reality which is separate from our everyday lives; discussions of "cyberspace" and "virtual reality," contrasted with activities "IRL" (in real life, a commonly used e-mail and chatroom acronym) suggest that one can "enter" the Internet world, thus leaving everyday life behind. It seems unlikely that those individuals who constitute and create the social world of the Internet are suddenly freed of their usual complement of values and behavioral norms. However, online interaction does present certain freedoms and opportunities which are generally unavailable in more traditionally created social connections. Current and future adolescents will be spending at least some of their time interacting with others in a "place" which imposes very few limits on speech, behavior, or relationships. The Internet has many liberties, each of which is likely to attract and affect teenagers in different ways.

Freedom from External Controls

Cyberspace is a place of anarchy. In spite of the role of the U.S. government in developing the technology, the Internet has become a decentralized and user-controlled communications medium. In fact, the Federal Communications Commission (FCC) acknowledges the potential for government regulation to hinder growth and development, and encourages governments to maintain a hands-off approach, in order to encourage further growth across the globe (FCC, 1999). The Net was originally developed by the government and by universities, to be used primarily for military research and exchange of research information. Thus, early personal uses (e.g., e-mail and chat, newsgroups) subverted the Net's original purpose by taking advantage of the absence of absolute authority and defined laws of use.

The development of "freeware" (e.g., Linux), operating systems and software provided online without charge and developed voluntarily by users and programmers worldwide (Linux International, 1999), exemplifies the "anarchic collective" ethos of at least a subset of frequent Internet users, undermining or ignoring typical approaches to product development and intellectual property. Linux continues to be freely available to anyone, and its popularity has led for-profit software developers (e.g., Corel, makers of WordPerfect) to provide Linux-based versions of their products, as well as the standard Macintosh and Windows platform versions. The Internet is, apparently, a "place" where the collective voice can rapidly gain influence.

Adolescents' participation in Internet "anarchies" such as freeware development has not yet been quantified. If that participation requires programming skills and a great deal of time, it will probably be restricted to a small group of teens. However, increasing awareness of the potential for involvement without age restrictions may lead to other uses of the Internet for "subversive" purposes. This defiant, activist aspect of Internet culture may have a certain appeal for adolescents seeking avenues of rebellion against authority. Because the Internet is still relatively new and very large, adolescents can participate in activities their parents have neither heard of nor imagined, and can feel like a part of something separate from their parents' influence.

Freedom to Take What You Want

Music piracy is a relatively common form of illicit online activity which requires only basic Internet know-how. MP3's are digitized recordings of music, much of which is copyrighted. They are made available by individuals, free of charge, on the Net; Internet businesses such as MP3.com and Napster have created programs that allow individuals to procure and provide MP3's more easily. Adolescents are getting involved in online music trading in increasing numbers. For instance, at the University of Illinois at Urbana-Champaign, whose computer networks provide Internet access to more than 26,000 undergraduates, the Internet security director identifies as many as 30 students per week engaged in music piracy (Wood, 2000). Recording companies and artists are attempting to fight this trend in court (Gray, 1999; Snyder, 2000). To settle one lawsuit, Napster was required to set up a paid subscription service for music trading, promising payment of licensing fees to music artists and publishers whose products are made available at the site (Borland, 2001). Napster faces additional lawsuits for copyright infringement, but the larger fight against online MP3 trading will be difficult to win. Trading on newer MP3 sites has far surpassed Napster's total trading volume (*Wired News*, 2001), and the total population of non-Napster services nearly quintupled between March and August of 2001 (Manjoo, 2001). Furthermore, many musicians encourage online trading, MP3 server sites are multiplying, and individual users can evade detections with ease.

The gap between legal mandate and practical enforceability is an ideal place for adolescent limit-testing to take hold. Indeed, students have labeled as censorship universities' attempts to limit their access to Napster, and thus their MP3 trading (Hilty, 2000). This above-ground resistance is coupled with the underground development of Napster-like programs and continued shifting of MP3 sites to avoid discovery by authorities. Popular music is a mainstay of adolescent culture, and the ability to download huge quantities of music, illegally and free of charge, offers adolescents a chance to connect with each other while still participating in a rebellious act. Assuming adolescents remain interested in popular music over the years, they will likely continue to make use of MP3's and other media as they become available online, whether or not the practice is legal.

Freedom to Make and Break Rules

The absence of centralized controls and enforcement techniques, in combination with a new and rapidly expanding technology, also makes room for fringe elements in the online community. "Cyberdelinquency" is not an uncommon phenomenon. Viruses are created by individuals for no apparent purpose other than to "gum up" the workings of large groups of anonymous individuals or organizations; similarly, a mode of hacking known as "smurfing" has evolved on IRC (chat) channels. This latter form is practiced by individuals sometimes known as "script kiddies," so labeled because they are usually adolescents who copy "scripts" created by more experienced programmers, without actually understanding how the program works. These scripts are used, among other things, to "invade" IRC channels being moderated by rivals. In this process, the "attacker" hacks into networked computers and manipulates them such that they send vast quantities of information to the victims' own computer, through which that victim controls a particular IRC channel. In this case, control includes the ability to permit or deny channel access to other users, so that the channel becomes a "clique" of sorts. Preventing such control allows the attacker to take over, subsequently denying access to the victim and other rivals. The recent distributed denial of service attacks on several major public Internet sites such as yahoo.com, allegedly made by a 17-year-old (CNN, 2000) are another, more pernicious example of this type of activity.

Although these attacks are not damaging to the individuals themselves (unlike physical fights, which are perhaps the closest parallel in regular adolescent interactions), except perhaps for blows to the ego, they wreak havoc on those computers and networks which are used as "weapons" in the attack. The chosen computers are not necessarily in physical proximity to the attacker or the victim (by virtue of the Internets' worldwide links, they can even be on other continents), they are simply vulnerable machines to which the attacker gains access. The result is a breakdown in network communications, sometimes across large sections of the network, because the data flow from hacked machines is so enormous that nothing else can pass through.

Not all "hacking" is intended to cause harm or even wreak havoc. *The Ultimate Beginner's Guide to Hacking and Phreaking* (Revelation, 1996), one of many online introductions to the ethics and practice of hacking, provides a typical definition of hacking as "the act of penetrating computer systems to gain knowledge about the system and how it works." Levy (cited in Denning, 1996) identifies two key principles of a so-called hacker ethic. The first is that "[a]ccess to computers – and anything which might teach you something about the way the world works – should be unlimited and total," and the second is that "all information should be free" (p. 141). These statements, which are echoed in numerous online discussions of hacking, seem to express some deeper philosophical basis than what we might assume for more traditional forms of delinquency, such as shoplifting and vandalism. Perhaps hackers with this particular bent, who are likely to believe that "malicious hacking is morally wrong" and are "concerned about causing accidental damage" (Denning, 1996) are different from those described above, who seem to have no qualms about causing problems for others. Certainly they are pushing the boundaries of our understanding of information, property, and the reason for limiting access to certain types of knowledge.

Hacking is not likely to become the next wave of delinquent behavior for adolescents. The relative number of individuals participating in this type of activity is probably extremely small and will remain so. Most people using Internet services are not particularly skilled in programming or hacking, nor are they interested in these capabilities. The average teenager, spending only about 40 minutes online per day, would not have adequate time to become a successful hacker. However, in the same way that a subset of adolescents engages in other negative behaviors, such as shoplifting or fighting, there will be a group of adolescents who are attracted to hacking. The stereotype of the socially awkward teenage male hacker may become less accurate as more adolescents begin exploring the Internet, and hacking may become slightly more common among adolescents.

Although anarchy, piracy, and hacking can have an enormous effect on their targets, especially in the world of online commerce, their negative impact on teenagers will probably be insignificant. Hacking has the most potential for the expression of antisocial urges, but it requires technical skill, planning and sustained attention, unlike the impulsive action of shoplifting or violence. Increasingly common knowledge of "hacker culture," the MP3 controversy, or non-commercial software development may lead adolescents to perceive more flexibility in social rules and laws, such that "received wisdom" can be questioned not as a reflexive act of defiance, but as an exploration of possibilities beyond the constraints of conventional thinking. This is not to say that hacking and copyright violation are not potentially problematic, simply that they are no more problematic than similar offline behaviors, and their online forms may have a broader social effect because of the Internet's ubiquity. For instance, Anderson (this volume) discusses the impact of communication technologies, including the Internet, on cheating and plagiarism, and the associated challenges to the teaching and enforcement of ethical standards.

Freedom to Explore Sexuality

The proliferation of sexual content and activity on the Internet is potentially appealing to adolescents, and a source of concern for the adults who guide their development. Taking advantage of the relative freedom of cyberspace, and the apparent willingness of some subset of the population to pay for the privilege of viewing sexually explicit materials, numerous entrepreneurs set up pornography sites. In addition, a subset of newsgroups (e.g., alt.sex.stories, alt.sex.bondage, alt.sex.spanking) have emerged which offer sexually explicit stories and/or downloadable digitized photographs of pornographic materials. A frequently-quoted statistic suggests that "more than 80 percent of all hits on the Internet are to pornographic sites" (Aitkenhead, 1998); the veracity of this statistic is somewhat questionable. However, when I entered the word "sex" into a standard Web search engine (in November, 1999), I had more than 17,000,000 "hits," the great majority of which appeared, based on a sample of the first 100 URLs, to be devoted to "adult content" rather than to education or philosophical discussions.

The Communications Decency Act (CDA) was passed in the United States in 1996, in an effort to censor such sexual content, but the CDA's final form was limited to criminalizing provision of "patently offensive" materials to individuals under the age of 18, and requiring "effective" measures to verify the age of potential viewers. While it was and is an admirable goal to provide young people some guidance as they explore the Internet and learn about sexuality, the CDA's requirements were impossible to implement effectively (access can be restricted to those users who confirm that they are over 18, but actual verification of a user's age is not possible), and the CDA was eventually struck down because it effectively censored free speech online (ACLU, 1997). A second version, the Child Online Protection Act, was also challenged and deemed unconstitutional (ACLU, 2000(A)), but in December 2000, Congress mandated public libraries and schools to use blocking software geared to prevent access to materials deemed "harmful to minors" (ACLU, 2000(B)). The legislative focus on minors is notable here, as it emphasizes the potentially disproportionate impact of Internet sexual content and freedom on young people, particularly adolescents, who may be likely to seek sexual content online as part of their individual explorations of sexuality.

The prevalence of pornographic materials on the Web can be a problem even for teenagers who do not intentionally seek them out. Adolescents using search engines on the WWW can gain access to more age-appropriate materials concerning health and sexuality; doing so is, in theory, no more difficult than finding "entertainment," including pornography. However, the sheer numbers of pornography sites far outweigh those of sites discussing sexual health (Shpritz, 1997). Even non-sex-related searches yield surprisingly high numbers of pornography hits. Twenty-five percent of 10–17-year-old Americans in a recent study (Finkelhor, Mitchell, and Wolak, 2000) said they had experienced undesired exposure to online pornographic materials, with Web surfing and searching as the primary vectors for the unwanted contact. Adolescents in this study were also confronted with pornographic materials via e-mail and instant messaging. The very openness and freedom that allow teens to learn about sexuality online may also foist sexual content upon unwary and naive youth. The Finkelhor et al. (2000) study showed that of those youth who had unwanted contact with sexually explicit material online, about one quarter were upset by the experience. Filtering software is designed to prevent these problems, but these programs and services have inconsistent success in preventing access to pornography (Magid, 2000). They may also intentionally or inadvertently filter out non-pornographic material such as family planning and sexual health. With the new federal mandate for libraries and schools to use filtering software, American adolescents' access to sexual material, whether pornographic or educational, may be quite limited for a time. However, pornography will likely continue to proliferate on the Web, and interested adolescents will probably continue to seek out or unexpectedly encounter online sexual material. Online filtering is a clumsy method for addressing this important issue, and the Internet is highly resistant to outright censorship. These factors, combined with adults' interest in guiding young people's introduction to sexuality, may hasten a shift from traditional but uncomfortable silences to more direct personal and cultural conversations about pornography and sexuality.

It is possible for adolescents (and others) to engage in sexual activity online; in addition to chat rooms devoted to "dating" and in some cases to more explicit sexual conversation, users have the opportunity to create a "private chat room" where they can converse unobserved by the rest of the chat room members. The same is true for MUDs and MOOs (see Appendix A, this chapter), in which people can enter rooms and "lock" them, subsequently engaging in a sexual exchange. Data are not yet available concerning the extent to which adolescents seek sexual information and contact online. However, this life stage is associated with sexual maturation, along with curiosity and concern about sex and relationships. As noted previously, adolescents currently favor social uses of the Internet, such as e-mail and chat. In combination, these characteristics provide ample motivation and opportunity for sexual exploration online. Whether or not teens are more likely than other age groups to engage in this activity, its impact may be stronger for adolescents and young adults who have only limited life (or sexual) experience in which to ground their online experiences.

Freedom to Explore Identity and Political Action

The Internet may spark a new wave of political activism among young people. Consciousness raising groups in the 1960s and 1970s combined the personal and the political in building a feminist social/political movement, and grassroots organizing was the modus operandi of young peoples' political change efforts during that era. Now the Internet has become a "meeting place" and a worldwide bulletin board for a vast array of cultural subgroups, political movements, and members of minority groups who would not normally have access to other people "like them." Personal and organizational Web pages, as well as topic-oriented support groups (both newsgroups and chat rooms) provide a variety of ways in which people can share information and support with a much wider network of people than they might otherwise be able to approach.

As adolescents explore their own values and identities, and struggle with issues that may not be easily discussed with parents or peers (e.g., sexuality, depression, and suicidality), Internet communication can provide information and emotional support in a relatively safe and anonymous way. !OutProud! (www.queer.com, www.outproud.org), for instance, is a site developed by the National Coalition for Gay, Lesbian, Bisexual, and Transgender Youth. The Web site offers an archive of coming out stories, publications discussing sexual orientation-related issues, lists of resources across the country, and perhaps most importantly, a message board. In the "high school" forum, discussion topics include gay-straight alliances, social activities, lesbigay student rights, and "queers should be shot," in which several homophobic statements have been posted and subsequently refuted by other readers.

Adolescents are already seeking social contact and information online, using chat rooms, e-mail, and WWW information searches. Once familiar with the Internet-based tools of connection and activism, adolescents are likely to begin creating online spaces for themselves, rather than waiting passively for desired forums to appear. Ethnic and sexual identities may be strengthened and established through online contacts, adding a new facet to the already complex picture of adolescent development and acculturation. It appears that the gay/lesbian/bisexual/transgendered community has already recognized the benefits offered by online communication, and is becoming a leader in Internet activism and support. Other traditionally oppressed or voiceless groups are also claiming space online. Online support groups and information will have an enormous positive impact on

Internet-savvy teenagers in decades to come. Young people who have no other avenues for discussing issues of identity and bigotry will be most likely to benefit. They will also be most vulnerable to misinformation and rhetoric masquerading as fact. This is a common problem on the Net, a forum largely devoid of content control and verification. As with pornography, the decades to come will likely require educators and parents to engage in direct, open conversation about historically uncomfortable or taboo topics, to support teens as they encounter the Internet's flood of information, opinion, and rhetoric.

Freedom of Self-presentation

My description of the Internet as a social realm has focused thus far on those aspects of the online "world" which parallel more familiar, "real-life" cultural and individual experiences. Clearly, though, the Internet is not simply a new location to which people can go and do the same things they have always done. Internet communication is qualitatively distinct from other forms of communication, even while it shares some features with those older forms (e.g., the text-only format of e-mail, Internet chat, and letter writing). Social relationships online are based in exchanges of text. Multimedia interaction, whether in games or in video conferencing, is a recent development, but technological limitations on bandwidth and (therefore) on speed of transmission make these forms somewhat unsatisfying at this point. Most multiuser adventure-type games (MUDs, MOOs, etc.) are text-based, such that entering a MUSH (see Appendix A, this chapter) combines elements of story telling, role-playing games (choosing an action and awaiting the result, as decided by the "dungeon master" or in this case the program itself) and social interaction. It is the combination of text-only communication and mutual anonymity that makes the Internet a truly unique social space.

Interaction on the Web can include elements of both letter-writing and telephone conversations. However, online interactions have a very different "flavor" from more traditional modes of long-distance contact, because one can communicate with complete anonymity to unknown numbers of unknown others. "Anonymous users can switch genders, appearances, and countless other usually integral aspects of the public self. People can also take on multiple identities" (Baym, 1995, p. 154). For adolescents experimenting with social selves, and struggling with the incongruity between an internal sense of emerging adulthood and an external experience of being treated "like a child," the potential for "maximum self-presentation by commission and omission" (Schnarch, 1997) may be particularly appealing.

According to Erikson, the main task of adolescence is to resolve an identity crisis, to "form a stable sense of self-identity" rather than experiencing "the self as a series of scattered, disconnected, and inconsistent poses and roles" (Alexander, Roodin & Gorman, 1980, p. 49). Reading the latter description might lead to the conclusion that adolescents experimenting with self-presentation on the Net would be developmentally damaged by the experience. However, identity-play on the Net is often done consciously and for fun; individuals must actively choose to represent their gender, personality, interests, or conversational style in a particular way. Tapscott's (1998) online observation and discussion with over 300 young people suggested that these Internet-savvy youth understand and accept that their Net acquaintances might be presenting a false front. Perhaps the power to choose and inhabit a different persona can be beneficial to adolescents. Net relationships are relatively risk free, and the consequences of various behaviors can be seen or experienced virtually, without affecting the person's offline life. This safe form of identity-exploration will become more common as adolescents gain access to and comfort with the social world of the Internet.

Adolescents who become familiar with the Internet will have access to a new realm of possibilities for behavior, learning, and social contact. The liberties presented here combine aspects of "real-life" behavior, such as theft, sexual experimentation, social support, and identity exploration, with unique features of life online: decentralized or non-existent government, anonymity, and rapid access to vast numbers of people and quantities of information. To some degree, then, online adolescent behavior will parallel "real-life" behavior from pre-Internet eras. A small group of teens will find ways to misbehave and test limits, though the limits are likely in many cases to be set by their parents rather than by online authorities. Many adolescents will use the Internet primarily for e-mail and chat; they may talk only with friends from school, but over time they will probably make friends online with young people from other places. Gathering information about sensitive topics in private, or claiming a different identity for an online conversation, will appeal to teenagers' interest in discovering the world beyond their own family, and discovering their own values and self-image. At the same time, longstanding approaches to the protection of young people from uncomfortable or confusing issues are likely to lose their effectiveness. Online exploration can expose adolescents to numerous viewpoints not generally shared in their own families or communities. Current trends toward more direct, open discussion of difficult issues, such as drug use and sexuality, will continue as concerned adults seek new ways to guide adolescents' exploration of behavior and values.

EFFECT OF ONLINE INTERACTION ON SOCIAL RELATIONSHIPS

The Internet is a "social space" whose customs and capacities combine unique freedoms with features of more traditional social systems. This combination of familiar and unfamiliar conditions can be fertile ground for changes in social behavior, norms and culture, both on- and off-line. Adolescents are already making the Internet a regular part of their learning and social lives; they will pioneer some of these new ways of thinking and being. Their online activity will, and already does, call into question the ownership of knowledge, the nature of platonic and romantic relationships, and the constitution and permanence of identity. Wallace (1999) discusses the psychology of the Internet for adults, identifying important areas of difference from offline life, such as impression management, identity and deception, aggression, and intimacy. These online differences will have a distinct and perhaps greater impact for adolescents, whose chief developmental task may be to learn about and experience a world outside the limits of adult supervision and family life. To assess the effects of online social experiences on adolescents in the future, we must consider specific social activities as they are carried out online.

Appearance, Gender, and Race

Although the ability of the Internet to transmit images is increasing rapidly, it is unlikely that text-based communication will ever be completely eliminated. Transmission of text requires less sophisticated equipment, is simpler and cheaper, and takes up less bandwidth than live transmission of visual or audio data. Telephone conversations complement letter writing, rather than replacing it; e-mail has complemented these earlier forms of communication, and visual transmission will do the same. To the extent that text-based contact represents a significant portion of all online communications, it is reasonable to explore the potential effects of text-based media on the lives and perceptions of adolescents. Considering the absence of visual cues, one might imagine a relative social utopia (especially for self-conscious teens) where one is included or excluded based on the ideas or personality they present online. However, the text-based and appearance-free world still has several problems. Verbal skills are suddenly at a premium in online conversation; a teenager may have difficulty masquerading as someone older, given a perhaps more limited amount of experience or vocabulary. Similarly, people who cannot read, or who do not speak English, will have limited access to the social worlds being created on line.

In spite of the potential for release from traditional visually-based categorization, gender and race still garner attention in online conversation. Upon entering a chat room or a newsgroup conversation, one will soon be asked "are you male or female?" or more simply "RUMorF?" (Kollock & Smith, 1999) if gender is not evident from one's screen name. Schnarch (1997) speculates that because more men are involved in online communication than women, "some men regularly sign on using women's names because they get to chat with more people" (p. 17), while "many women users report that they attempt to pass as men so that they will be 'taken seriously,' or to avoid what many participants suggest is an unusually high level of sexual harassment' (O'Brien, 1999, p. 91). O'Brien's observations run contrary to the "gender-free utopia" vision of the Internet; she suggests that "it is theoretically implausible that the charting of the new frontier of cyberspace will consist of original forms" (O'Brien, 1999, p. 95).

Indeed, based on a qualitative study of 47 adolescent Internet users, Clark (1998, p. 166) reports that girls, seeking to "strengthen their position in the [online] dating interaction . . . reported that they adopt new physical personae, describing their looks in such a way as to appear more attractive to the males." Clark suggests that this takes some power away from the young men involved, as visual cues are not available to allow them to evaluate the girls' appearance; however, these same girls, whatever their appearances may be, will eventually be interested in face-to-face interactions with boys. Their online presentation supports the dominant view that physical attractiveness is paramount, rather than subverting that viewpoint, a strategy which may prove more effective in face-to-face relationships.

Burkhalter's (1999, p. 73) research involved observation of numerous Usenet (newsgroup) discussions; he asserts that racial stereotyping occurs online as well, but in a way which reverses the usual form. "Stereotyping in face-to-face interaction follows from an assumed racial identity. Online interaction differs in that the imputation tends to go in the other direction – from stereotype to racial identity" such that statements reflecting "typical" Black or White sentiments will lead readers to assume the writer's ethnicity accordingly. Burkhalter's (1999) discussion also points out that perceived discrepancies between a writer's stated ethnicity and his or her expressed views are likely to result in direct challenges to that individual's claimed racial identity. Thus an adolescent whose social time is spent online will still encounter the constructions of gender and ethnicity so common, and to some so objectionable, in offline/face-to-face interaction.

However, as Internet communication becomes more common, it is possible that people will develop separate sets of expectations and behaviors for their interactions on- and off-line. In this "separate worlds" scenario, one would attend to a speaker's gender or skin color, in face-to-face interaction, because of cultural habit and the human tendency to seek visual categorization cues. This same person might then go online and engage in a discussion or an interactive game, and never think to question the gender or race of the other participants; these cues may become irrelevant over time in our Internet communications. One source of this irrelevancy is the somewhat superficial nature of many online connections; newsgroup participants may become familiar with each others' verbal styles, but may never know the details of their lives. Thus questions about race or gender might be set aside until an interaction becomes more personal and connected: when a discussion moves people from acquaintance into friendship. Gender will, of course, always be more obvious online for those people using their real names, but even this may be confounded as the online population becomes more international in character. Furthermore, the relative unimportance of gender to online interaction may lead to diminished interest in that categorization.

Even with separate sets of expectations and curiosities for on- and off-line communication, it is quite likely that online communication styles will increasingly influence offline interactions. Bruce (1997) discusses the common misconception of technology and social reality as completely distinct entities, with technology "acting upon" a passive culture or vice versa. More accurate, he argues, is a picture of bidirectional influences between technology and social relations. The direction of influence appears to be largely unidirectional at this time, from traditional to newer modes (e.g., online resumes look very much like paper resumes; online newspapers have only begun to look different from their doorstep counterparts). As Internet communication becomes more familiar, the influence may work in both directions, thus leading people to question the importance of gender and race to their categorizations of people in their day to day lives.

Deception and Exploitation

Computer-mediated communication's capacity for "identity play" has negative connotations as well. Online interaction has great potential for deception, especially regarding one's own identity. In single interactions or posts to newsgroups, misrepresenting one's identity is probably harmless, unless it involves claiming another's identity. However, the same deception in an ongoing relationship can be quite damaging to the deceived person should they discover the truth; for instance, Van Gelder (cited in Robson & Robson, 1998) describes one such situation in which the deceived victims felt violated by a man ("Alex") who pretended to be a woman ("Joan") in an online discussion group. Joan became close to several group members, and set up dates for some of them with "her friend," Alex. Presumably the women trusted their date more because he was introduced by a female mutual friend. The betrayal was eventually discovered, leaving Alex's real-life dates and Joan's online friends feeling deceived and exploited. Adolescents, particularly those with limited social skills or limited support networks in their day-to-day life, may be particularly vulnerable to this sort of manipulation, which may extend to even more abusive forms of exploitation (e.g., kidnaping, sexual abuse, child pornography) in extreme cases. Finkelhor et al. (2000) report that in one year, 19% of American youths surveyed had received unwanted sexual attention online, such as requests for intimate sexual information or online sex.

Although online activity could increase vulnerability to this type of attention simply by increasing the numbers of people with whom youth have contact, these risks may be reduced in the future by adolescents' increasing familiarity with the unique qualities of online interaction. Computer-mediated communication provides limited cues for assessing trustworthiness, or any other characteristic. Online interaction plays havoc with typical human approaches to social connections. Even in face-to-face interaction, people jump to erroneous conclusions about others based on limited evidence, such as preconceived categories of people or perceived similarity to oneself (Wallace, 1999). Removing important sources of information such as vocal register and body language make it even harder to assess another person's character. This may be less of a problem for adolescents in the future, accustomed as they will be to the differences between Internet and face-to-face interactions. Even now, Internet-savvy youth do not necessarily expect trustworthiness from online connections (Clark, 1998). To the extent that these low expectations for trust imply the adoption of self-protective behaviors, young people in years to come may be less likely than their current-day counterparts to be deceived or exploited, and less traumatized when those problems do occur.

Online Socialization and Communication Skills

CMC offers the possibility of "lurking" (reading the messages posted without adding any messages of your own) on newsgroups. Lurking provides a chance to observe the social terrain, learn some of the customs, and decide whether the current discussion is too hostile, too boring, or too cliquish to be an appropriate point of entry. This might be contrasted with a high school party or dance, at which a "wallflower" would be noticeably disadvantaged. By lurking, an adolescent could simply observe and learn from the interactions of others, without ever participating directly, just as young people seek information about social interaction through observing adults around them (parents, siblings, movie and television characters, teachers, strangers).

Online communication may eventually serve as a "socialization ground" for adolescents, especially those who are shy or uncomfortable with their peers in face-to-face interaction. This text-based social learning may not be beneficial. Consider the adolescent who creates and enjoys a strong persona online, who feels confident and assertive in his or her newsgroup communication. She or he may have plenty of practice in verbal argumentation and discussion, but still have no idea how to read social cues such as boredom, interest, or flirtation. Misunderstandings online are solved primarily by "throwing verbiage at the problem," but this method would be useless in face-to-face interaction without an accompanying understanding and utilization of non-verbal cues. On the other hand, Wallace (2000) points out the possibility that online experiments with alternate behaviors may reap social rewards, leading to an offline experiment with the same attitude or style. If the online context is one that encourages developing personal relationships, like a MUD or chat room, this positive result may be more likely. Unlike direct involvement, the vicarious learning provided by lurking in online conversation may actually discourage offline social interactions, because the risks are so much higher. However, entirely supplanting face-to-face contact with online interaction (or lurking) may be akin to the extremely unlikely possibility of Harlow's monkeys choosing an animated wire mother over one with at least some semblance to a real, flesh and blood, mother.

As Internet video transmission becomes more feasible, some arenas which are currently text-based (e.g., chat rooms) may make "face-to-face" interaction possible. However, asynchronous newsgroups and multiuser chat rooms and dungeons would be rendered unwieldy and slow if visual capabilities were added. In addition, video capability is likely to be expensive, and thus will not be available to a great number of users; assuming that newsgroups and chat rooms continue to be fairly democratic and cheap, users might resist the addition of video, which would eliminate so many people from the conversation. If video links do become more commonly available, online social contacts with adequate video capacity will come to resemble regular, face-to-face contact, just as online video conferencing closely resembles in-person meetings. The greatest difference will be in turn-taking, which in face-to-face conversation is somewhat messy, with frequent overlaps, interruptions and false starts. Video conferencing requires more rigidity about speech turns, as technical limitations prevent truly synchronous transmission of image and sound. In practice, this rigidity tends to limit social comfort, rapport and conversational efficiency, and could therefore hinder the ease of communication and intimacy which characterizes text-based online relationships.

At least for now, it appears that the qualities of computer-mediated communication which make it unique can be beneficial to a degree, especially in the sense of providing opportunities for young people to observe and participate in social interaction without the perceived risks and insecurities attending face-to-face interaction with everyday peers. These benefits, though, can become hindrances to the extent that they become an expected or necessary part of a person's social interactions. Identities which work online may not be so welcome at a school dance, and conversational skills honed in the somewhat aggressive and flame-ridden world of newsgroups may not get a person elected class president. On the other hand, these CMC characteristics are relatively new to our culture. Fifty years' time may bring CMC values further into the mainstream, with the limitation that they are at least partially a result of the anonymity and "blindness" of current Internet communications.

Interest-based Connections and Hidden Identities Online

The enormity and anonymity of the Internet lead to a situation in which "the vast array of people to whom we are not physically drawn, yet with whom we might connect quite well if given the opportunity, become available to us" (Cooper & Sportolari, 1997). Online, any individual with Internet access can seek out other people in a fairly targeted way, whether through Web searches for particular text, such as "skateboarding," or through newsgroup participation. Some IRC channels are also devoted to specific topics, regions, or institutions, thus providing at least an initial presumption of shared interest. Of course users will meet people they like or dislike regardless of shared interests, just as they would in face to face interaction. However, the problem of "what to talk about when you meet someone new," which may be particularly salient for socially self-conscious teenagers and young adults, is in part solved online through categorized groups, chats and Web sites. "The Net increases one's chances of connecting with like-minded people due to the computer's ability to rapidly sort along many dimensions simultaneously" (Cooper & Sportolari, 1997, p. 9).

Anonymity, interest-oriented searches for newsgroups and chat rooms, and the opportunity for lurking are all qualities of Internet communications that are particularly suited to individuals who may be stigmatized in some way, whether through physical attributes (obesity, disability) or through invisible differences (hidden disabilities, homosexuality, or sexual interests). "In virtual groups . . . people can admit to having marginalized, or non-mainstream, proclivities that they hide from the rest of the world. For the first time, they can reap the benefits of joining a group of similar others: feeling less isolated and different, disclosing a long secret part of oneself, sharing one's own experiences and learning from those of others, and gaining emotional and motivational support" (McKenna & Bargh, 1998, p. 682).

In two studies of newsgroups and their participants, McKenna & Bargh (1998) found that Internet newsgroups have a clear and consistent effect on the "transformation of an individual's social identity" (p. 691). In the process of identity transformation, individuals with marginalized identities (e.g., homosexuality or disability) are strongly affected by the response of other newsgroup members to their own messages. Active involvement (as opposed to lurking) in a newsgroup focused on that marginalized identity "led to increased importance of the group identity, which in turn increased self-acceptance of that identity" (p. 691). Group identity importance also increased the likelihood of coming out to family and friends offline, and decreased individuals' sense of social estrangement, while active newsgroup participation was found to decrease social isolation (p. 688). These results suggest that participation in identity-relevant newsgroups may be of great benefit to individuals whose characteristics, whether visible or kept secret, may make them vulnerable to social stigma in their own communities.

McKenna and Bargh's (1998) first study involved analyzing threads of conversation in a group, looking at the ways in which group responses affected individual participation; this study did not include demographic information. The second study, however, involved the administration of questionnaires to over 100 respondents, all of whom were participants in one of three newsgroups. The participants were adults, ranging in age from 18 to 68 years, with an average of 37 (McKenna & Bargh, 1998, p. 687); although adolescents were not included in this study, the dynamic identified by the authors is useful in understanding the possibilities of Internet involvement for the development and strengthening of identity. For teenagers, who are perhaps at a lifetime peak of sensitivity to social approval, increased access to a supportive social network and decreased "aloneness" with the stigmatized identity could be crucial in maintaining a healthy sense of self.

Weinrich (1997) interviewed a group of "homosexual pioneers" of computing and the Internet (p. 59), who generally agreed that "[o]ne of the most common benefits of the Internet to the gay community . . . is that it permits geographically dispersed minority individuals to interact with one another as if they were a local majority" (p. 62). Winzelberg's (1997) exploration of the functions served by an electronic support group, in this case a group discussing eating disorders, revealed that members of the group used "similar helping strategies to those that are found in face-to-face support groups. Members provided emotional support, information, feedback, and acknowledged that they were experts on their problems" (p. 404). Although it would be foolish to believe that newsgroups could supplant face-to-face support completely, it would also be foolish to suggest that these groups are not serving an important purpose. Adolescents are often reluctant to reveal some of their most difficult problems to adults or even to their peers; at times this isolation and silence can lead to increased difficulties (e.g., substance abuse and suicide for closeted gay teens). A supportive electronic community, providing the benefit of anonymity and the emotional support of people with similar experiences, could be of great benefit in that situation.

Online communities can also provide a network for organizing, disseminating information pertinent to particular groups, and promoting social change. The !OutProud! site for queer and questioning teens exemplifies the social and political benefit of online support for adolescents. In a 1997 online survey (Kryzan & Walsh, 1998) , the developers of the! OutProud! site obtained nearly 2000 responses from people ages 10–25 years, using advertisements in queer-oriented print publications and online sites. The respondents, two-thirds of whom were between 15 and 19 years old, were more active Internet users than adolescents in other, broader surveys. Most (70%) had been using the Internet for at least one year, and 79% reported being online at least one hour a day. Echoing McKenna and Bargh's (1998) results, 68% of survey participants agreed that "being online helped them to accept their sexual orientation," and of that group, over half said that the Internet had been "crucial" to accepting their sexual orientation. The Internet has contributed something unique and important to these respondents' identity development.

The following posts appear to be typical contributions to the !OutProud! site, based on my reading of the message boards. The first is from the high school forum's "chat" section, and the second is from the social activities forum's "anyone wanna talk" section. I have removed names and address information, which were included in the original posts but probably not intended for a large, non-gay-specific public audience.

Hi!! It's just me again. I was just wondering if you guys/gals have noticed the majority of homophobia in your school . . . and how many teachers don't do anything about it. That's the case with me. Well, what I wanted to say is that you guys/gals should go to www.advocate.com . . . and go to idea exchange. There is a lot of support and friendship there. Also, there is a lot of great advice. Just ask away and about 5 people will answer you every time. There is probably hundreds of people on there . . . but, I have yet to hear from them all. Have a nice day!!! (http://www.outproud.org/forum?outproud-14@ˆ1724@.ee6b691/0, posted 3/5/99).

Hi, my name is ****, i am a 16 y/o Bisexual. I am looking for anyone to talk to around Washington State. I just want someone to hang out with, either on the computer or in real life. It is so hard to find anyone to talk to. I don't care if you are interested in being "more than friends," i would love to talk to even a sweet bi/gay boy, just someone who knows what i am going through.   (http://www.outproud.org/forum?outproud-13@ˆ 1727@.ee6b671, posted 10/7/99).

These messages show how the Internet can facilitate social connections, social support, and activism among young people who otherwise feel isolated because of their sexual orientation.

The Nature of Intimacy and Dating Online

Although one may be able to find solace or social support online, it is a matter of debate whether these connections constitute intimacy, or in what way time spent online affects overall social connectedness. Robson and Robson (1998), reviewing research and theory on intimacy and applying it to Internet-based relationships, focus on the issue of self-disclosure, suggesting that appropriate timing, amounts, and patterns (reciprocity) of self-disclosure are sufficient to constitute intimacy. In this view, according to the authors, "people do seem to be able to develop intimate relationships, healthy or not, using computer communication" (p. 36). Of particular note in a discussion of Internet communication is the suggestion that "self disclosure should be matched to the intimacy level of the relationship" (Duck, 1988, cited in Robson & Robson, 1998); I have observed that many "Netizens" thrive on rapidly blooming, intimate (i.e. self-revealing) conversations, but when these online relationships turn into face-to-face meetings, a sudden discomfort often accompanies the realization that the chemistry both individuals felt in e-mail or chat is missing from the face-to-face relationship. At the same time, one may realize that "I don't *know* this person, and s/he knows my whole life story!" Whether true intimacy was achieved prior to meeting then comes into question. This reaction may become less common as people become accustomed to the nature of computer-mediated relationships. Separate sets of individual and cultural expectations for on- and off-line relationships are likely to develop with increased experience online.

Schnarch (1997) asserts that the Net, because it allows for self-editing, "is a relatively poor stimulus for the self-confrontation and core self-disclosure that epitomize intense intimacy" (p. 17). He goes on to suggest that the positive sentiments one may gain from others in this context will not be validating because they are responses to a false online self, constructed specifically to minimize perceived personal flaws; the validation is not for one's true, whole self, but for an idealized public image. It is Schnarch's position that online chat is not a sufficient forum for the development of relationship skills or intimacy, in large part because of the limited personal risks involved in relatively anonymous, edited communication. Cooper and Sportolari (1997), on the other hand, state that "the Net is a model of intimate yet separate relating" which "can facilitate positive interpersonal connections, including the healthy development of romantic relationships" (p. 7). They suggest that CMR (computer-mediated relating) may be particularly useful to people who are anxious about entering relationships, or who need to experiment with "putting normally inhibited parts of themselves forward" (p. 11).

Perhaps intimacy is not valued by teenagers in online relationships. Clark's (1998) conversations with adolescent Internet users suggested that teens' online dating relationships are "pure relationships," sought out and maintained not because of social pressure, economic necessity, or expected permanence, but "solely for the gratification they provide to the persons involved" (p. 176). Rather than recoiling at this proposition, as many adult observers might, Clark reminds her readers of the context in which today's teens (and adolescents of the coming century) are developing. Specifically, teens perceive themselves to be at greater risk, emotionally and physically, and are less attached to the image of relationship permanence that suffuses earlier generations' beliefs. "[T]rust and 'authenticity' are *not* central to teen chat room relationships; 'fun' is. In fact, one important aspect of the 'fun' is in working within the 'mysterious' element . . . of not knowing the other person in the on-line relationship at all" (p. 179).

Online dating may provide adolescents some shelter from the perceived risks of face-to-face relationships. Clark's (1998) respondents appear to have little expectation for long-term connections or face-to-face meetings, perhaps because the potential for "playful dishonest" so clearly implies that the relationships are not between two "real" people. Thus online dating may be so transient that "breakups" are not a possibility, because "breakup" implies commitment that may not be a goal in this context. If online breakups do occur, they may be less painful than the face-to-face version. They are not witnessed by the couple's peers, nor do they necessarily imply a failing of either person's "true self" to be a worthy partner. Furthermore, they do not presage a long, lonely wait for a new relationship to arise; chat room connections are made quickly, unhindered by the appearance-focus and inhibition of face-to-face relationships. The Internet is providing a forum in which adolescents can move beyond traditionally defined "intimacy" and "dating," creating relationships for their own sake. If this were to become a trend in adolescent relationships, it would provide teens in the future a clearer perspective (compared to current-day or past adolescents) on the nature and desirable qualities of intimate relationships. Having relationships "just for fun" would allow practice in the skills of communicating to make a relationship work, without the pressures of long-term commitment and sexual contact.

Online communication offers adolescent users the opportunity to stand outside of normal social relationships: to observe the effects of various verbal maneuvers, to question the relevance of standard categories (gender, ethnicity, sexuality) for identity, and to "date" without the emotional risks of commitment and sexual involvement. Adolescent members of traditionally oppressed minority groups may find additional benefits in the ability to share concerns with a large community of similar individuals, avoiding the risk of public identification with that group. Teens in general will probably become accustomed to using and playing with online anonymity before video connections are sufficient to replace or adequately supplement text-based interaction. As young people explore this free social space, we will see continued change in their self-perception, their identity development, and their relationships. In addition to the presumed benefits of these changes, certain mental health risks have come to light in the past few years of Internet expansion. The following section of this chapter explores the potential impact of Internet life on the mental health of adolescents.

IMPACT OF INTERNET USE ON MENTAL HEALTH

Turning Inward: Isolation and Depression

The adequacy of Internet relationships, and the potential benefits and disadvantages of Internet use, have already come into question. Kraut and colleagues (1998), in a longitudinal study of 73 families, found that Internet use was associated with declines in social connections with family and friends, and increases in depression and loneliness (p. 1017). The study may be less than suitable to the current purpose, as the study sample included more adults than children. In addition, the conclusions drawn, though accurate, may not completely represent the results of the study; for instance, the authors emphasize the decrease in connections with people, but do not equally emphasize their finding that perceived social support (having someone you can talk to, or get help from) was not significantly related to Internet use. The study does not present the pre- and post-Internet use "amounts" of loneliness, social support, and so on; without this information it is difficult to determine the relative impact on study participants of reported changes in the factors measured. The study has been subject to other critiques (e.g., Rierdan, 1999; Shapiro, 1999), but it does raise important issues about the effects of Internet use on social and psychological functioning.

A second study now suggests that Internet use is associated with increases in perceived social isolation. The mechanism by which this change in perceived social connection occurs is not yet clear; it is too soon to blame it on "Internet use" per se. Nie & Erbring (2000) released a study of "Internet and Society," based on questionnaires administered to nearly 2,700 households. The preliminary report focuses on the inverse relationship between time spent online and time spent in three categories of social activity: talking to family and friends on the phone (which could have been replaced by email contact, as the authors acknowledge), spending time with family and friends, and attending events. However, the majority (79–91%) of Internet users in the study reported no change whatsoever in time spent on these activities. On the other hand, the percentage of respondents reporting a decline in social activity does appear to increase dependably with the amount of time spent online (from 15% of users spending less than one hour online per week to 55% of those with more than ten weekly hours online).

It seems possible, however, that some of the problems being identified here have to do with respondents taking time to adjust to occupying two very different kinds of social reality. People might, for instance, feel very connected to the people they meet online, and develop the sort of intimate conversation which is somewhat typical of Internet users; this could make their relationships overall seem less satisfying ("except for this one person, nobody really understands me"). In these circumstances, loneliness would be a logical result of spending time away from one's incredibly close online relationships. Over time, these same individuals may learn to take for granted the remarkable differences between online and offline conversations and relationships, and recognize the benefits and drawbacks of each. If Kraut and colleagues (1998) were to re-administer their questionnaires to the same people in five years or so, I suspect they would see substantial improvement in people's social connections and experience of loneliness.

It is also important to ask whether those individuals who spend a great deal of time in online activities may be doing so specifically because they are unhappy, lonely, or otherwise "maladjusted." One particularly cynical observer states that "Internet friends are a self-selecting group of melancholics. Happier souls are, by definition outside, busy getting on with real life" (Aitkenhead, 1998, p. 13). This may be supported by Nolen-Hoeksema's (1998) work on the link between ruminative coping style and depression. Rumination involves focusing on one's depressed feelings and negative circumstances, and is associated with increased duration and severity of depressive episodes. The wide audience of "listeners" in online support and newsgroups may be quite attractive to ruminators, thus leading to an increased population of depression-prone individuals online. Adolescents who are predisposed to depression or isolation might spend a great deal of time finding solace online, meanwhile becoming increasingly isolated from the family attention and community care they require. However, blanket statements about "how much is too much" will be less useful to adolescents, families, and educators than will some guidelines about staying in touch with teenagers in a world of ever-increasing sensory stimulation and emotional risk.

In a personal anecdote intended to counter the assertions of Kraut and colleagues (1998), Silverman (1999) details positive aspects of online communication as she experienced it. She refers to a feminist theory of women's development, which posits that "When we feel we are unheard in our relationships, we experience depression" (p. 780–781), and asserts that for her group, listening to and being heard by others were essential ingredients of the newsgroup experience. Thus, Silverman argues, online communities can be a great boon to participants. Being heard is not necessarily the modal experience in newsgroups, and Silverman's group was formed by women who already knew each other and shared a profession (mental health practice) and a viewpoint (relational theory and feminism). To the extent that adolescents may find other like-minded teens online, or choose to create an environment (be it a MUD, an IRC channel, or a newsgroup) to reflect their own interests and values, they may also benefit from participating in online communications. This statement would hold equally true for everyday, offline activities. If a young person feels excluded and "unheard" at school, she or he is likely to feel unhappy, and creating or joining a club would probably alleviate some of that unhappiness. Some of the "discoveries" people have made about the Internet, particularly in terms of its social functions, serve more to emphasize its current similarities to other social media than to warn us about new and unforeseen dangers.

Acting Out: Hacking, Trolling, and Flaming

As a social medium, the Internet may appeal to some adolescents as a forum in which to exercise antisocial or oppositional tendencies. In general, use of computer-mediated communication is associated with higher frequencies of a variety of verbally aggressive behaviors such as insults, swearing, and hostile comments (Wallace, 2000). The capacity to exit a conversation or "location" immediately after insulting or harming another may encourage these behaviors in otherwise placid individuals. "Trolling" on newsgroups, in which a person makes inflammatory comments in order to provoke heated arguments, may be an example of an Internet-specific "antisocial" behavior; "flaming" (viciously verbally berating someone, usually in the "public" space of a newsgroup rather than in private) is another, more familiar, online negative behavior. While trolling and flaming are generally discouraged by online community members, the "perpetrator" can completely avoid rebuke simply by logging off or deleting critical responses. Hacking, which involves programming for the purpose of breaching security systems and gaining access to information, is probably the most likely outlet for anti-social tendencies. Hackers are reputed to be mostly teenaged and young adult males, who may be acting out a more secretive and less impulsive version of the externalizing disorders (e.g., conduct disorder, antisocial personality) commonly seen in offline life.

Impulse Control Problems: Internet Addiction

Internet addiction is a topic that has gained attention in recent years, although the controversy about the validity of this "disorder" has not yet been resolved. Young (1996) reports finding reliable differences between "dependent" and "non-dependent" Internet users. Dependents spent an average of 39 hours a week online, compared with five hours a week for non-dependents, and dependents spent much of their Internet time seeking social contact (through chat rooms, newsgroups, and MUDs), while non-dependents were more likely to use the Net for e-mail and Web searches. Criteria for this behavior problem are based on the American Psychiatric Association's (APA) criteria for the impulse control disorder of pathological gambling: in both cases, they include preoccupation with the desired activity, the felt need to do the activity for increasing amounts of time, futile attempts to stop the behavior, impairments in relationships or at work as a result of excessive involvement in the activity, and so forth (Young, 1999). Pathological gambling has a typical onset for males in early adolescence and "later in life" for females (APA, 1994, p. 617); if Internet addiction is in some ways parallel to a gambling disorder, it may crop up in adolescent males as the Internet becomes an even more common aspect of everyday life.

However, given our culture's recent propensity for labeling any and every behavior as a disorder (e.g., shopping, using credit cards), it remains to be seen whether the existence of this particular "disorder" will be supported by further research. The patterns of Internet use described as "addiction" in research and online anecdotes seem to fit APA criteria for impulse control disorders. Griffiths (1999) argues, though, that Internet-addicted individuals are attracted not to being online per se, but to the social "rewards" one can access in this way, such as building new relationships or debating issues, without the risk of face-to-face conflict. The unique qualities of Internet communication described earlier may lend a particular appeal for individuals who are having difficulty with their everyday social relationships. In other words, compulsive Internet use is most likely to be a risk for people who are dissatisfied with some aspect of their daily lives, particularly if online interaction appears to solve the problem they encounter offline.

Whether the compulsive Internet use is a true impulse control disorder or a short-lived but intense fascination with the new world of online communication, it is likely to be a problem for some and no problem for many. Particularly lonely, isolated, or socially unskilled adolescents may be more prone to this type of "addiction," but it may also provide them something (i.e., social support and contact) they are lacking in their normal life; in that sense, Internet "addiction" may be very different from compulsive shopping, gambling, or overworking. This is not to say compulsive online activities are not damaging, simply that the risk is probably fairly small. In spite of Young's (1999) warnings about health risks such as lack of exercise, lack of sleep, and carpal tunnel syndrome, the dangers for an Internet addict are small relative to those for an alcoholic or heroin addict. To the extent that the Internet has addictive qualities, compulsive use patterns are probably most likely for people already predisposed to addictive behaviors or impulse control problems. Concerned parents and educators can make use of the warning signs presented by Young (1999) to assess young people in their care. If Internet addiction is a reality, it seems most likely that a small percentage of adolescents will develop this disorder, just as a small percentage show signs of any other psychological disorder.

The mental health risks of Internet use may stem in part from the unique forms of relationship and communication available online, but the risks themselves are not new or unique. The Internet simply provides a new forum for the expression of problems which would previously have been expressed in other ways. If the stereotype of the socially awkward male hacker is accurate, then hackers, without the Internet, would be socially isolated, possibly depressed and actively antisocial young men. Internet "addicts" have found a way to connect with people online which is apparently captivating to them, and which may be a substitute for some missing aspect (e.g., self-esteem, validation, emotional intimacy) of their real-life social lives. Without the Internet, they might spend "too much time" writing to pen-pals or reading fantasy novels. As the Internet continues to grow and reach more people, it will be important to keep track of "risk factors" for these problems; over time, though, they will likely become no more or less of an issue than any of the mental health problems encountered in young people today. Rather than getting caught up in dire predictions of Internet-related mental health problems for teenagers, we need to look at the entire complex of Internet capacities and the unique social space they create, with an eye toward understanding what adolescence will be like when this "new world" is visited as commonly as any physical gathering place.

IMAGINING THE FUTURE

Looking forward, it seems clear that teenagers will continue to use and explore the Internet. As the Internets' capacity and ubiquity increase, teens' online time will increase significantly as well. Homework, chatting, organizing activities, playing games, watching or listening to broadcast media: all these activities are, or will soon be, supported by the Internet. The social functions of online communication will probably continue to be most attractive to teenagers. It is the uniqueness of the social space created by the Internet, rather than the access to information or the ability to do homework online, that will most affect adolescents' experience of themselves and the world around them. Several aspects of adolescents' future Internet use and its impact are envisioned:

- Adolescents will spend more time online in the future than they do currently. The Net will become more familiar and more appealing, and more people will be online, making it potentially more interesting.
- As adolescents spend more time online, they will become more aware of current events and of the world beyond their own community; this awareness will be somewhat constrained by the limited access of a subset of the world's population.

- Increased awareness, and the opportunity for teens who are part of stigmatized groups to communicate with similar others, may lead to increased activism, which will evolve beyond e-mail chain letters and newsgroup arguments to more focused social action.
- Sexual experimentation online will continue; this is most likely to have a negative impact on the teenagers of today and the next decade or so. The cultural myth that love and sex are necessarily connected will be shaken by newer, less intimate online sexual practices. However, as our culture learns what to expect, and what not to expect, from online relationships, this will cause fewer emotional difficulties and surprises.
- Similarly, the issues of social isolation and depression, as related to the Internet, will fade as people grow accustomed to having different sets of expectations for online and "real life" relationships.
- Internet "addiction" or overuse will continue to be an issue, whether it becomes an officially designated mental disorder or not. However, the number of adolescents affected by this will be relatively small, and the damage will be minimal relative to that caused by other mental health and behavior problems. Increasing familiarity with Internet use and overuse will allow earlier recognition and intervention for this problem.
- Gender and race will continue to be salient features of "real-life" interactions, and they will become less relevant but not absent features of online communication.
- Spending time online is becoming a norm for many adolescents; as this trend continues, those activities which are somewhat rare now (such as MOOs and IRC) will become more commonplace. Playing with identities will become an expected part of this process.
- As playing with identities becomes more common, adolescents' sense of identity may become more fluid, such that identity crisis may be replaced by a calmer sense of identity exploration, and the concept of a single "permanent" identity may be replaced by that of multiple layers of identity or multiple social selves.

Reconsidering the most polarized views of our Internet future, we see that some aspects of the pessimistic outlook are worth attending to: Shy, isolated adolescents may be at risk for "addiction" to online relating, to the detriment of offline social relationships and potential support. On the other hand, those same shy adolescents could blossom with the opportunity to observe social interactions and experiment with not-so-shy ways of relating. Youngsters with lots of time and few friends may take the opportunity to experiment with hacking, though this will remain a rare activity. Although increased time online must mean decreased time with family, this does not necessarily imply increased isolation. On the contrary, teenagers who identify with marginalized groups will likely find increased connection and social support online.

Perhaps most important for adolescents is the broadened conception of identity and relationships made possible by Internet communication. Although users of any age can be influenced by these changes, the effect will likely be the most profound for teenagers. Adolescents' energy is geared toward connecting with people, learning about and developing the self, and exploring the world; if that exploration includes the Internet, teens will emerge into adulthood with very flexible senses of identity, sexuality, and relationships. Particularly in Western, industrialized nations, the Internet could change the very experience of adolescence, enhancing its exploratory nature and diminishing its isolation and discomfort.

APPENDIX A: TERMINOLOGY

The *Internet* and the *Net* are synonymous terms for the total technology and infrastructure upon which a variety of forms of electronic communication and information storage are based. *Computer-mediated communication* (CMC) refers to the various processes by which the Net can be used to make connections among individuals; *computer-mediated relating* (CMR) is one term for the online relationship process. *E-mail* (electronic mail) is an asynchronous method of correspondence, allowing individuals to send, receive, and store messages in electronic form. *Usenet newsgroups* archive "posts" (e-mailed messages from individuals) on a particular topic, such that readers worldwide can access a full list of posts, and contribute their own messages, at their convenience; newsgroups are divided and indexed by topic and named with some shorthand representing the topic matter (e.g., soc.support.youth.gay-lesbian-bi is a social-oriented group, focused on providing social support, specific to gay/lesbian/bisexual young people; the alt.politics hierarchy covers a wide range of political value systems and topics in at least 16 separate groups). The *World Wide Web* (WWW) is the first and only CMC tool (thus far) that allows for visual and auditory content in addition to text. *Hyperlinks* are connections from one WWW "page" to another; Web "pages" can be constructed and made available by individuals, businesses, or organizations and may provide any type of information or imagery, as well as links to related pages or sites of interest to the original page's developer.

Internet Relay Chat **(IRC)**, *chat rooms*, and *interactive communication* all refer to methods of text-based, direct (i.e., synchronous) communication between individuals; these forms allow for users to see each other's contributions to the conversation as they are written, and thus parallel regular, *face-to-face* **(FTF)** conversation. *MUDs* (Multiuser Dungeons or Multiuser Dimensions), *MOOs* (Multiuser Object Oriented environments) **and** *MUSHes* (a play on words for a derivative of MUDs; sometimes said to stand for "Multiuser Shared Hallucination") are all games or worlds, usually created by individuals and provided free of charge via IRC-type connections, which combine elements of role-playing and adventure games with interaction among users. For example, users' online characters can, via keyboard commands, "go to" a particular room, "see" certain items (described in text on the user's computer screen), and "use" the items for a desired effect (e.g., "wave wand," "drink potion"). These worlds have until recently been entirely text-based, but hypermedia MUSHes, which include graphics and sound (making them similar to an advanced, interactive video game), are now possible as well.

References

Aitkenhead, D. (1998, September 4). Sad, lonely? Log off and get out! *New Statesman*, p. 13.

ACLU (1997, June 26). Supreme Court rules: Cyberspace will be free! ACLU hails victory in Internet censorship challenge [Online]. Available: http://www.aclu.org/news/n062697a.html

ACLU (2000(A), June 22). Appeals Court rejects Congress' second attempt at cyber-censorship [Online]. Available: http://www.aclu.org/news/2000/n062200b.html.

ACLU (2000(B), December 18). ACLU promises legal challenge as Congress adopts bill imposing Internet blocking in libraries [Online]. Available: http://www.aclu.org/news/2000/n121800a.html.

Alexander, T., Roodin, P., & Gorman, B. (1980). *Developmental Psychology*, New York: Van Nostrand.

American Psychiatric Association (1994). *Diagnostic and Statistical Manual of Mental Disorders* (4th ed.). Washington, D.C.: Author.

Barlow, J. P. (1999, September). The aesthetics of cyberspace. Lecture presented as part of CAS/MillerComm Series, Beckman Institute of the University of Illinois at Urbana-Champaign, Urbana, IL.

Baym, N. K. (1995). The emergence of community in computer-mediated communication. In Jones, S. G. (Ed.), *CyberSociety*, 138–163. Thousand Oaks, CA: Sage.

Borland, J. (2001, September 24). Napster reaches settlement with publishers. *CNET News.com* [Online]. Available: http://news.cnet.com/news/0-1005-200-7283716.html.

Bruce, B. C. (1997). Literacy technologies: What stance should we take? *Journal of Literacy Research*, 29(2), 289–309. Available: http://www.geocities.com/Athens/Parthenon/3605/chip.html.

Burkhalter, B. (1999). Reading race online: Discovering racial identity in Usenet discussions. In Smith, M. A. & Kollock, P. (Eds.), *Communities in Cyberspace*, 60–75. London: Routledge.

Cartlidge, S. P. (1998). International review [Introduction], *Educational Technology Research and Development*, 46(3), 102.

Clark, L. S. (1998). Dating on the Net: Teens and the rise of "pure" relationships. In S. G. Jones (Ed.), *Cybersociety 2.0*, 159–183. Thousand Oaks, CA: Sage.

CNN (2000, March 8). Teenager charged with computer hacking. [Online]. Available: http://www.cnn.com/2000/TECH/computing/03/08/hacker.arrest.02/index.html.

Cooper, A. & Sportolari, L. (1997). Romance in cyberspace: Understanding online attraction. *Journal of Sex Education and Therapy*, 22(1), 7–14.

Denning, D. E. (1996). Concerning hackers who break into computer systems. In Ludlow, P. (Ed.), *High Noon on the Electronic Frontier*, 137–163. Cambridge, MA: Massachusetts Institute of Technology, [Online]. Available: http://www.cpsr.org/cpsr/privacy/crime/denning.hackers.html.

FCC (1999). The Internet. In *Connecting the Globe: A Regulator's Guide to Building a Global Information Community*, pp. 50–51. [Online]. Available: http://www.fcc.gov/connectglobe/sec9.html.

Finkelhor, D., Mitchell, K J., & Wolak, J. (2000). Online victimization: A report on the nation's youth. Durham, NH: Crimes Against Children Research Center. [Online] Available: http://www.unh.edu/ccrc/Victimization_Online_Survey.pdf.

Georgia Tech Research Corporation (1998). *GVU's 10th WWW User Survey* [Online]. Available: www.gvu.gatech.edu/user_surveys.

Gray, D. F. (1999, November 1). Music industry campaigns against Net pirates. CNN [Online]. Available: http://cnn.com/TECH/computing/9911/01/music.pirates.idg/index.html.

Griffiths, Mark (1999). Internet addiction: Fact or fiction? *Psychologist*, 12(5), 246–250.

Hilty, W. (2000, March 3–9). Bandwidth on the run. *Orange County Weekly*, 5(26), [Online]. Available: http://www.ocweekly.com/ink/00/26/machine-hilty.shtml.

Jones, S. G. (1995). Understanding community in the information age. In Jones, S. G. (Ed.), *Cybersociety*, 10–35. Thousand Oaks, CA: Sage.

Kollock, P. & Smith, M. A. (1999). Communities in cyberspace. In Smith, M. A. & Kollock, P. (Eds.), *Communities in Cyberspace*, 3–25. London: Routledge.

Kraut, R., Patterson, M., Lundmark, V., Kiesler, S., Mukopadhyay, T., & Scherlis, W. (1998). Internet paradox: A social technology that reduces social involvement and psychological well-being? *American Psychologist, 53*(9), 1017–1031.

Kryzan, C. & Walsh, J. (1998). !OutProud!/Oasis Internet Survey of Queer and Questioning Youth. [Online] Available: http://www.outproud.org/survey/report.pdf.

Larson, R. W. & Verma, S. (1999). How children and adolescents spend time across the world: Work, play and developmental opportunities. *Psychological Bulletin, 125*(6), 701–736.

Linux International (1999). Linux International Home Page. [Online]. Available: http://li.org.

Magid, L. (2000, March). Filtering programs useful but far from perfect. [Online] Available: http://www.safekids.com/articles/filtering2000.htm.

Manjoo, F. (2001, October 10). Another day of Napster nattering. *Wired News* [Online]. Available: http://www.wired.com/news/politics/0,1283,47437,00,html.

McKenna, K.Y.A. & Bargh, J.A. (1998). Coming out in the age of the Internet: Identity "demarginalization" through virtual group participation. *Journal of Personality and Social Psychology, 75*(3), 681–694.

Nie, N. H. & Erbring, L. (2000). Internet and Society: A preliminary report. Palo Alto, CA: Stanford Institute for the Quantitative Study of Society. [Online]. Available: http://www.stanford.edu/group/siqss/ Press_Release/Preliminary_Report.pdf.

Nolen-Hoeksema, S. (1998). Ruminative coping with depression. In Heckhausen, J. & Dweck, C. (Eds.) *Motivation and Self-Regulation Across the Life Span*, 237–256. New York, : Cambridge University Press.

O'Brien, J. (1999). Writing in the body: Gender (re)production in online interaction. In Smith, M. A. & Kollock, P. (Eds.), *Communities in Cyberspace*, 76–104. London: Routledge.

Revelation (1996). *The Ultimate Beginner's Guide to Hacking and Phreaking* (Online). Available: http://www.multimania.com/tnh/text/starthak.txt.

Rierdan, J. (1999). Internet-depression link? *American Psychologist, 54*(9), 781–2.

Roberts, D. F., Foehr, U. G., Rideout, V. J. & Brodie, M. (1999, November). Kids and the media at the new millennium: A comprehensive national analysis of children's media use. Menlo Park, CA: Kaiser Family Foundation. [Online]. Available: http://www.kff.org/content/1999/1535/

Robson, D. & Robson, M. (1998). Intimacy and computer communication. *British Journal of Guidance and Counselling, 26*(1), 33–41.

Schnarch, D. (1997). Sex, intimacy, and the Internet. *Journal of Sex Education and Therapy, 22*(1), 15–20.

Shapiro, J. S. (1999). Loneliness: Paradox or artifact? *American Psychologist, 54*(9), 782–3.

Shpritz, D. (1997). One teenager's search for sexual health on the Net. *Journal of Sex Education and Therapy, 22*(1), 56–57.

Silverman, T. (1999). The Internet and relational theory. *American Psychologist, 55*(9), pp. 780–784.

Snyder, J. (2000, May 3). RIAA CEO talks about legal proceedings against MP3.com and Napster. CNN [Online]. Available: http://www.cnn.com/2000/TECH/computing/05/03/riaa.cio.speaks.idg/index.html.

Subrahmanyam, K., Kraut, R., Greenfield, P., & Gross, E. (2001). New forms of electronic media. In Singer, D. G. & Singer, J. L., *Handbook of Children and the Media*, 73–99. Thousand Oaks, CA: Sage.

Tapscott, D. (1999). *Growing Up Digital: The Rise of the Net Generation*. New York: McGraw-Hill.

United States Census Bureau (1999). *Computer Use in the United States: October 1997*. [Online]. Available: http://www.census.gov/population/www/socdemo/computer.html.

Wallace, P. (1999). *The Psychology of the Internet*. Cambridge, UK: Cambridge, University Press.

Weinrich, J. D. (1997). Strange bedfellows: Homosexuality, gay liberation, and the Internet. *Journal of Sex Education and Therapy, 22*(1), 58–66.

Winzelberg, A. (1997). The analysis of an electronic support group for individuals with eating disorders. *Computers in Human Behavior, 13*(3), 393–407.

Wired News (2001, September 6). Napster eclipsed by newcomers [online]. Available: http://www.wired.com/news/business/0,1367,46596,00.html.

Wood, P. (2000, February 26). Bootleg music taxing university computers. Champaign-Urbana News-Gazette [Online]. [Available: http://www.news-gazette.com/ngsearch/story.cfm?number-6687.

Young, K. S. (1996). Internet addiction: The emergence of a new clinical disorder. Paper presented at the 104th annual meeting of the American Psychological Association, August 11, 1996, Toronto, Canada. [Online]. Available: http://netaddiction.com/articles/newdisorder.htm.

Young, K. S. (1999). Internet addiction: Symptoms, evaluation and treatment. In L. Vande Creek & T. Jackson (Eds.), *Innovations in Clinical Practice: A Source Book*, Vol. 17, 19–31. Sarasota, FL: Professional Resource Press. [Online]. Available: www.netaddiction.com/articles/symptoms.htm.

8

Approaching Policy for Adolescent Development in the 21st Century

James Youniss and Allison J. Ruth

The chapters of this book provide a wealth of information about major economic, demographic, political, and cultural conditions that could have an impact on adolescence in the century we have just entered. Eschewing catchy "futurism" with lists of predictions about tomorrow's world, the authors offer careful analyses of the issues that adolescents are likely to face and the kinds of policy decisions that need to be made to deal with education, work, and other issues, intelligently and equitably. We know that the details of how adolescents live their lives and the place of adolescence in the life course have changed markedly over the past two hundred years since the Industrial Revolution (Gillis, 1981; Kett, 1977). We know also that change of an equally dramatic sort has occurred even during the 20th century (Modell, 1989). What we don't know is what further changes will occur as we face yet another transformation in the large social context that constitutes Western society and its globalizing economic and political outreach.

The authors of these chapters present a wealth of evidence that should spark reflection and spur action by researchers, educators, youth advocates, practitioners, and policy makers. It follows from this material that we cannot simply continue the kind of work we have done for the past several decades. If we do, we will have missed the opportunity to create new, more supportive institutions for adolescents' development and allowed unfortunate inequities to expand, dividing further youth who happen to be born in more or less auspicious circumstances. The question we face is, how to begin this process of choosing among the alternatives that will determine the future of youth and the long-term well-being of our society?

The aim of this commentary is to encourage the kind of reflection that will initiate this process. This chapter opens with a review of the preceding chapters that describes their unifying themes and the implementations for social policy that follow from them. This is followed by a brief sketch of specific policy issues that pertain to education and schooling, just one of the areas that demands close attention. The third section of this chapter inspects what may be called a culture war against youth. The purpose here is to present evidence that undermines that war by showing how competent the present cohort of adolescents is and why it is worthy of our commitment of resources. The last section is focused on a scientific model we might choose to adopt to support the above efforts. It is grounded in a view of youth as co-constructors of society. The historical record shows that this is much more than a politically correct cliché; when adults have recognized youth's potential and worked with youth, intelligent change has been brought about for the good of youth and for the long-term gain of society. Although many of the issues to be discussed can be applied internationally, the primary focus here will be on the United States.

Much more could be said about these chapters, but it is assumed that readers will draw from their rich treasury for years to come. Moreover, these chapters constitute only one part of a larger project, which is currently producing more work. These publications will cover topics that are as equally important to an understanding of youth as the present chapters are. For example, they will expand on the need for policy that can effectively address social inequalities, and an entire volume will be devoted to youth from various cultures and the ways that globalization is affecting their lives (Brown, Larson, & Saraswathi, 2002).

With the end of the cold war in 1989, the world entered a new age of uncertainty. The subsequent search for order involves inspection of presuppositions regarding economics and politics, culture and religion, and family life and moral principles. At the same time, we have experienced a generational shift as the veterans of World War II have passed the torch on to younger leadership that has yet to be tested. One could hardly imagine a more opportune moment for beginning the kind of reflection that will help this leadership, including scholars and policy makers, to know how best it can bring youth into our world as partners in the inter-generational task of making history.

A UNIFYING THEME

This section presents a synthesis of the major concepts that give a unifying coherence to the chapters of this volume. The purpose is to offer readers one way to form a coherent and optimistic reading of this vast and diverse material. For rhetorical purposes, discussion is focused on 10 connected elements that give an overarching portrait of the conditions that are apt to control the shape of adolescence in the coming decades.

1. There is a rising bulge in our nation's demographic age profile; it is already upon us and will continue for the next several decades. Should anyone doubt the importance of sheer numbers, they need only recall the 1960s and 1970s when institutions were unprepared for the adjustments needed to accommodate the first wave of youth of the baby boom generation. We will soon face, again, the possibility of disruption that comes with large numbers as youth's needs press our institutions, especially our schools, and make a call for a fair share of the nation's resources.

2. The coming numbers will be accompanied by an increase in ethnic diversity as the offspring of the large 1970–2000 immigrant flood reaches adolescence. If immigration itself also continues, then the diversity factor will take on even greater momentum, for instance, in pressing further the tensions that threaten common values on which our civil society is based. Diversity is also likely to pose challenges for tolerance and inter-ethnic understanding.

3. Numbers and diversity will not affect all sections of the nation evenly. It is anticipated that particular sections of the country will be most affected; for instance, New York, California, Illinois, Florida, Texas, Pennsylvania, New Jersey, and Michigan. As was seen in the 2000 presidential election, the nation's political outlooks are already divided by geography. The anticipated unevenness in regional population issues may exacerbate these differences. This poses a special problem for the design and funding of federal programs. Some individual states or regions may feel the strains of diversity, whereas others may not. This is not an ideal condition for garnering consensus on federal programs, in contrast to the greater agreement regarding child labor laws, compulsory education, and juvenile justice at the start of the 20th century.

4. The foregoing changes occur in a context in which the nature of work and the economy are shifting. Within the past 50 years, the

nation has passed from an industrial to a post-industrial economy with the newest version of the latter based in information-communication technological (ICT) advances. ICT will open up a new array of commerce and work, and will also serve as a tool to make an impact on other parts of the economy. Not everyone, however, can work in the ICT sector. Accommodations must be made to this reality and to that part of the population, which will function independently from ICT, for example, parts of the so-called service sector. Issues of importance include the imbalance of wages, the inherent importance of work, and the kinds of satisfaction that are derived from various types of labor.

5. The combination of numbers, diversity, and ICT puts new pressure on education, which must find appropriate forms to meet these emerging needs. Since the 1980s, schools have been pushed into the unfortunate position of defending themselves for having "put our nation at risk." This has led to political rhetoric regarding accountability and achievement testing that skirts issues of learning and education in their fuller sense. This rhetoric seems to escalate yearly, but not necessarily to the advantage of youth. As many observers have noted, education for the future requires moving beyond the acquisition of discrete skills that are apt to become outmoded quickly in the face of innovative technology. That is why astute observers have called for the kind of learning that allows persons to reprogram themselves periodically in what promises to be a continuous educational process through much of the life span. Thus, our goal ought to be education for self-regulated re-programmable learning through the life course.

6. Parents, who for some time have found it dysfunctional simply to transmit familiar work skills and social outlooks to children, will continue to find themselves best suited to roles in which they provide guidance and supervision. Their major function will be to provide access to educational, work, and value resources that will be functional in the future, rather than preservative of the past. For 40 consecutive years, surveys of adolescents' perceptions of parents have shown relatively peaceful parent-adolescent relations, in contrast to the proverbial conflict that might have prevailed at one time. They have also shown a general agreement on values, even during the 1960s and '70s when "rebellion" was thought to be at its height. Agreement and lack of conflict may already indicate a shift in the parental role to broker from that of

stern teacher. This role is highly likely to remain functional in the coming decades as social change continues apace and adolescents seek adult guidance.

7. The foregoing elements are complicated by the fact that we now live in a global context in which information and financial capital move rapidly from one location to another, shortening distances and shrinking differences in outlooks. We have already witnessed the chaotic consequences that follow when whole industries, like steel or auto production, move out of a locality, or when capital shifts quickly from one investment sector to another. Not only are economies and lives in particular places affected, but often these events initiate migration of people that ultimately affects the equilibrium in distant societies.

8. The role of government has been the subject of debate as the liberal consensus earlier in the century gave way to neo-conservatism later in the century, but recently shifted again in another direction called neo-liberalism. Meanwhile, government retains many essential functions with respect to education, health care, and juvenile justice, to mention a few that are directly pertinent to youth. As was noted above, state and regional differences are apt to create problems for enactment of policy at the federal level. Moreover, with uneven geographic distribution of diverse adolescents, there may be difficulty in getting government to take a positive perspective toward youth, one that would encourage investment of resources in their development instead of being focused on punishment of deviations. This issue also calls for researchers to focus on how they choose to characterize youth and which of youth's many sides they emphasize. Meanwhile, government faces crucial decisions about which segments of the population merit support, for instance, whether it focuses on provision of social security and medicare for the elderly, or education and access to health care for youth.

9. As reflection on this theme and the respective empirical bases from which it was derived proceeds, it becomes apparent that no single social science discipline can adequately address adolescence as it needs to be conceptualized. We need to stop using "interdisciplinary work" as a cliché, and begin to form collaborative endeavors that do justice to the issues that are at stake. For example, any adequate analysis of health care provision would gain from the joint efforts of economists, public health scholars, sociologists,

and psychologists. Just as researchers have recognized that discrete behavior categories, say, drug use and pregnancy, are best seen as related, we need to take seriously the fact that the forces accounting for behavior are best understood when expert perspectives are wielded together through cooperative work. Yet another problem will be to maintain the view that youth are actors in their own fate, when, at the same time, we are considering the impact of larger social structural forces of economics and politics.

10. The last item in this scheme is overarching and the most open to debate. In reviewing the forces that operate to shape adolescence as a social phenomenon and personal experience, one is struck by the critical ethical issues. For example, with the prominence of ICT in the areas of work, education, and culture, questions of access and competence cannot be ignored. Denial of access, whether by design or neglect, is tantamount to relegating some youth to secondary status in the competitive job market. For another example, educational issues implicated in the various articles cannot be viewed simply as a matter of providing funds for youth programs. Such funding is, per force, connected to the allocation of resources to other segments of the life span. Increases in educational funding cannot be separated from seeking political favor through reductions in taxation. These matters bear on the concept of inter-generational equity for which an ethical calculus is every bit as crucial as an economic accounting.

EDUCATION POLICY AND THE FUTURE

This section focuses on some policy implications for education that follow from the authors' analyses. In describing various scenarios that emanate from key economic, political, demographic, social, and technological trends, the authors alluded directly or implicitly to the role schools and education, more broadly, would play in adolescents' development in the future. Extensions of schooling and growth in the education sector comprise the most obvious phenomena that differentiate adolescence in the 20th century from previous times. If the implications drawn from these chapters are correct, then education's role is likely to expand even further in the present century. However, the forms education might take are complex, and the challenges its expansion pose for society are formidable. The present discussion highlights these forms and challenges.

The Importance of Schooling. The chapters on work and technology emphasize the role that schooling has played in adolescence throughout the 20th century. During the past 100 years, schools became the major venue for adolescents' daily rounds of learning, preparing for adult work, socializing, and enculturation. Whereas in previous centuries most adolescents were found at work sites alongside adults on farms as well as manufacturing places, the 20th century gave schools a new prominence in adolescents' lives. It seems clear that schools will continue to be a key institution in which the daily rounds of adolescence are conducted, although changes in the surrounding context dictate that schooling itself must also change by diversifying its forms and offerings.

Much preparatory work needs to be done before our society is prepared to make the needed commitment to education. For the past 20 years, public discussion has been warped by a critique of school management, teacher accountability, and student discipline. A seminal document that was commissioned during the Reagan presidency, "A Nation At Risk" (1983), painted a bleak portrait of our failing schools, when compared with an abstract standard of an indefinite golden age, and with other nations with smaller, more homogeneous populations. An irony is that during this presumed educational dark age, the graduates of this system were creating the new technology age which became the basis of the world's post-industrial economy. Personal computers, the Internet, telecommunications, and the like, have formed a thriving economic sector in themselves and have become the major means to productivity in other domains, such as education, micro-biology, and agriculture. Somehow in the face of these obvious achievements, the media and political rhetoric have been allowed to caricature our schools as poorly managed holding places for incompetent teachers and unmotivated students. In addition, they have been permitted to turn sporadic incidents of school violence, tragic though they are, into general events that characterize the larger syndrome of failure. In fact, schools are relatively safe environments that have been becoming even more safe in recent years (Kober, 2000).

Some observers of the negative attacks on schools (Berliner & Biddle, 1996), view them as part of a broader "culture war" whose goal is to rid us of the liberal philosophy that guided the growth of schools and progressive attitudes toward children and youth through the first two-thirds of the century. They see the attack aimed also at teacher unions, which represent this same progressive impulse. Berliner and Biddle note, among other things, that for years, the media reported successive declines in SAT scores when, in fact, these scores remained constant and actually rose for the increasing number of minority students who took these tests. The SAT data parallel results from the National Assessment of Educational Progress (National Center for Educational Statistics, 1998), which show either no change or improvement on reading and math scores for the nation's 3rd, 7th, and 11th graders, compared with the early 1970s. These data also are in accord with the significant reduction in drop out rates for adolescents, which since 1972 have taken a downward direction for white, black, and Hispanic students (wirt, 2000).

Fifty years ago, at mid-century, about 50% of American youth had obtained high school degrees. Today, roughly 88% of American youth receive high school diplomas, 66% of whom go on for post-high school education. Throughout the century, females continued to increase their level of education, and by the late 1990s, females' educational achievements have equaled or surpassed those of males. In 1998, 87% of females received high school diplomas, compared with 90% of males, and 30% of females received bachelors' degrees, compared with 32% of males. (National Center for Education Statistics, 2000). These are remarkable accomplishments that should embolden policy makers. Throughout the 20th century, our nation has made an enormous investment in education which has taken up an ever increasing portion of our gross national product (Meyer, Ramirez, & Soysal, 1992). If the political and economic status the United States has achieved is not thought to justify this investment, then it can be concluded only that education's critics are not in touch with empirical data or are misanthropic youthophobes.

SCHOOL AND WORK

The past, of course, is less important than what lies ahead and what needs to be done educationally to prepare for society's needs tomorrow. The authors of the chapters have described a series of challenging policy issues. One task is to connect school and employment more directly and palpably (e.g., Hamilton, 1990). This may occur on its own in the future as the life-course sequence of schooling-then-work, shifts to a more flexible going back-and-forth between periods of schooling and periods of work (Kerckhoff, this volume). The need for a stronger connection is evident in the difficulty some immigrant groups experience with the present system. For example, the high school drop-out rate for Hispanic immigrant youth is double the rate for Hispanic youth born in the United States. Whereas dropping out has declined for whites and blacks since 1972, it has declined less for Hispanics. These trends are related to family income, a link that should only prod policy makers to move more forcefully to connect education to employment.

A second challenge pertains to the kind of workforce the nation needs. During the past two decades, the number of jobs in industry has declined whereas jobs requiring more social and cognitive skills have increased (Anderson, this volume; Kerckhoff, this volume). There are two messages in this shift. The obvious one is that new kinds of skills beyond traditional, behavioral conformity and regularity (e.g., Kohn, 1977) are needed. The other is that the nature of work can change rapidly, as we have witnessed over the past century, in shifts from agriculture to industry, then to white collar and professional, and now to service and technology. With the advent of this last development, theorists now differentiate education that instills specific skills from education that teaches students how to learn. Castells (2000) calls the latter re-programmable learning which is essential for the rising workforce that may need to adapt to multiple shifts in the nature of work during its lifetime. This, unfortunately, is not the kind of learning that public officials emphasize when they speak of holding schools accountable through the mechanism of yearly achievement testing. It is, rather, learning which leads to the capacity for self-regulated and self-motivated knowledge and skill acquisitions that will be needed to adapt to future changes in the economy and social environment.

A third challenge is to instill communication and interpersonal skills. Part of the 1970s–1980s Asian economic miracle (Fussell & Greene, 2002) was paced by the resurgence of Japanese businesses after the ravages of World War II. They became a model for the West that had tended to view production and marketing as mechanical processes in which individuals were interchangeable parts. One of the lessons learned from Japan was that productivity rose when workers operated as a team with upper management in which all members had a voice. This lesson was picked up to considerable gain by Western managers and is now a core part of the ICT sector. Whereas at one time social and communication skills could be checked at one's locker when entering the workplace, the nature of work's organization today and in the foreseeable future makes these skills essential to manufacturing as well as service work.

Education and Citizenship. There has always been more to education than preparatory skills for employment. Enculturation and citizenship development are equally important and even more pertinent for the coming decades when ethnic diversity will continue apace (Fussell & Greene, 2002). Citizenship has become an issue high on the agenda of political scientists who already see a decline in the civil society that is essential for our democracy (e.g., Edwards & Foley, 1997). Schools offer an obvious opportunity for addressing this problem because they reach all youth and at an age that is seminal for life-long civil engagement (Youniss, McLellan, & Yates, 1997).

One of the central issues within the civil society debate concerns the formation of common values and acceptance of procedures that enable different perspectives to be debated and mutual understanding to be achieved through open discussion. Ours is a democracy based on the assumption that different interests are inevitable, but each has a right to be entered into the political system. Maintenance of this system requires use of fair procedures and tolerance of differences so that all sides on any issue receive a fair hearing. Both private and public schools can play an important role in sustaining this system by socializing children and youth through regular enactment of these basic elements as Dewey and others have argued (Kahne & Westheimer, 1997).

Immigration and diversity, of course, are hardly new to our society. At the dawn of the 20th century, William James (1909) considered heterogeneity of immigration and the separation between classes to be a problem that might be solved through community service. It would be a device for providing youth in advantaged positions with first-hand experience of diversity so that they would come to appreciate and respect people living in different circumstances. During the 1920s, Dewey (Kahne & Westheimer, 1997) and Dunn (1929), among others, encouraged educators to incorporate service into the normal curriculum so that civic responsibility would become part of everyone's educational experience. It is probably not by chance, then, that as immigration and diversity once again are visible forces in society, schools have reinstated service as an important educational mission (Boyte, 1991). The challenge is to take this function seriously by developing programs of service that are as sophisticated as the academic curriculum and as professionally structured as, say, athletics or the arts.

Funding Schools

A special issue that hovers over the topic of education is cost and the allocation of public resources. As Fussell (this volume) has shown, the youth cohort will grow in size, but so will the size of the elderly cohort as the baby boom generation reaches retirement age later in the present decade. As was seen in the 2000 presidential campaign, candidates for public office put much emphasis on social security and medical care for the elderly, as they make an obvious appeal to them as a bloc of voters. When seen from this broader perspective, economic allocation becomes a matter of equity among the generations. The ultimate resolution must be settled by a negotiation between generations as each has a legitimate call on public resources (Fussell, this volume; Wisensale, 1999).

In what Hobsbawm (1995) has called the golden era of the welfare state, the post-World War II period witnessed the establishment of a compact in which both education for the young and financial security for the old became priorities in the United States and Western Europe. Both were thought possible during this moment of reconstruction and economic growth. Now, 50 years later, demographic patterns have changed the ratio between workers and retirees, thereby threatening the compact and pressing nations to make new choices about taxation and distribution of public funds. With both segments of the population increasing, balances need to be struck among education costs, social security costs, and the inter-generational distribution of health care (Fussell, this volume; Ozer, et al., this volume; Peterson, 1999).

Schools and Society

When schools were confronted with similar circumstances in the late 19th century, communities pulled together to reform education. New organizational systems were modeled after the then new commercial corporation (Tyack, 1974). Local civic leaders sought to upgrade schooling by taking control away from politician-patrons and by hiring superintendents with instructions to establish professional standards that would apply uniformly throughout each city. Today, several constituents claim responsibility for our schools. They include federal, state, and local governments, administrators and teachers, teacher unions, university scholars, local business leaders, various representative parent groups, and numerous interest groups that represent minority families and students with special needs. As the daily news attests, these constituents are frequently in conflict over control of funds, educational goals, and strategies for achieving them.

As was noted, despite the high-pitched rhetoric, our schools must be doing something right as students are achieving academically and leading healthy as well as socially and morally constructive lives. Nevertheless, schools face daunting challenges in developing re-programmable learning skills, fostering the values of tolerance and mutual respect, and training students for the spectrum of types of work that are anticipated while preparing them all for active citizenship. It will be essential that these various constituent groups find a new principle that will allow them to work together cooperatively rather than competitively. One feasible strategy would be to change the basis of funding so that all schools within metropolitan areas or states would receive equal funds from a common tax pool. Because most schools are funded through local taxation, there are large disparities in per student expenditures across tax districts of the inner cities and adjacent suburbs. A legal and moral case for equalization has already been made (e.g., Miller, 2000). The near-future circumstances facing schools add urgency that can be met only if the various interest groups comprehend that we need to educate youth for the sake of the society we want to sustain.

A POSITIVE PERSPECTIVE ON YOUTH

The future, or history, does not simply happen. Macro-social forces do not generate effects on their own, but become operational insofar as people respond and reproduce them strategically with policy and planning. This is the basis of several of the authors' pleas that we look at the future as a matter of choice by starting with a clear sense of history and constructing a clear vision of the kind of society we want in the future (e.g., Cullen & Wright, this volume; Fussell, this volume). Part of any policy decision requires choice in how we allocate resources, to which age groups, and in which forms. The aim of this section is to address how we might understand youth so that an adequate investment is made in their's and society's future.

Gilliam and Bales (2000) have used the concept of framing to describe one problem that impedes investment in youth. The media, for whatever reasons, have chosen to cultivate an image that emphasizes the problematic nature of youth, stressing incidents that play up excessive violence, sexuality, and risktaking. Repetition of this frame has made "difficulty" an almost automatic paired-associate of the term "youth". Reports on, for example, failure to meet academic standards, increases in drug usage, or rises in the rate of teenage pregnancy, become taken-for-granted stories that override facts and wrongly characterize a whole generation. The power of this media-driven image is illustrated in Gilliam and Bales's finding that when given empirical evidence to the contrary, for instance, regarding youth's proclivity for community service, adults either deny the facts or say that these positive examples must be exceptions to youth in general.

The authors of these chapters have compiled an impressive list of facts which indicate that this generation of adolescents is anything but problematic and that the developmental potential manifested in its positive behavior is more the rule than the exception. The national 30-year upward trend in academic achievement and the accompanying 30-year decline in drop-out rates have already been reviewed. These data take on broader meaning when they are viewed in light of other statistical indicators. For example, rates of juvenile property offenses, which constitute the bulk of youth crime, are down and have been on the decline since the mid-1970s (Cullen & Wright, this volume). Rates of violent crime, which include threats as well as direct physical assaults, rose from the mid-1980s to mid-1990s, but thereafter plummeted sharply. Recent declines in crime are especially evident for urban minority youth who were largely responsible for the earlier rise in violence. The data also clearly contradict the labeling of juvenile offenders as super predators and should put to rest the hyperbolic cry that youth violence has become an epidemic that bodes poorly for the nation's future.

The statistics on physical and mental health reported by Ozer, and colleagues (this volume) are equally emboldening. It is clear that the vast majority of adolescents are healthy. Sexual experimentation is on the decline as is teenage pregnancy, which has reached its lowest rate since 1969. Again, the data contradict the perpetrated image of hedonistic youth who are caught up in a conscienceless drive to seize the moment for personal pleasure. These data are congruent with reports on the percentages of adolescents who use marijuana or alcohol, as both have declined since the early 1990s. In fact, today's adolescents use marijuana to a lesser degree than their parents did when they were adolescents in the mid-1970s. And alcohol use, as indicated by the annual Freshman Survey (Sax, Astin, Korn, & Mahoney, 1999), is, at 50%, the lowest since 1981.

This evidence coincides with reports on the proportion of high school students who do community service. All of the national surveys conducted in the 1990s show that more than one-half the respondents have done service the previous year, with about one-half of these having done service on a regular basis (e.g., Nolin, et al., 1997). At the same time, today's adolescents have a deep regard for traditional values, for instance, in believing that religion is "very" or "pretty" important in their lives. According to Fogel (2000), this generation of youth is on the forefront of a national awakening to religion as a source of meaning that connects everyday life to transcendent values. This renewal of interest in the religious-spiritual dimension ranges from the more traditional and fundamentalist to the more spiritual, non-denominational type.

Empirical data consistently portray this generation of adolescents as achieving, responsible, competent, and grounded in traditional values. What is not so obvious, but quite important, is that these indicators apply to minority as well as to white middle-income youth. When adults' perceptions of teenagers have been probed, a distinction is often made between teenagers in general and the particular teenagers known to the respondents, say, their relatives or neighbors. The insinuation is that whereas the latter, who are known well, are fine young people, adolescents in general are troubled and are not doing well. This distinction may be responsible for pessimism about minority youth and may be perpetuated by the media's persistent negative framing. Since minority youth are likely to have fewer resources than the more advantaged white majority to cope with macro-forces that impinge on people's work lives and daily environments, it is important that policy be directed specifically to them. But this policy should be strategically applied so that it addresses real problems and does not waste funds and campaigns on concocted images that feed faulty racial and class stereotypes.

Direction for policy comes from one encouraging line of research that addresses community effects on juvenile crime, teenage pregnancy, and the like. These studies report that rates of negative behaviors differ across neighborhoods that are identical in ethnic composition and poverty rates, but vary in residential stability, density of personal networks, and presence of formal institutions such as churches or voluntary associations (e.g., Brooks-Gunn, et al. 1993; Sampson, Raudenbush, & Earls, 1997). It is possible that these characteristics and the generally positive trends among minority youth are partly the result of a decade-long strong economy that has brought work even to minority inner city families. Work, according to Wilson's (1996) thesis, may account for residential stability, the formation of social networks, and the spawning of organizational presence. It would follow that policy initiatives might gainfully be focused on making work available, providing reasonable housing, and infusing at-risk communities with supporting institutions.

In this manner, we would be choosing to create positive environments, which strengthen families and produce cohesive neighborhoods that sustain rather than impede adolescent development.

Males (1999) has attacked the media and government for their unwarranted negative presentation of youth to the American public. He has compiled a mass of results that overlap with the statistics that are presented in this volume. It should now be apparent that facts alone will not alter this negative image which has become deeply ingrained in society's reflexive association of "adolescence" with "problems," and "youth" with "troubled." The punitive approach adopted by government policy makers toward juvenile offenders is one example of the consequence of this perception. The punitive model did not simply arise one day when people spontaneously tired of the progressive's rehabilitation ideal. As Cullen and Wright (this volume) argue, the punitive approach evolved through a complex historical process that included the attempt to provide youth with rights within the justice system. It likely also owes a special debt to events of the past 50 years which include youth protests of the 1960s and 1970s, racial antipathies after the passage of civil rights legislation, and to the widening of the gap between economic classes. This is not the place to speculate further, but having identified the problem of youth framing, social scientists ought to take responsibility to counteract this misleading frame by helping to form policy that addresses actual problems while it builds on adolescents' real strengths.

YOUTH AS PARTICIPANTS IN SOCIETY'S DESTINY

The social science literature on adolescence has been relatively neglectful of the role that youth have played in shaping their own lives and, in the process, reforming society. This is an omission of some importance which diminishes the role youth have played in history and promotes the misdirected thesis that macro-conditions are determining in their own right. In fact, history is replete with instances in which youth's collective actions have helped to confront macro-forces by moving societies in alternative directions and, in the process, altering the course of history. Recent cases of note include youth's participation in the civil rights movement in the American South during the 1950s and 1960s and Chinese students' protest for democracy at Tianemen Square in 1989. Less well-known but equally telling were the roles that youth played in government reform in Mali (Brenner, 2000) and nationwide campus protests against sweat shop labor that produces clothes sold at U.S. universities (*The Nation*, 2000; AFL-CIO Web site, 2000).

Youth's participation in the unfolding events of the civil rights struggle are perhaps the best documented of these various events. We know that black college students at colleges in Florida and North Carolina collectively put themselves at risk for jailings and physical assaults by protesting publicly and persistently for equal rights. We know also that these protests were supported by churches and political organizations that provided resources and bridged the protesters to networks of interested parties in distant geographic regions. Further, it is known that white college students participated in the movement by going to the South to help register voters, join in public protests, and provide instructional classes for children in areas where schools were shut down to avoid court-ordered integration. It is understood that both black and white students were affected by their experiences. When they returned to their campuses, they re-focused collective action on various local reforms. The evidence is clear that student participants, compared with their fellow non-participants, were, 25 years later, still activists who are committed to social reform, vote at exceedingly high rates, are involved in local political movements, and are active members of voluntary associations. In retrospect, it is possible to see that this collective movement involved both youth and adults who worked together through established organizations, some of which came into being explicitly for the sake of this movement, while others, such as churches, were already nationally rooted (Fendrich, 1993; McAdam, 1988).

Civil rights is an obvious but not unusual case. American youth have taken the lead in several collective movements throughout the 20th century. Sometimes they sought to better their own position, say, in obtaining rights on college campuses in the 1930s and again in the 1960s. Other times they acted to help others who were in need, for example, in helping to unionize Kentucky coal miners in the 1930s, or today, to promote literacy in inner-city children through programs such as America Reads or serve impoverished children through Teach for America. Still other times they acted to highlight broader principles of justice such as in signing the Oxford Peace Pledge between World Wars I and II, protesting against official racial segregation, or boycotting products made with overseas sweatshop labor. Braungart (1980) and Cohen (1997) have described aspects of these various movements, confirming many of the points made above with regard to civil rights. A comparable range of movements led by youth is found outside the United States, for example, in China, Iran, Mali, Mexico, Palestine, Russia, Senegal, and South Africa (e.g., Lippsett, 1969).

Youth engaged in these movements are usually older than adolescents and are frequently of college age. However, their actions often attract adolescents who participate alongside them, for example, as occurred with the Palestinian adolescents during the Intifada (e.g., Barber, 1999). In a typical case, adolescent social activism is less radical, as it occurs through more traditional means than protests or boycotts. It is found as participation in school government, in associations like 4-H, or in community service of various sorts. In these activities, youth take active stances toward societal traditions, often with the clear idea of promoting civic or ethical principles, and frequently in collaboration with adults in formal organizational settings. These are not trivial acts for these very reasons. In taking explicit action regarding traditions that stand for moral, religious, or political values, adolescents enter society as its agents, not just its recipients. The proof of its importance can be seen in the long-term effects on participants vs. their non-participant peers. Later in adulthood, participants in school government (e.g., Verba, et al., 1995) or 4-H (Ladewig & Thomas, 1987) still differ from non-participants in their civic-moral activism, in voting, and in their voluntary membership in community associations. Community service is so varied in type and quality that it would be difficult to specify long-term effects that last to adulthood. Still, having done service during one's high school years is a strong predictor of doing service later, and when service type was known, it too predicted voting and political involvement after high school (Youniss & Yates, 1997).

There is another more subtle way in which youth may be pictured as active agents in determining the future. At various moments during the last 200 years, changes in the economy and the structure of work have caused serious disruptions to family life and youth's passage through the life course. During the period 1780–1820, for example, the manufacturing of textiles in England was shifted from the home to mills. This move radically altered the family as a production unit and broke the tie through which fathers transmitted work skills to their sons, changing the traditional role of fathers in the socialization process. In the face of forced change in work, families made several adaptive responses, for example, by taking their sons to the mills as assistants, later destroying machines, and after that, by accepting compulsory education laws so that schools substituted for fathers in preparing sons for work and providing social control and socialization (e.g., Smelser, 1959; Rule, 1982).

Other examples of disruption occurred in the United States during the period from 1880–1920 when industrial labor gave way to new kinds of white collar work within the corporation and, more recently, as white collar work has given way to its ICT successors. In the former instance, fathers found that the skills they had developed in blue-collar jobs were not needed in the corporate world of white-collar labor, as accountants, clerks, marketers, and managers. Again, families adjusted by recognizing the importance of school which provided their sons with adaptive literacy and numeracy skills (e.g., Sennett, 1974). In the more recent case, parents have agreed to extend the educational careers for their sons and daughters in order to give them advantages for entering the competitive job market (Fussell, this volume). Reduced levels of high school drop outs may signify the same sort of adjustment for non-college youth.

Perhaps the most compelling case for the active role of youth pertains to changes in the life course of women during the past century. Degler (1980) provides a description of the period 1820–1900, when women initially adopted the two sphere doctrine which separated family and home as their domain from the male domain of the outside world. By the end of the 19th century, women had reduced their fertility by one-half and extended their interests outside the home, where they joined together in organizations to effect change in society. Therein lie the roots of a key element in the progressive movement described by Cullen and Wright (this volume). During the 20th century, women continued to change their life course even more radically as they reduced fertility further, extended their schooling to outreach that of men on average, and blended marriage with independent careers in the workforce (e.g., Glick, 1977; Goldin, 1983; Modell, 1989).

It is important to look beyond macro social forces when trying to project into the future and to realize that youth are agents in the course of their own and society's destiny. From heroic acts of revolution and protest to everyday strategies such as remaining in school or delaying marriage a few years, young people can alter the structure of their youth and re-shape the entire course of their lives. Obviously, youth do not do these things just on their own, but utilize the resources that families, institutions, and society provide for them. The historical evidence for this form of agency is strong, thus calling our attention to youth as participants in the making of history. It seems evident that a focus on macro-forces should be complemented with analysis of micro-sociological processes insofar as macro-structures depend for their existence on reproductive processes and become functional through everyday interactions among humans (e.g., Giddens, 1991).

CONCLUSION

It is a rare moment when academic researchers can step back from their work to reflect on the past century of studies of youth in order to prepare for the future. The perspective set forth in this concluding chapter might further that reflection and make it more fertile. The authors of these chapters merit praise for identifying the many social conditions that youth are likely to confront in the coming decades. What will happen in the future, however, will depend as much on these conditions as on the actors who confront and transform them in the course of living their lives. Indeed, the story of youth during the 20th century can be told only from the double perspective of youth responding to changing social-economic conditions in strategic ways that allowed them to maintain purpose while leading meaningful lives.

The choices social scientists and policy analysts make are best viewed from the perspective of providing youth and families with the kind of personal and community resources they can use in strategically confronting the social and economic conditions they will face. There are many ways to construe youth and adults' role in individual development. The one offered here assumes that each generation of youth has an obligation to inspect society and move forward as best it can given the historical conditions that arise. In this regard, youth must remake history every generation. It is our complementary obligation as the older generation, then, to provide youth the resources they will need in this task. While we cannot predict the future, we surely know how to help youth meet and confront it successfully. That is our choice and opportunity.

References

AFL-CIO (2000). Enraged, outraged, the next rage. [Internet Web site reference.] (Available at http://www.aclu.org)

Anderson, R. E. Youth and information technology. This volume.

Barber, B. K., (1999). Youth experience in the Palestine Intifada. *Roots of Civic Identity*, In: Yates, M., & Youniss, J., eds. New York: Cambridge University Press, 178–203.

Berliner, D. C., & Biddle, B. J. (1996). *The Manufactured Crisis: Myths, Fraud, and the Attack on America's Public Schools*. Reading, MA: Addison-Wesley.

Brenner, L. (2000). Youth as political actors in Mali. Unpublished manuscript, School of Oriental and African Studies, University of London.

Brown, B., Larson, R., & Saraswathi, T. S. (2002). *The world's Youth: Adolescence in Eight Regions of the Globe.*, New York: Cambridge University Press (In Press).

Boyte, H. C. (1991). Community service and civic education. *Phi Delta Kappan*, 72 (10), 765–67.

Braungart, R. G. (1980). Youth movements. In J. Adelson, ed., *Handbook of Adolescence*, 560–597. New York: Wiley.

Brooks-Gunn, J., Duncan, G. J., Klebanov, P. K., & Sealand, N., (1993). Do neighborhoods influence child and adolescent development? *American Journal of Sociology*, 99 (2), 353–395.

Castells, M. (2000). *End of Millenium*. Oxford: Blackwell.

Cohen, R. (1997). *When the Old Left Was Young: Student Radicals and America's First Mass Student Movement, 1929–1941*. New York: Oxford University Press.

Cullen F. T., & Wright, J. P. Criminal justice in the lives of American adolescents: Choosing the Future. This Volume.

Degler, C. (1980). *At Odds: Women and the Family in America from the Revolution to the Present*. New York: Oxford University Press.

Dunn, A. W. (1929). *Community Civics*. Boston, MA: D.C. Health.

Edwards, B., & Foley, M. W. (1997). Social capital and the political economy of our discontent. *American Behavioral Scientist*, 40 (5), 669–78.

Featherstone, L. (January, 2000). The new student movement. *The Nation*.

Fendrich, J. (1993). *Ideal Citizens*. Albany, NY: State University of New York Press.

Fogel, R. W. (2000). *The Fourth Great Awakening and the Future of Egalitariansim*. Chicago, IL: University of Chicago Press.

Fussell, E. Youth in aging societies. This Volume.

Fussell, E., and Greene, M. E. (2002). Adolescence in the 21st century: a review of global demographic trends. In B. B. Brown, R. Larson, & T. S. Saraswathi, eds. *The World's Youth: Adolescence in Eight Regions of the Globe*. New York: Cambridge University Press. In Press.

Giddens, A. (1991). *Modernity and Self-Identity: Self and Society in the Late Modern Age*. Cambridge, UK: Polity Press.

Gilliam, F. D., & Bales, S. N. (2000). *Strategic Frame Analysis: Reframing America's Youth*. Washington, DC.

Gillis, J. R. (1981). *Youth and History*. Tradition and change in European age relations, 1770–Present. New York: Academic Press, Inc.

Glick, P. C. (1977). Updating the family life cycle. *Journal of Marriage and the Family*. 391, 5–13.

Goldin, C. (1983). The changing role of women. *Journal of Interdisciplinary History*. Spring, 13, 707–733.

Hamilton, S. F. (1990). *Apprenticeship for Adulthood: Preparing Youth for the Future*. New York: Free Press.

Hobsbawm, E. J. (1995). *The Age of Extremes: A History of the World, 1914–1991*. New York: Pantheon Books.

James, W. (1909/1971). *The Moral Equivalent of War and Other Essays*. New York: Harper and Row.

Kahne, J. & Westheimer, J. (1997). In the service of what? The politics of service learning. *Phi Delta Kappan*, 77 (9), 593–99.

Kerckhoff, A. C. The transition from school to work. This volume.

Kett, J. F. (1977). *Rites of Passage: Adolescence in America: 1790 to the Present*. New York: Basic Books.

Kober, N. (2000). *Do you know the good news about American education?* Center on Education Policy and American Youth Policy Forum: Washington, DC.

Kohn, M. (1977). *Class and Conformity (2nd ed.)*. Chicago, IL: University of Chicago Press.

Ladewig, H. & Thomas, J. K. (1987). *Assessing the Impact on Former 4-H Members*. College Station, TX: Texas Tech University.

Lipset, S. M., ed. (1969). *Student Politics*. New York: Basic Books.

Males, M. A. (1999). *Framing Youth: 10 Myths About the Next Generation*. Monroe, ME: Common Courage Press.

McAdam, D. (1988). *Freedom Summer*. New York: Oxford University Press.

Meyer, J. W., Ramirez, F. O., & Soysal, Y. N. (1992). World expansion of mass education. *Sociology of Education*, 6 (2), 128–49.

Miller, M. (1999). A bold experiment to fix city schools. *Atlantic Monthly*, 284 (1), 15–31.

Modell, J. (1989). *Into One's Own: From Youth to Adulthood in the United States 1920–1975*. Berkeley, CA: University of California Press.

National Commission on Excellence in Education. (1983). A nation at risk: The imperative for educational reform. Washington, DC.

Nolin, M. J., Chaney, B., Chapman, C., & Chandler, K. (1997). Student participation in community service activity. Washington, DC: National Center for Education Statistics.

Ozer, E. M., Macdonald T., & Irwin C. E., Jr. This volume.

Peterson, P. G., (1999). Gray dawn: The global aging crisis. *Foreign Affairs*, 78 (1), 42–55.

Rule, J. (1982). *The Labouring Classes in Early Industrial England 1750–1850*. London: Longman.

Sampson, R. J., Raudenbush, S. W., & Earls, F. (1997). Neighborhoods and violent crime: A multilevel study of collective efficacy. *Science*, 277, 918–924.

Sax, L. J., Astin, A. W., Korn, W. S., & Mahoney, K. M. (1999). *The American Freshman: National Norms for Fall 1999*. (1999). American Council on Education: University of California, Los Angeles, CA.

Sennett, R. (1974). *Families Against The City; Middle Class Homes of Industrial Chicago, 1872–1890*. New York: Vintage Books.

Smelser, N. J. (1959). *Social Change in the Industrial Revolution*. Chicago: University of Chicago Press.

Tyack, D. B. (1974). *The One Best System: A History of American Urban Education*. Cambridge, MA: Harvard University Press.

Verba, S., Schlozman, K. L., & Brady, H. E., (1995). *Voice and Equality: Civic Volunteerism in American Politics*. Cambridge, MA: Harvard University Press.

Wilson, W. J. (1996). *The Truly Disadvantaged: The Inner City, the Underclass, and Public Policy*. Chicago, IL: University of Chicago Press.

Wirt, J. G. (2000). The Condition of Education, 2000. National Center for Education Statistics: Washington, DC.

Wisensale, S. K. (1999). Grappling with the generational equity debate: An ongoing challenge for the public administrator. *Public Integrity*, 1, (1), 1–19.

Youniss, J., McLellan, J. A. & Yates, M. (1997). What we know about generating civic identity. *American Behavioral Scientist*, 40 (5), 620–31.

Youniss, J. & Yates, M. (1997). *Community Service and Social Responsibility in Youth*. Chicago, IL: University of Chicago Press.

Index